FULL
COUNT

FULL COUNT

Four Decades of Blue Jays Baseball

JEFF BLAIR

Vintage Canada

VINTAGE CANADA EDITION, 2014

Published in Canada by Vintage Canada, a division of Random House of Canada Limited, Toronto, in 2014. Originally published in hardcover in Canada by Random House Canada, a division of Random House of Canada Limited, in 2013. Distributed by Random House of Canada Limited.

Vintage Canada with colophon is a registered trademark.

www.randomhouse.ca

Library and Archives Canada Cataloguing in Publication

Blair, Jeff
    Full count : four decades of Blue Jays baseball / Jeff Blair.

ISBN 978-0-345-81254-4

    1. Toronto Blue Jays (Baseball team)–History. I. Title.

GV875.T6B53 2014   796.357'6409713541   C2013-900615-X

Cover and text design by Andrew Roberts
Cover image: Hats from the collection of Garrett Gaulberto; photograph by Andrew Roberts
Interior images: Roberto Alomar, photo by CHRIS WILKINS/AFP/Getty Images; Joe Carter, photo by JEFF HAYNES/AFP/Getty Images

Printed and bound in the United States of America

10 9 8 7 6 5 4 3 2

To family, for their understanding and support
To Hal Sigurdson, for being the first to believe

CONTENTS

INTRODUCTION 1

1 THE FOUNDING PRINCIPLES 12

2 THE MOUNTAINTOP 24

3 THE WORLD SERIES 40

4 TOUCH 'EM ALL 54

5 THE NEST EMPTIES 68

6 THE VILLAGE IDIOT 84

7 ONE LAST FLOURISH 102

8 MONEYBALL NORTH 114

9 STRANGE DAYS 134

10 THE BIG PLUNGE 146

11 THE SHIP IS SINKING 168

12 TOUCHE LES TOUS(?) 184

13 THE NIGHTMARE DREAM 204

14 OVER-HYPED . . . BUT BETTER
THAN THIS 228

15 THE GAME GROWS UP 238

REFERENCES 263

ACKNOWLEDGEMENTS 267

INDEX 269

INTRODUCTION

IN THE END, A PITTANCE WAS ALL WE HAD. NOTHING more, really. The Toronto Blue Jays celebrated the 20th anniversary of back-to-back World Series victories by winning the winter of 2012–13 and not much else. Jose Reyes, Mark Buehrle, Josh Johnson, Melky Cabrera . . . and R. A. Dickey, the National League Cy Young Award winner. All of them were acquired by general manager Alex Anthopoulos in a whirlwind makeover that took the team's payroll to an all-time high ($119,277,800) and led to Las Vegas odds-makers listing the Blue Jays as a 15–2 favourite to win the World Series. In the end, it all added up to 74 wins.

And Canadian baseball fans thought 2012 was bad? That season was nothing, compared to 2013. They thought it was tough in 2012 when the promise of a young, go-go team, the return of a popular logo and jersey that energized a once-dormant fan base, and the very real chance the team had a homegrown star in Brett Lawrie—not to mention the best spring training record in the majors—turned into a season of dysfunction that ended with manager John Farrell being traded to the Boston Red Sox for infielder Mike Aviles (and then, in 2013 taking his new—and old—team to the World Series, and winning).

The baseball gods had a different kind of betrayal in store for Blue Jays fans in 2013. This time, it was the betrayal of all that promise. It started in spring training when Lawrie, the native of Langley, British Columbia, strained his left oblique during a practice with Team Canada ahead of the World Baseball Classic. As if that wasn't enough of a harbinger, the home opener in front of 48,857 at the Rogers Centre was distinctly anti-climactic. Catcher J. P. Arencibia had three passed balls with knuckleballer Dickey on the mound, reinforcing the notion that he could not catch the team's new ace (despite working with Dickey in the off-season in Nashville, Tennessee, and at the World Baseball Classic with Team USA). He would soon be replaced in Dickey's starts, first by Henry Blanco and then Josh Thole. The rest of the team wasn't much better. The Blue Jays stumbled out of the gate, going 10–17 in April and losing Reyes (who'd quickly become a key part of the team's emotional core and was its lead-off hitter) when he suffered a left ankle sprain attempting to steal second base in a game in Kansas City on April 12. Just 10 games into the season, the Blue Jays found themselves without Reyes for 66 more. "A nightmare," manager John Gibbons said as he sat in his office later that night. By then the Blue Jays were already in last place; they never made it higher than fourth in the American League East, and the last time they were *there* was April 19.

At least there was no clubhouse implosion, as there had been in 2012. General manager Alex Anthopoulos, who'd gone off the board in bringing back Gibbons for a second term as Blue Jays manager after Farrell's exit, announced in August that Gibbons would be back in 2014. Farrell's departure was just baseball business—in Anthopoulos's words, a "perfect storm" of circumstances. But it was still taken by the fans as a slap in the face, as evidence of the team and its city getting short shrift. All in all, this has been some two-year period, some way to celebrate those back-to-back championships.

Not that there had been any formal celebrations planned in the first place. "As an organization, I think there was a sense that we lived too much in the past," Blue Jays president and chief executive officer Paul Beeston said when asked about it at the end of the

2012 season. "You could see people feeling that way. We talked about doing something about the anniversary. But there really was a sense we had to move on."

The fans, however, were still hoping to see that anniversary excitement translate to the field. When the Pittsburgh Pirates clinched a playoff spot on September 23, it ended a drought of 21 seasons without a playoff berth and left the Kansas City Royals (28 years, all the way back to 1985) as the only team with a longer drought than the Blue Jays. In what must surely count as a small mercy, the Royals did not make the playoffs, despite flirting with wild-card status into the final two weeks of the regular season. Other "cursed" franchises had also moved on. In 2012, the Washington Nationals nearly made the World Series, something they'd never managed to do as the Montreal Expos. Baseball fans with sympathies leaning toward the Expos looked on with mixed feelings as the Nationals briefly turned into the best story in the game, clinching their playoff spot at a canter and doing so with a combination of precociousness— teenager Bryce Harper, electric-armed pitcher Stephen Strasburg— and an incredible sense of self. Meanwhile, commissioner Bud Selig got to keep all the politicians happy and add another star to his legacy by shepherding the game back to the nation's capital.

But what about Canada? Even leaving the Montreal mess aside, the story of baseball in this country has been at best mixed in the years between Joe Carter touching 'em all in 1993 and the Blue Jays losing 'em all in 2013. Triple-A franchises in Ottawa, Calgary and Edmonton have disappeared—the only remaining affiliated minor league franchise in the country is the Vancouver Canadians, the Blue Jays' short-season Single-A affiliate in the Northwest League (who, by the way, won their second consecutive title in 2013)—and in their place, independent league teams in Winnipeg and Quebec City have established themselves in niche markets. The Canadian Baseball League was founded in 2003. It died that year too. At least

70 Canadian cities and towns have been the home of minor league baseball teams down through the years, with the high-water mark coming in 1913, when no less than 24 towns and cities had minor league baseball. We are nowhere near the high-water mark now. Not even close.

The Blue Jays did not escape damage from the 1994 players strike, even though the impact in Toronto did not seem as immediately profound as it appeared to be in Montreal. Attendance began a slow, steady decline that picked up speed as the club settled into a kind of middle-class hell. Once the biggest spenders in the game, the Blue Jays saw American League East rivals the New York Yankees and the Boston Red Sox dwarf their payroll. At the same time, the sale of the team's owner, John Labatt Limited, to Interbrew SA, a soulless Belgium-based brewery with no interest in a sports franchise, started to soften the strong leadership structure that had made the Blue Jays the Cadillac of franchises. The inevitable player exodus was followed by an exodus of management, including general manager Pat Gillick and president Paul Beeston. The SkyDome became an empty shell on many nights, and the sense that the team was spinning its wheels grew. Attendance, which had peaked at 4,057,947 in 1993, fell below 3,000,000 in 1995. By 2002 it was down to 1,637,000, rebounding to 2,536,562 in 2013.

The Blue Jays have finished in second place just once since 1993, in 2006, and have seldom threatened for a playoff spot. (In fact, the Expos came closer than the Blue Jays during that time, in 1996.)

And so, there is much at stake in 2014. Baseball keeps bringing us back after breaking our hearts. In some ways, after all, Paul Beeston is right: history has often been a burden for the Blue Jays. The club's marketing department said a reunion held in 2009 to celebrate the career of Cito Gaston pretty much sufficed for the 1992 team. Besides, there had been criticism levelled frequently in recent seasons over the fact that the club seemed locked in a schmaltzy time warp, with "Flashback Fridays" that continually brought back the same old faces, trotting them out to be introduced during the game to the theme song from *Welcome Back, Kotter.* One season, some of the team's veteran players wore T-shirts emblazoned with "Turn The Page Tuesdays." A clear message, you'd have to think.

And for all the significance of that first World Series win, it was 2013 that marked the 20th anniversary of one of the seminal moments in Canadian sports history. Such moments are indelibly stamped on our consciousness. One could argue that other than Paul Henderson's memorable performance in the 1972 Summit Series against the Soviet Union (the crash behind the net, the stick-to-it-iveness of jumping back up into the play and heading for the crease), the only act that comes close is Carter's World Series–winning homer off Mitch Williams.

Those were the heady days of four million fans per year packing the SkyDome to see a team that crossed the $50 million threshold before any other club. In 1992–93 the Blue Jays were, according to Beeston, "at the head of the game's big-market caucus," putting more money into revenue sharing than any other team—all while playing a brand of baseball that was not only exciting but exquisite in its professionalism. Four players from those World Series teams would go on to the Hall of Fame—Paul Molitor, Dave Winfield, Rickey Henderson and Roberto Alomar—and the manner in which Pat Gillick put the team together is the standard against which subsequent Blue Jays general managers are measured.

Carter and Mitch Williams have been videotape twins since that homer, and in mid-August of 2012 the former Phillies pitcher took part in Carter's annual charity fundraising golf tournament at Eagles Nest Golf Club in Maple, Ontario. They have developed something of a friendship and are at ease in each other's company, in the manner of most professional athletes after time erodes the rough edges of competition.

Still, as Carter rounded the bases on that October night, few of the 52,195 at the SkyDome or the millions more viewing the game around the world would have detected the dying embers of a remarkable franchise or grasped hold of the reality of the upcoming players strike. "Touch 'em all, Joe. You'll never hit a bigger homer in your life," was the call of the late Blue Jays broadcaster Tom Cheek and, like most signature calls, it rang true.

Carter never did hit a bigger home run. Nobody in Canada did. But something else happened in the aftermath of Carter's heroics— something that has, despite some appearances to the contrary, made the game in many ways as strong as ever in this country. In 1997, a member of the Montreal Expos and a native of Maple Ridge, BC, named Larry Walker won the National League's Most Valuable Player Award with the Colorado Rockies. And things kept happening. In 2003, relief pitcher Eric Gagne from Mascouche, Quebec, pitched for the Los Angeles Dodgers. He was one of the biggest deals in Hollywood, winning the National League's Cy Young Award as part of a three-year run of dominance that saw him convert a major league–record 84 consecutive saves. In 2006, a slugging first baseman from New Westminster, BC, won the American League Most Valuable Player Award. Justin Morneau of the Minnesota Twins was, in fact, considered the heir apparent to Walker until 2010, when a first baseman from Richview Collegiate Institute in Etobicoke, Ontario, flirted with the Triple Crown en route to winning the National League Most Valuable Player Award. Joey Votto, a cornerstone of the Cincinnati Reds, came within one vote of being a unanimous selection.

In and around all that, Canadian players started being chosen in the first round of the amateur draft—high up in the first round. The first Canadian-born player chosen in the first round was David Wainhouse, a pitcher selected 19th overall in 1988 by the Montreal Expos. By the time the Texas Rangers selected Langley, BC–born catcher Kellin Deglan with the 22nd pick overall in the 2010 draft, a total of eight other Canadian-born players had been selected in the first rounds of various drafts. The 2012 draft was not considered particularly outstanding for Canadian-born players, yet 27 players were chosen by 17 different teams.

The game's growth at home translated into international success at competitions such as the Pan Am Games, and, on one memorable afternoon in 2006, a team of Canadian players that included major leaguers and minor leaguers beat a team of US stars 8–6 in Phoenix, Arizona, sending shockwaves through the inaugural World Baseball Classic. In 2013, there were 23 Canadian-born players on major league rosters at one time or another. Meanwhile, the eyes of scouts throughout the game were on Gareth Morgan, a 6-foot-4, 17-year-old outfielder from Toronto who has played on the Canadian junior team since he was 14 years old, is expected to be a high pick in the 2014 draft and is creating a buzz among scouts that has not been seen by any of his predecessors.

As Beeston points out, it is "one helluva story: the game gets better in Canada, regardless of how we do. Almost in spite of us." And it has: the history of Canadian baseball no longer stops with discussion of Hall of Famer Ferguson Jenkins, the Chatham, Ontario, native who was one of the most dominant pitchers in the majors at a time when domination meant throwing 300 innings in a season and not missing a game with injuries. Nor does it stop with Melville, Saskatchewan's Terry Puhl, a mainstay of some very good Houston Astros teams of the 1970s and '80s. It no longer means padding the discussion with references to the first Canadian big leaguer, Bill Phillips, who came from Saint John, New Brunswick, and made his debut for the Cleveland Forest Cities on May 1, 1879.

We're talking about a time when pitchers still threw underhanded, until 1884, and Phillips, like all players, was allowed to call for a pitch.

No, there's much more that Canadian baseball fans can talk about. Speak, by all means, in reverential tones the name of Tip O'Neill, whose moniker graces the award given by the Canadian Baseball Hall of Fame to the Canadian player judged to have had the most outstanding season. O'Neill hit over .300 in seven of his 10 big league seasons and finished with 1,385 hits. And why not also celebrate cameo appearances by some of the sport's biggest names on Canadian soil: Babe Ruth hit his first professional home run (his only minor league home run) on September 5, 1914, at Toronto's Hanlan's Point, in the midst of throwing a one-hitter for the Providence Grays against the Toronto Maple Leafs; Nap Lajoie and Wee Willie Keeler spent the dusk of their careers wearing Maple Leaf colours, while Ed Barrow managed and was part-owner of the Maple Leafs before becoming one of the architects of the New York Yankees dynasty; and everybody knows that Jackie Robinson broke the professional colour barrier playing with the Brooklyn Dodgers' Montreal Royals affiliate. We can take pride in these achievements without feeling as if we are talking about something borrowed from another country.

Not that that should have ever been the case. There are published accounts of games in southern Ontario as far back as 1838, albeit a game played with a unique set of Canadian rules. It was in cities such as Hamilton (home to the first organized team in Canada), London and Guelph, and—of course—Toronto where much of the game's early history was written. But baseball is a game played across the country: in the Maritimes, where senior men's baseball is still a going concern; in the Prairies, where Canada Day hardball tournaments were a small-town staple; and in British Columbia, where the BC Premier League vies annually with the Ontario Baseball Association, and takes turns churning out the year's top-ranked Canadian prospect.

They have played for pay for decades across Canada. Just ask Gillick, the architect of those Blue Jays championship teams, who played in the Foothills-Wheatbelt League in the 1950s as a left-handed pitcher for a team based in Vulcan, Alberta. Gillick earned $250 per month, plus room and board, and that was enough to entice him to hitchhike from California to Alberta.

Better yet, ask Walter Lee Gibbons, who went by the nicknames "Dirk" and "Bubblegum" and kicked around the Negro Leagues from 1941–49 before heading north to play in North Dakota and Manitoba. Gibbons, who now lives in Tampa, Florida, was honoured in 2008 when the Tampa Bay Rays made him their "pick" in a special draft of Negro League players held in conjunction with baseball's entry draft. Two years earlier, Gibbons was inducted into the Manitoba Baseball Hall of Fame. Robinson's breaking of the colour barrier was an event of profound historical significance, but it had a flip side too: as major league teams (grudgingly, in some cases) opened their doors to the better players from the Negro Leagues, older or less-accomplished Negro League players were left with a game facing financial hardship due to the loss of its stars. Gibbons was one of many who came north to play—for better money, in some cases. After playing for the Brandon Greys in 1949, he returned to the US to serve in Korea, before travelling back to Manitoba to play four more years in the Man-Dak League, including stops in Brandon and with the Winnipeg Giants.

On every night of the major league season, there is tangible evidence that Canada is a country that does more than play hockey. This often surprises our American brethren—there are writers who raise their eyebrows in surprise whenever Votto admits that not only was he never much of a hockey player, he can barely skate—and you will still hear babble about baseball being played with a hockey mentality. Those stereotypes will never die, but the sport stands very much on its own in Canada, even as the Blue Jays try to rekindle the glory of those two years when they were the best in the game.

There is a saying about baseball: the game waits for no one. There's certainly evidence to support the theory. While the Jays and their fans have been biding their time (waiting, it seems, for the waiting to end), baseball in Canada has indeed moved on. Over 20 years after that second World Series win, the Blue Jays are still playing catch-up to Canadian baseball, instead of the other way around. Who would have imagined that as Joe Carter was touching 'em all?

FULL
COUNT

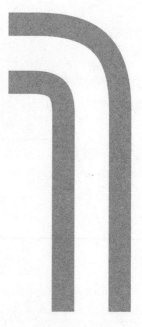

THE FOUNDING
PRINCIPLES

IT IS ONE OF THE LEAST REMEMBERED MEMORABLE moments in the history of the Toronto Blue Jays, but for Paul Beeston it is crucial to understanding what made the team special even before it won back-to-back World Series and became one of the game's defining franchises through the '80s and mid-'90s. The moment? The day that Peter N. E. Hardy, *paterfamilias* of the club, seized control.

On this, the 20th anniversary of Joe Carter's walk-off World Series home run, and after a winter in which the Blue Jays saw their manager's head turned by "a dream job" with the archrival Boston Red Sox, it is timely to remember the day that Peter Hardy came to own the Dream Team. It was certainly something Beeston was fond of talking about on October 23, 2012, the day after the Blue Jays announced that they had released John Farrell under cover of a trade. Forty-eight hours after he'd hung up with the Red Sox, Beeston was, shall we say, not particularly happy with events. He worked over an unlit cigar feverishly in his Rogers Centre office and urged his visitor to go find the 1985 "Dream Team" edition of *Sports Illustrated*. These were happy times he was talking about. Better times.

"They got all these guys in the picture—George Brett, Cal Ripken, all of them—and there's Peter Hardy. They're calling him the 'Dream Owner' or the 'Dream Executive' which was funny as hell because he didn't even own the fucking team," Beeston said, laughing. "I mean, these were the days of Steinbrenner. The Yawkeys. Ewing Kauffman. Those people. And there's Peter. The best owner."

It was the damnedest thing. The Blue Jays were owned largely by John Labatt Limited, the Canadian Imperial Bank of Commerce and Howard Webster, who came from a well-heeled Montreal family and was publisher of the *Globe and Mail* newspaper. It was a serious-minded group, yet there was also a raffish quality about it, best summed up by Beeston, the chartered accountant from

Welland, Ontario, who was known for wearing loafers with no socks, and Hardy, his bearded, fellow cigar smoker. There was a hail-fellow-well-met quality to the pair, and that quality gradually put its imprimatur on the team, though not before it suffered through some early growing pains under the first president, Peter Bavasi. Hardy was chairman of the board of Labatt, and was on the ground floor of the successful bid to bring the Blue Jays into existence in 1976 before going on to become the team's chief executive officer and chairman of the board.

It was no wonder people thought he was the owner. In point of fact, Hardy and Beeston did for the business end of the operation what people such as Pat Gillick and the venerable Bobby Mattick and Al LaMacchia did for the on-field part of the club. The Blue Jays had lean years—they finished dead last for the first five years of their existence—before taking a leap forward in 1984, when they finished second in the American League East, 15 games back of a Detroit Tigers club that started the season 35–5 en route to winning 104 games and taking the World Series. Until then, the Jays had been known mostly as an organization that did things the right way, that treated people properly up and down the chain of command and employed shrewd judges of talent. The classic example of that proficiency was found in the manner in which the Blue Jays used the Rule 5 draft—where players who aren't protected on 40-man rosters within three to four years of their original signing are made available to teams for $50,000, with the proviso that the player has to stay with the major league team or be offered back to his original club for $25,000. In those early years, the Jays used the Rule 5 draft to bring in core pieces such as Willie Upshaw (1977) and George Bell (1980). Later, Kelly Gruber and Manny Lee would join the team by a similar route. Gruber was very much a key piece of that first World Series–winning team.

Former Blue Jays catcher and manager Buck Martinez understood very early in his Blue Jays tenure just how attuned the minor league system was to the needs of the major league team, and how vital it was to become in building a sustainable club. Current bullpen coach Pat Hentgen–in some ways the patron saint of Blue Jays pitchers–remembers looking around him during his first couple of spring trainings and "wondering if I wouldn't be better off in another organization, the pitching was so deep."

Martinez knew the feeling. "We'd see guys in spring training and go, 'Who the hell is that?' Pedro Hernandez? These guys are everywhere," he said. "And when Gillick brought up a guy who'd been under Bobby Mattick's tutelage, he could play baseball. I mean, Bobby would not let you leave the field until you'd learned something. Now, you have guys getting days off in the minors. Hitting in shorts. All that nonsense."

Martinez paused. "We have let standards slip in this game. I still believe the team that brings back infield drills during batting practice will dominate baseball, because you want outfielders and catchers who can throw, and too many times now it seems that guys go into a game not knowing what base to throw to. I didn't do that as a manager, and I regret it."

DOING THINGS DIFFERENTLY

But there was another aspect to the foundation the Blue Jays were laying in those early years, and it explains why the organization enjoyed such favourable reviews within the industry. As Hardy explained to Stephen Brunt in *Diamond Dreams*: "Baseball over the years had a master-servant relationship–the idea that you do, or you're gone. It would be abusive. Scare tactics kept people in line. That was fine, I guess, when the twentieth century started out, but baseball was still living with that tradition. That's the way it's done, that's the way we'll continue to do it, and that was their method of operation."

The Blue Jays did it differently. They dealt with players differently and even dealt with agents differently, developing relationships that often blurred what could have been battle lines.

"We had this thing that we would do everything face to face," said Gillick, the team's general manager from 1978 to 1994. "I mean, we were going after Goose Gossage one year as a free agent. He was represented by Jerry Kapstein, who was based in San Diego then, and as part of the negotiations we had to change the offer two or three times. On each of those occasions we flew to San Diego from Toronto to give them the change. Not by phone or anything else. We did it face to face. It was just our way."

There was an openness to the Blue Jays and a respectful approach from ownership that stood out at a time when the game did not enjoy the degree of labour peace with which it is now blessed. Each year, Hardy would speak to the players and tell them whether the team made money or lost money. Martinez was acquired by Pat Gillick on May 10, 1981, in a trade with the Kansas City Royals for outfielder Gil Kubski. He was told that he was being brought in to help the pitchers pitch and help Ernie Whitt catch. He also received a car—a Honda, to be exact. In the beginning, the cars had Blue Jays emblems on the doors. Then, they were removed. "I'm sitting there when I hear this, and I'm thinking to myself, 'A car? Really? Haven't had that happen to me before,'" Martinez said, chuckling. "But that's the way the Blue Jays did things.

"It was a rainy, dreary day when I got there, and I was at old Pearson Airport thinking, 'What the hell have I gotten myself into?' I remember Gillick saying 'We are going to be a good organization. "You came from Kansas City and Milwaukee and know what a good organization is all about.' The thing that always stood out in my mind was Peter Hardy and Peter Widdrington [the former Labatt CEO who was chairman of the board when the Blue Jays won their back-to-back World Series] and how they took six of us—players and wives—out to dinner to a place called La Scala. He would sit us in a private room and just ask us, 'What can we do to make this a good place to play?' Wives too. That was the big difference, because wives had always been excluded. They wanted to make it a destination. I mean, Lenny Bramson [president and CEO of Telemedia, the network that had Blue Jays radio rights] would have a media party and you'd have 25 players climbing all over each other to go to it. They had those promotional caravans, and it was a big deal when the Blue Jays came to town. Come to the Brandon Wheat Kings game, the Jays are in town.

"They built up a following. But it also made the players believe there was a long-term commitment. To me, that's the challenge of getting it all back: to make the players believe they're a part of it. That's why continuity is so important; it creates an identity and stays with it. That's what Widdrington and Hardy insisted on."

Attention was paid to detail even at the minor league level. Beeston and Hardy would make two trips each year to each farm team. "The thing is," Beeston said, "a guy would see us when he was in Single-A, then in Double-A and then in Triple-A. That's how you establish a culture. It was all part of the way Peter did business."

Adds Gillick: "It was a great ownership group and it started with Don McDougall [president of Labatt when the Blue Jays were founded], down to Mr. Widdrington and everyone else. They were not involved in ways that cut into your autonomy. But at the same time, you knew that if you needed anything they were there."

Duane Ward and Tom Henke were an effective bullpen tag team during the franchise's glory years, and Ward is still an active member of the Blue Jays alumni, overseeing baseball camps throughout Canada. Born in a small oil-and-gas town in New Mexico and now living in Las Vegas, Ward still tells people that his "heart lies north of the border." He wasn't always so certain. Acquired in a trade for

Doyle Alexander in 1986 from the Atlanta Braves—who'd chosen him with the ninth pick overall in the same 1982 amateur draft that produced Dwight Gooden and Shawon Dunston—Ward remembers having a similar reaction to Martinez upon his arrival.

"God almighty," Ward said. "That's what I thought, but it took me about two months to realize I'd gone from the penthouse to the *presidential* penthouse. The Braves are a class organization, but the Blue Jays . . . the way they treated you when you got there was something else. I mean, you'd see Gillick in the clubhouse here or there, but Beeston, Mr. Widdrington and Mr. Hardy? They were there all the time. The owners. They'd always ask you if everything was good, how was the family, could they do something for you. Constantly."

And that didn't change once the Blue Jays became successful. A pitcher for the Detroit Tigers named Jack Morris first took note of what was going on in Toronto during the 1984 season, when the Tigers saw that the Blue Jays had answered their 35–5 start with a 30–14 run of their own. "I got the sense then that these guys were dang close," Morris said. "From that point on, I just kind of felt that they were a team you always had to keep an eye on. You knew where they were." Morris would, of course, end up doing more than merely keep an eye on the Blue Jays. In 1992, he joined them as a free agent.

THE TURNING POINT

Martinez believes the naming of Bobby Cox as manager in 1982 was the on-field turning point for the franchise. By then the Jays had a well-developed farm system of athletes with speed and pitching. They had also developed some swagger, to the point where Martinez remembers Willie Wilson of the Kansas City Royals standing at the plate screaming at Blue Jays pitchers, then yelling at nobody in particular to "tell those motherfuckers to stop throwing at me." Martinez and Willie Upshaw had a system for tipping off the location of the opposing catcher's glove, with Martinez saying "C'mon, Willie," if the glove was positioned inside, or "Hey, Upshaw, c'mon," when the glove was outside. Alfredo Griffin took to stealing the catcher's signs when he was at second base and relaying them with such flourish that his teammates had to tell him to tone it down. It was a team of players thinking about what they could do to win, and Cox was the perfect guy for that group at that time—a guy whose first meeting with Martinez, at the end of spring training in his first year, consisted of these words: "I don't know you guys very well but you had a good spring. Ernie [Whitt] had a good spring. You're going to platoon and go out and have a good year." They were in the process of developing that inner belief common to good teams in any sport.

"I thought when we started this whole thing in 1976 that we would have a free pass for three or four years, that it was years five, six and seven where you'd start to feel public pressure," Gillick said. "At that point, people would be looking for improvement. So we had to get the foundation right in those first couple of years. It was different than the things I had to do in my other jobs later on—whether it was Baltimore, Seattle or Philadelphia. In those cities, it was all about filling in holes here and there as opposed to developing right from the bottom." Gillick, of course, would go on to win a third World Series with the 2008 Phillies.

FICKLE GODS

In 1985, the Blue Jays finally made it to the post-season, finishing 99–62 before blowing a 3–1 lead to the eventual champion Kansas City Royals in the best-of-seven ALCS (American League

Championship Series). In the first of what would seem to be many snubbings by the baseball gods, it was the first time in 16 years that the league championship series was best-of-seven instead of best-of-five. A year earlier, a 3–1 lead would have been enough to move on.

"By '83 we could out-hustle everybody and out-play everybody, and Bobby used everybody," said Martinez. "We had a great mix. Lloyd Moseby, George Bell, Alfredo [Griffin], Jesse Barfield . . . a great mix. And they all grew up together and came to the big leagues together. Hell, in 1984 we thought we'd played better than the Tigers after that great start that they had."

Cox would leave the Blue Jays after the 1985 season and return to Atlanta to become general manager of the Braves, the team that had fired him in 1981. Cox had kept his home in Atlanta, and it wasn't hard to hear echoes of Cox in the explanation John Farrell gave for leaving Toronto for Boston with another year remaining on his contract. Boston was Farrell's dream job; Cox, who was on his second marriage, wanted to return home. Baseball has tampering charges that prevent teams from pursuing employees of other clubs, but the Blue Jays had a much-ballyhooed "handshake" policy that allows coaches and front office executives to make lateral moves, the understanding being "if you don't want to be here, we don't want you here." That was all fine when the Blue Jays were winning and the grass wasn't greener any place else, but when Beeston returned as president and chief executive officer under the ownership of Rogers Communications, it seemed quaint, a sign of weakness. And when rumours first surfaced after the 2011 season that John Farrell was being courted *sotto voce* by the Boston Red Sox, Beeston said publicly that it was no longer the case.

Jimy Williams was the choice to replace Cox, and it was a sensible move because he was familiar to the organization, and as Cox's third-base coach was the on-field executor of the manager's will, an omnipresent lieutenant. But as good as the Blue Jays were, the core of the team was still in transition, and Williams' demeanour had a tendency to make every baseball decision seem a black-and-white choice, fraught with tension and hinting at agendas that likely didn't exist. The Blue Jays took a step back in 1986 when the roots of a legendary feud between Williams and George Bell were laid, a feud that burned enough that Williams could still cut off a conversation about it 20 years later. Then Toronto suffered through a galling collapse in 1987: up three-and-a-half games with seven left to play, Williams' Jays dropped all of their remaining matches to finish in second place with a 96–66 record that left them two games out.

"That was a major meltdown," said Ward. "I mean, to not even squeak out one win? That happens and you know the stars aren't aligned."

Williams' time with the team ended with a 12–24 start in the 1989 season, and the Blue Jays stayed in-house again, naming hitting coach Cito Gaston as manager. The hiring was made on an interim basis, and it was clear almost immediately that Gaston was far from Gillick's first choice for the permanent posting. That would have been Lou Piniella, a broadcaster with the New York Yankees who had previously spent three years as a manager for George Steinbrenner. Piniella would go on to win three Manager of the Year awards and rank 14th on the all-time wins list when he left the game, but at the time, Steinbrenner was asking for three players in a trade. "Not even a trade for a manager, a trade for a fucking broadcaster," Paul Beeston said, laughing. The Yankees clearly valued Piniella more as a broadcaster than the Blue Jays valued Farrell as a manager; the Jays settled for one mediocre Boston infielder named Mike Aviles.

Gaston remained as the Blue Jays' manager through their halcyon years, staying with the organization as a senior advisor and coming out of retirement to take over the team in the dying days of general manager J. P. Ricciardi's tenure. As was the case with most minority players of his time, Gaston viewed much of the criticism he faced with the Blue Jays—and he faced a ton of it—through the prism of past racial battles won and lost. That was wholly understandable, and anyone who heard the stories told by Gaston and his contemporaries, or by people like Tommy Harper and Felipe Alou and Frank Robinson, might agree.

Gaston's style gave his critics much to chew over. He was criticized for sometimes being insensitive to young players and putting too much faith in older players, although it's easy to find as many counter-examples of that as it is to find examples. Beyond that, Gaston was a firm believer in not fixing what wasn't broken; his lineup was usually static because it didn't need much tinkering during the World Series years. And when he gave players a day off, it was a day off, regardless of whether a favourable late-inning matchup presented itself.

Yet with the odd exception, that same style is lauded by his former players.

"Cito wasn't my choice, but that's what was good about the Blue Jays organization," Gillick said one day in October 2012, as he prepared to watch some Philadelphia Phillies prospects in the Arizona Fall League. "It wasn't a closed shop. The understanding was you didn't try to intimidate people when they were giving their opinion. You had to listen to people. I used to tell guys: 'You can't listen if your mouth is going.'

"The fact is that hiring Cito worked out perfectly under the circumstances," Gillick said. "Lou was my first choice because I thought we needed somebody with experience. I just thought that given the way we had played in 1989, it was going to be difficult for somebody who had coached that group to take charge of it.

"Look, you always have differences between your manager and GM. But in hindsight, I have to say that I really understand and appreciate Cito Gaston as a manager. It's one thing to put pressure on guys, another thing to put what I'd call 'finger pressure' on them. Cito could do that."

Blue Jays fans who believe that the team's history begins in 1992 might be surprised to learn that the 1989 team is in some ways Gaston's favourite. Gaston did not want a hitting coach hired to replace him, feeling it was counterproductive to introduce someone new mid-season. But by the season's end, pitching coach Al Widmar wasn't healthy—he'd had a variety of back and neck problems—so Gaston put his hand into that aspect of the game as well. "I just thought I knew the hitters better than anybody they could have brought in," said Gaston. "It was a challenge, because when you're a hitting coach guys are more willing to talk to you. You become a manager? They don't come to talk to you anymore.

"But, man, to me that 1989 team was a lot of fun. Maybe the most fun to manage of the teams I had. We didn't have the power we had in later years but we could manufacture runs. George Bell was hurt with a bad shoulder, and he spent a lot of time just hitting to right field, so you had to do some things. I found out a lot about myself that year."

Years later, during the 2012 season, when asked whether Gillick always had Gaston's back, whether he was always supportive of the manager, Paul Beeston paused. "I don't think I have to answer that question," he said. "Peter Hardy was. I was. The board and coaches were. And the players were."

In 1992 and '93, the baseball world would find out just how much support Gaston had.

THE
MOUNTAINTOP

ROBERTO ALOMAR STOOD ON A STAGE IN A GREEN field in Cooperstown next to the Clark Sports Center alongside the man who brought him to Toronto, Pat Gillick. On a blistering hot afternoon, Alomar spoke about his heart being half Puerto Rican, half Canadian.

It was July 24, 2011, and Alomar was being inducted into the Baseball Hall of Fame, the first player to wear a Blue Jays hat on his plaque, which reads in part: "Set the standard for a generation of second baseman with a quick, powerful bat, a smooth, steady glove and seemingly endless range." When Alomar retired following a stillborn spring training audition with the Tampa Bay Rays in 2005, he'd won 10 Gold Gloves in 16 seasons (most all-time among second basemen) and hit an even .300 with 2,724 career hits, 210 home runs, 1,134 runs batted in and 474 stolen bases. Five of those Gold Gloves came during his five-year career with the Jays, when he hit .307 and racked up 206 of his steals.

Gillick was also being inducted as a builder, in no small measure for his work in putting together those back-to-back World Series winners in Toronto. Gillick had had a decent curve during his playing days, but nothing like the third member of the Class of 2011, Bert Blyleven of the Minnesota Twins. Blyleven, too, had Canadian roots of sorts: when his family emigrated from the Netherlands, the family name was spelled Blijleven, but was anglicized during their time in Saskatchewan. Blyleven's father had come to Canada to join his brother as a farm labourer near Melville, and the young Bert recalled living in Saskatchewan for four years. Canada was all over the place at Cooperstown that weekend.

THE BIGGEST BLOW

It almost goes without saying that Joe Carter's walk-off, World Series–winning home run is both an iconic Canadian sports moment and an iconic Canadian cultural moment. But if you put every member of the 1992 and 1993 Blue Jays in one room—whether players or executives or coaches—they'd tell you that it was in fact Alomar who struck the biggest blow in the history of the franchise. It happened in the late afternoon shadows on a pleasant fall day at Oakland–Alameda County Coliseum. Dennis Eckersley—who had a hand in much of the warped history that had surrounded the Blue Jays franchise for a five-year span—looked in at Alomar, who was standing at the plate in the top of the ninth. Devon White was on third base after an error by Athletics outfielder Rickey Henderson, and the Athletics held a 6–4 lead with none out. The Blue Jays were up 2–1 in the best-of-seven ALCS, and had fought back in Game 4 from a 6–1 deficit.

Eckersley would go on to win an unusual double in post-season awards balloting, capturing the American League Most Valuable Player Award and Cy Young Award after a remarkable season. It was a year in which pitching dominated the majors, with one of every seven games a shutout, and Eckersley had more than done his part, going 7–1 with a penurious WHIP (walks and hits per innings pitched) of 0.913 and an earned run average of 1.91 with 51 saves. Eckersley was well on his way to being a first-ballot Hall of Famer, and in fact was *also* on the dais in Cooperstown on the day Alomar was inducted, standing out in a group of Hall of Famers who were welcoming the newest members of their fraternity, Eckersley's longish hair just a shade lighter and the perpetually tanned face still the same. But on that day in October 1992, Alomar got the better of him.

A few days after Game 4, Joe Giuliotti, a long-time baseball writer for the *Boston Herald*, would report that Eckersley had confided to friends about a nagging pain in the elbow at the end of the season. Giuliotti knew Eckersley from the pitcher's days with the Red Sox, and he felt he was on solid ground when he took comments from the reliever ("I could say my arm's a little tired or something's bothering me or I've lost velocity, but that would be making excuses and I don't make excuses") to suggest that he was something less than 100 percent effective when he threw a 3–2 pitch to Alomar. Alomar did not dispute the idea; Eckersley, Alomar said, had had difficulty keeping his pitches down and he wasn't throwing as hard as usual. Alomar went to the plate believing that Eckersley's fastball was flat and that his slider had little life.

He was right: Alomar drove a pitch that he thought was a slider that bit back over the right-field wall. Eckersley said it was a high fastball, but whatever: his three-game total was 17 batters faced and eight hits allowed and either way it was sweet, especially after Eckersley's fist-pumping celebration of Ed Sprague's eighth-inning strikeout, spiced with words directed at the Blue Jays dugout. That would fuel a war of words for the rest of the Series, with old warriors such as Jack Morris chiming in on the Jays' behalf. Athletics manager Tony La Russa and Eckersley both returned verbal shots. "Let Devon White try to make a living getting base hits off Dennis Eckersley and he'll be carrying a lunch pail," said La Russa. Morris called Eckersley's antics "Little League stuff," and when the two men met on the field before Game 5, Morris didn't back down when Eckersley questioned him about his participation in the banter. "He's a competitor, so he probably understands—yet he buries me," Eckersley told reporters. "Cheap shot."

Eckersley was a familiar nemesis from 1989, when the Blue Jays were staring at elimination in Game 5 of that year's ALCS (the team's first trip). La Russa, looking at a 4–2 lead in the ninth inning, called on Eckersley to close. At that point, Cito Gaston strolled out and asked umpire Rick Reed to check Eckersley. The Blue Jays had heard from clubhouse attendants—and some of their players believed they'd seen anecdotal evidence—that Eckersley was using an emery board to scuff the baseball, which was against the rules and could alter the path and movement of the baseball. Eckersley passed inspection, but Gaston, La Russa and several of the Athletics players become embroiled in a verbal confrontation that some say nearly boiled over into something physical.

So there was that. Three years old, but a scab still fresh enough to be picked open. There is a fear that resides deep down in every major league team until it wins its first World Series—the fear that it could find itself like the Chicago Cubs, that it is a team cursed, a team that for whatever reason has run afoul of the baseball gods. Play 162 games a year and spend all those days with the same group of people and things that might otherwise be viewed as distractions become just another trend waiting to develop. Put it this way: there isn't a Blue Jays player alive from 1991 who doesn't believe that their team was far superior to the Minnesota Twins, who won the ALCS 4–1 over the Jays and then went on to beat the Atlanta Braves in seven. Even though the Twins had a better regular season record than the Blue Jays (95–67 compared to 91–71) the Blue Jays had gone 8–4 against the Twins.

And there was also, of course, the epic collapse down the stretch in 1987 and that blown 3–1 lead to the Kansas City Royals in the 1985 ALCS. That's a lot of stars crossed for a franchise that had been around for just 15 years.

Enter Alomar.

"That was the bigger blow of the two, between Robbie's homer and Joe's homer," Gillick said the day before his induction. "Because it got us to the mountaintop."

Duane Ward, who formed a monstrous two-headed bullpen with closer Tom Henke, picks a different analogy. "The stone that broke the window," is how he refers to it. "Suddenly, it didn't seem so impenetrable," Ward said. "But at the same time, it wasn't like we just all of a sudden looked at each other and said, 'Yeah, we can do this.' By that time in those playoffs, we weren't even thinking of going home . . . but that did take the wind out of Oakland's sails, no question."

The Blue Jays went on to win the game in the 11th inning on a sacrifice fly by Pat Borders. Then, after the Athletics beat David Cone on three days' rest in the fifth game, the Jays put the series away with an emphatic 9–2 win in Game 6 at the SkyDome.

But it wasn't just the homer itself that proved decisive; it was the atmosphere surrounding the blast. Creating an image that predates Carter's run to the pitcher's mound after the 1992 World Series win, or his hop and fist thrust after his homer off Williams in 1993, Alomar tossed aside the bat and proceeded to round the bases. The Blue Jays had done so many things right in assembling their teams in recent seasons only to run into blind corners in September. And when that happened, it was the Detroit Tigers, Milwaukee Brewers, Kansas City Royals, Minnesota Twins and the Athletics that often seemed to play the bully.

Alomar often gets asked what that homer felt like, not just the raw emotion of it, but the physical sensation too. The answer is he didn't feel a thing, and that's how he knew it was gone. Hit a ball that hard and that well and you don't feel it. "All I remember," he said, "was Joe [Carter] in the on-deck circle saying 'run, run.'

"I wasn't here in 1989, but I didn't really feel pressure whenever I played this game," said Alomar. "I don't know if I ever felt pressure in baseball. I always felt like this is what I was born to do. But that was a big comeback. If we had lost that game, I believe we would have lost that series. But after I hit it and we came back to win the game, it just seemed like from that point on we could beat those guys. And once that happened, everything just seemed to click."

CHANGING TIMES

Despite the vitriol and back and forth that came to characterize the series, there were some in the Athletics clubhouse who were quietly sitting back and taking note. For many, the sense that this was a team to watch started in Game 3, when Dave Winfield drove in the winning run after an early deficit. Dave Stewart, considered one of the best big-game pitchers of his generation, told reporters before the fourth game that this was a different Blue Jays team than the ones that had lost the ALCS in three of the eight preceding seasons. "We haven't changed," he told the *New York Times*. "They've changed."

They surely had. Alomar and Joe Carter had joined the Blue Jays in what until the winter of 2012 would be the biggest trade in franchise history—on December 5, 1990, when Pat Gillick sent Tony Fernandez and Fred McGriff to the San Diego Padres—just three days after Devon White was acquired along with reliever Willie Fraser from the then California Angels for Junior Felix and Luis Sojo. Playing in their first full season in the SkyDome, the 1990 Blue Jays had gone into the final eight days of the season with a one-and-a-half-game lead over the Boston Red Sox atop the AL East and, faced with a nine-game road trip to end the regular season, proceeded to lose six of their last eight games, signalling that it was time for a change—despite an 86–76 record just one season removed from their appearance in the ALCS and loss to the Athletics.

They also had some big-time attitude brought by Winfield and Morris, which became apparent in Detroit on Monday, April 6, 1992, Opening Day. Dave Winfield stood up in the middle of the visitors' clubhouse and said, "I don't know what the rest of you motherfuckers are going to do, but if you get on base I'm going to drive your ass in." That's according to Gaston, anyhow. Several variations of the speech and the locale are recited to this day by members of that team, but the message was very much as the skipper remembered it.

At the age of 40, Winfield saw the club as a last, best shot to add the one commodity missing from his resumé: a World Series. He signed a one-year, $2.3 million contract a week before Christmas, 1991. All these years later, the ability to attract Morris, Paul Molitor (in 1993) and, to a certain degree, Winfield as free agents is held as proof by true believers that the only way to overcome the view of Toronto as little more than a free-agent fallback position is to put a winning team on the field.

Winfield hit 26 home runs and drove in 108 in 1992, with an OPS (on-base plus slugging percentage) of .867 that was 40 points above his career average. He would go on to drive in Alomar and Devon White with a two-out double in the top of the 11th inning in the Blue Jays 4–3 win over the Atlanta Braves in the sixth and final game of the World Series, bringing Toronto its elusive first world title. "I've been reinvented a couple of times," Winfield would tell Steve Jacobson of *Newsday* in February 1996, after finally announcing his retirement. "Bad guy, frank and insightful, loser, winner. Then—you become a leader."

The Blue Jays started the 1992 season with a three-game sweep of the Tigers en route to a season-opening six-game win streak, and finished the campaign with another three-game sweep of the Tigers. They won five of their last six games, putting up a 96–66 record that left them four up on the Milwaukee Brewers. It was not a good Tigers team that year, but considering the impediment the Tigers had been in the past, there was a message in the manner in which that finishing kick was delivered: Juan Guzman allowed just one hit over eight innings in the 3–1 win on October 3 that sealed the deal.

Winfield was hardly a beast during the 1992 post-season, however. The double was one of five hits in 22 World Series at bats and the only extra-base hit of the lot; it delivered two-thirds of his RBI production in the Series after he'd managed just three RBIs in the ALCS against the Athletics, when he hit two homers. But it was enough for New York Yankees owner George Steinbrenner to later apologize for his derogatory reference to Winfield as "Mr. May" during the 1985 season. Winfield played a little more than eight years for the Yankees and was a seven-time All-Star, but his poor performance in the 1981 World Series loss to the Los Angeles Dodgers (1-for-22, including a bizarre request for the ball after he singled to break an 0-for-18 slump in the Series) resonated in a city that measured its baseball players by post-season heroics.

It was odd in some ways that Winfield would find deliverance in the city of Toronto, where he was previously best known for facing legal action after killing a seagull with a thrown ball at Exhibition Stadium in 1983. But considering that he and Gaston had roomed together while teammates with the San Diego Padres, the decision to come north should have been no surprise. He became a trusted ally for Cito.

"If there was anything going on in the clubhouse that I wasn't aware of, he made sure he took care of it," Gaston said. "Jack [Morris] also was a guy who would patrol the clubhouse. I didn't mind guys sitting in the clubhouse because the bench was so small out there, but you had to have the game on the TV and if somebody had golf on, Jack was right on them. Jack was not a big golf fan, you might say."

Buck Martinez believes the acquisition of Morris and Winfield was yet another product of Pat Gillick's shrewd abilities to assess a team on the fly. "These guys always had an ability to decide on what they wanted or needed and then simply refuse to deviate from it," said Martinez. "I mean, in Morris they had a guy who had just thrown one of the greatest games in World Series history.

They went out and got a guy who had won in different cities and different circumstances, somebody who understood how to win. He had seen the Blue Jays since 1983 and had those great rivalries with us, and he said, 'Hey, that's a pretty good place to play.'"

Morris loved the city of Toronto and pitching in the SkyDome, and was smart enough to see the Blue Jays were a team on the cusp—that they were ready to take the big step forward.

What surprised Morris, he now admits, was Cito Gaston's ability as a leader—something Morris said he'd never realized as an opponent. "Cito was way different than Tom Kelly [the Minnesota Twins' manager] or Sparky [Anderson], way more quiet," said Morris. "But he controlled his team, and·I found I really appreciated the calmness he brought to situations. Cito understood what he had in the clubhouse, and he had the ability to do little things without getting in the way."

Gaston's handling of Morris on Opening Day in 1992 would set the tone. Morris was pitching against the Tigers at Tiger Stadium, where he'd become one of the most dominant pitchers of the '80s and won a World Series in 1984. As with any long relationship, there were wrinkles: Morris was one of the players most aversely affected in baseball's second round of collusion, when he received no free-agent offers in 1986 and was forced to re-sign with the Tigers. He was eventually among a group of players that received financial redress when the Major League Baseball Players Association successfully pursued ownership for damages resulting from what was seen to be a means of artificially restraining salaries. In his Blue Jays debut, Morris needed 144 pitches to throw a complete game five-hitter against his old teammates and put away a 4–2 Blue Jays win, earning a hearty clap on the back from Gaston and, a couple of days later, a call to come into the manager's office.

"Jack never wanted to come out of the game," said Gaston. "He had 130-some pitches and still didn't want to come out. So, I let him go. I let him go. Then we got back here in Toronto, where we had a decent clubhouse where you could talk to the players. So I brought Jack into the office and said, 'Big guy, let me tell you what's going to happen here: You get us to the seventh inning and we have two guys who are going to take it the rest of the way. That's Duane Ward and Tom Henke.' As soon as I told him that he was fine. But, see, that was Jack. If he was going to lose, he was going to lose himself.

"See," Gaston continued, "the big thing with ballplayers is if you treat them like men, they act like men. They knew I had rules; I just didn't have many of them. And they went by the rules. Now you like to have the same rules for everybody, but sometimes you have to bend a little bit for guys."

Morris and Winfield, Alomar said, both brought respect to the team. "Jack came here because he wanted to win World Series; he thought pitching for us was a chance to pitch in big games. When you see somebody do that for that reason, well, you start to think."

While Morris wanted to win more championships, Winfield wanted to win his first, and if that meant holding some feet to the fire, well, so be it. It was August 1992 when Winfield told a Toronto newspaper that the crowds at the SkyDome need to be noisier. "Winfield Wants Noise" was the headline in the *Toronto Sun*, and it soon appeared on T-shirts, mugs—everywhere. "The fans became a big part of our success here," said Alomar, smiling. "What else can you say about Winfield, man? He's in the Hall of Fame.

"Dave was something like a father figure to us," Alomar continued. "We looked up to him, and knew that he hadn't had a chance to go to the World Series after 22 years or so. He wasn't only a great player but a great person. And that's what we had: great players who cared for each other."

The additions dovetailed nicely with the existing Blue Jays. "Robbie, Joe Carter . . . Wardo [Duane Ward] . . . you didn't have to tell these guys anything," said Gaston. "I mean, you'd bring Ward into a game and you didn't have to remind him how to pitch guys or who was coming up. In fact, if you did, he'd get pissed at you."

Taken together, it was a nurturing environment for Alomar, whose acute understanding of clubhouse sensibilities and the inner game of baseball allowed him to soak it all in. There was a subliminal quality to Alomar that went beyond his wondrous athletic abilities to his baseball instincts, the grounding of which was provided by his father, Sandy Alomar Sr., a long-time major league player, coach and scout. Alomar's brother, Sandy Jr., had a long and successful career as a catcher and was rumoured to be a serious candidate for Blue Jays manager both when John Farrell was being courted after the 2010 season and when John Gibbons was brought back for a second time in the winter of 2012. The siblings are both considered to be expert in what might be called the game's darker arts: stealing signs, finding things pitchers do to tip off the pitch they're throwing—a slightly more pronounced flare on the web of the glove on a certain grip, for example. Gaston would sit in the dugout and Alomar would walk by him on the way to the bat rack or stroll over for a quick chat from the on-deck circle and say, "I'm going to hit a breaking pitch this time." And he would. In 1993, when Alomar was nip and tuck with Kenny Lofton of the Cleveland Indians for third spot in the batting race on the final day, he and Gaston kept in touch about whether he'd come out of the game to protect his edge or need a hit to gain an edge. Tiring of all the drama, Alomar told Gaston, "I'll just get a hit this time." And he did.

Alomar just shrugs, now, when asked about his baseball IQ. "That came from my dad," he said. "He always told me not to be afraid to ask questions, that there was no point in letting your ego get in the way of finding out things from people who knew. He always told me to be smart. So I'd watch for a pitcher's weaknesses. I'd pick a hitter in a game that I thought was most like me and watch what they did.

"There is a thing I remember when I first joined the San Diego Padres," Alomar continued. "I used to watch Tony Gwynn a lot, and I remember one day in spring training when I was at the minor league camp I saw how he'd stay after a game and just go into the cage and hit baseballs. That's all. Just hit baseballs. So I learned from that. I learned that you can learn something more every year about your game. Baseball players are not perfect. Not even the ones that are really good. But what we do, I think, is go with what we know will help our team win games."

There were many plaudits directed toward Alomar on that weekend in Cooperstown in 2011, but perhaps the most telling came from another inductee with a Hall of Fame and Canadian pedigree. Roland Hemond had also been honoured that weekend with the Buck O'Neil Lifetime Achievement Award for "extraordinary efforts to enhance baseball's positive impact on society." In his early eighties at the time, Hemond had served as a mentor to general managers such as David Dombrowski and Doug Melvin. Although he was born and raised in Rhode Island, his family had French-Canadian roots: his mother was a seamstress born in Quebec, and the family spoke mostly French at home until Hemond was six years old. Knowing there would be Quebecers in the crowd—long-time Montreal Expos broadcaster Dave Van Horne was being honoured with the Ford C. Frick Award for broadcasting excellence—Hemond even sprinkled in a few words *en français*.

Hemond was a GM with the White Sox and Orioles for 23 years, but he'd been a minor league executive with the Angels and Braves, and a senior advisor with the White Sox and Diamondbacks. So he knows ballplayers. Hemond is also part of the Hall of Fame's Golden Era Committee. This group of veteran Hall of Famers and baseball writers decides on the candidacy of players who have played for at least 19 years after 1947 and have been retired for at least 21 seasons without being on baseball's ineligible list. Retired managers, umpires and executives are also considered if they've spent 10 years in baseball.

The connection to Alomar came about when Hemond was charged with making the case for Joe "Flash" Gordon, a second baseman with the great New York Yankees teams of the 1940s. Gordon was a nine-time All-Star, member of five World Series champions, and won the 1942 American League Most Valuable Player Award despite the fact that this was the same season in which the Boston Red Sox's Ted Williams won the Triple Crown. The way Hemond tells it, he was searching for a way to put the career of the legendary Yankee second baseman into context. He thought about Alomar.

"I knew a lot of people on the committee hadn't seen Joe play, so I told them he was like Robbie Alomar," Hemond said. "Not many people knew that Gordon was a really good gymnast when he was at the University of Oregon. So I told them he really was acrobatic, just like Robbie."

Gordon was inducted into the Hall of Fame in 2009.

In some ways, Alomar had been an afterthought for Blue Jays GM Pat Gillick as he was negotiating with then Padres GM Joe McIlvaine at the 1990 winter meetings in the Chicago suburb of Rosemont. The focal point of the discussions had been a Carter-for-McGriff swap, although, truth be told, Gillick was likely looking for a way to move Tony Fernandez, a tremendously gifted shortstop who had worn out his welcome with the Jays. Gillick regaled the folks in Cooperstown all weekend with the story of how he'd tried to get Alomar once before—when he'd attempted to sign the then 16-year-old while he was in Puerto Rico, only to be beaten by the Padres, who had employed Alomar's father as a scout and coach.

Gillick actually claims his eye was drawn to Alomar even earlier, when the seven-year-old future star would run around Yankee Stadium while his father was with the team, for whom Gillick worked as player development coordinator.

Alomar, who is now an advisor to the Blue Jays, sat in the press box at Rogers Centre a year and a half after his induction and smiled as he thought about that day in Cooperstown. He and Eckersley spent some time together during the weekend, he said, but he never brought up the homer. "I didn't want to disrespect him," said Alomar. "I have too much respect for the game and the players." Of course, as Alomar said, Eckersley never brought it up either. And in some ways, that tells you all you need to know.

THE WORLD
SERIES

THERE IS LITTLE EDGE TO JACK MORRIS'S VOICE ON this cool fall day. There is no game to be pitched, just some television work with the MLB Network—go figure: Jack Morris, media personality—on the horizon. The playoffs beckon, the way they most always did when Morris pitched, the way they used to in Toronto, only to leave a sense of destiny unfulfilled until Roberto Alomar drove years of frustration over the wall at Oakland–Alameda County Coliseum in Game 4 of the 1992 ALCS, setting the stage for the first World Series between the Blue Jays and the Atlanta Braves. Morris is still a man of opinions, but on this day in 2012 they are delivered with caveats. Phrases such as "I don't mean to toot my own horn," or, if you can believe it, "I don't want to say this and make it sound, you know, critical."

He is on the radio now, for heaven's sake, leaving a job with the Minnesota Twins broadcast team to become Jerry Howarth's partner in the Blue Jays radio booth. Yes, that Jack Morris, who once grabbed the microphone from Blue Jays broadcaster Buck Martinez during a clubhouse celebration and said, "I don't know what this guy thinks he knows about anything. He doesn't know what he's talking about."

"Weirdest thing I ever saw," Martinez said about Morris's outburst after the Jays clinched the division in Milwaukee in 1993. "We didn't talk for awhile, but when they got to the World Series he gave me a bottle of champagne and apologized."

Morris not wanting to toot his own horn is doubly surprising because the topic is Dave Stieb, a frequent duelling partner through the 1980s—when Morris always seemed to be one of the things preventing the Jays from having something tangible to show for doing things the right way. Stieb, meanwhile, appeared destined to put together a brilliant career—one that finally included a no-hitter—yet still leave with a strange sense of unfulfilled expectations, failing to stop people from wondering if there wasn't something more to him. It was Morris who tuned up for one of the most memorable pitching performances in post-season history, beating the Jays twice in the 1991 ALCS before throwing 10 shut-out innings in Game 7 of the World Series, a 1–0 win for Morris's Minnesota Twins. It was also Morris who frequently chided Stieb for being a "quitter," for allowing himself, at least in Morris's opinion, to be taken out of games once he had secured the victory.

Morris was many things, but more than anything else, he was resilient. He won 254 games in 18 big-league seasons, won three World Series rings and was a five-time All-Star. He was so good that in addition to putting up the most innings and wins of any pitcher in the '80s, he also *gave up* the most hits, earned runs and home runs during that same decade.

When Blue Jays general manager Pat Gillick signed the then 36-year-old free agent Morris on December 18, 1991, to a contract worth $10.85 million guaranteed over two years (with a third-year option for $5 million), it was seen in baseball circles as an admission by the Blue Jays that they were soft, lacking the royal jelly of truly excellent teams. Morris might have at one time viewed them in the same way, but by the time of his signing, he came to see in the Jays the same potential he'd once seen in Minnesota, the team he'd joined following the 1990 season, after 14 years with the Detroit Tigers. He'd seen the Twins sign designated hitter Chili Davis to go along with young arms such as Scott Erickson and Kevin Tapani. Later, it was Toronto that had the young arms, and they added Winfield. At the time of his signing, Morris said that he probably could have received more money from the Boston Red Sox, but Toronto was a better competitive environment.

"As good as Dave Stieb was . . . and I don't want to say this and make it sound critical [see!] . . . they needed one more guy to go with him," Morris said diplomatically, when asked what he believed had prevented the Blue Jays from seizing a title before 1992. "And even though they had a couple of guys who were pretty good, guys like Mike Flanagan and Jim Clancy, they really didn't have anybody who could push Stieb as that perennially dominant guy.

"You know, we had Erickson and Tapani in Minnesota and they were good arms. They had the same thing in Toronto: a younger David Wells, Todd Stottlemyre, Juan Guzman, Pat Hentgen. Like the Minnesota guys, I think they kind of looked at me as this old fart and wondered what I was about. I loved that role; I was, like, 'try to hang with me if you can.'"

The Blue Jays were more than up to the task through the first half of the season, putting together the best record at the halfway point of any team in club history. But Juan Guzman developed soreness in his right shoulder and Stieb, after undergoing off-season back surgery, was no longer the pitcher he once had been. By the end of August, the Blue Jays' lead over the Baltimore Orioles was down to one-and-a-half games, with Morris doing yeoman's work. That's when Gillick traded Jeff Kent, who would go on to have a Hall of Fame–calibre career as a second baseman, and outfield prospect Ryan Thompson to the New York Mets for David Cone.

"Funny," Morris remarked. "For years, Toronto didn't spend crazy money on free agents and then it was like—boom!—two years in a row they went out and got anybody they needed. And it wasn't like they just bought anybody, the way teams do now."

Cone wasn't a purchased player, but his acquisition suggested that Gillick and the Blue Jays brain trust believed they were on the clock—and in many ways they were. Indeed, a conventional wisdom had developed that president and chief executive officer Paul Beeston was one of the game's power brokers, and there was a sense that change was in the air. Howard Webster, one of the original team owners, passed away in 1990, and Labatt Breweries had purchased his stake in the team. Meanwhile, the network television contract with CBS Sports was set to expire after the 1993 season, and during the 1992 World Series, ESPN announced that it was exercising a $250 million option for 1994–95 to get out of its deal after 1993, paying a $13 million walk-away fee. As if this weren't enough, labour Armageddon seemed imminent for the 1994 season. Gillick and Beeston could be forgiven for thinking their window of opportunity might soon be closing.

Beeston, however, denies that this was ever a concern. "We," he intoned, "are not that fucking smart."

Gillick concurred. "The way I've always done things is, take a look at the particular team, try to figure out how big the window is, then try to piece in guys to take that particular group of players over the hump, whatever that hump is," Gillick said. "When I went to the Baltimore Orioles [1996–98], it was, 'Okay, we have a two-year window here—three at most—to get something done.' In Seattle [Gillick was with the Mariners from 2000–03] we had Alex Rodriguez and Jay Buhner and Edgar Martinez. There's a shelf life to that group, either because of age or because of contract. That's why we did so much adding in '91, '92 and '93."

IN CANADA, EH?

The Blue Jays, who went 96–66 during the regular season, went on to win the World Series in six games, and in the process continued to show some of the swagger they gained in exorcising their ALCS demons. But there were ample signs along the way that the stars may not be aligning, for those who worried about such things, starting with the upside-down Canadian flag mistakenly carried out before Game 2 at Atlanta–Fulton County Stadium by the US Marine Corps Color Guard, before which Canadian-born singer Tom Cochrane also botched the singing of "O Canada." It was a strange brew, this mix of imminent doom and national sensitivities, that would surface during a series of missed calls but originally manifested itself in a perceived lack of respect—Major League Baseball famously apologized to Canada during the telecast of the game—that was almost as annoying as the Atlanta fans' "tomahawk chop." Both Kelly Gruber and Alomar took great delight in mimicking the motion at key points in the games in Atlanta—Gruber's grinning gesture after sealing a Game 2 win with his catch of Terry Pendleton's pop-up was particularly brazen, as was Alomar's tomahawk chop in Game 3 as he ran home with the winning run.

But the Braves, managed by the familiar Bobby Cox, took Game 1 by a score of 3–1, in the process handing Morris his first loss in seven career World Series starts. Damon Berryhill's three-run homer proved to be the difference as Morris also saw a streak of 18 consecutive scoreless World Series innings come to an end. It had been a disquieting post-season for Morris, who had lost Game 1 of the ALCS to the Athletics despite pitching a complete game, and was saved from a loss in Game 4 only when the Blue Jays won in extra innings.

"Personally, I was just spent," said Morris, who tossed $240\frac{2}{3}$ innings for the Blue Jays during the regular season en route to becoming their first 20-game winner (he was 21–6). It was the third consecutive year in which Morris topped the 240-inning plateau. "Plus, Atlanta was good. They were in the Series back-to-back years. I guess that's one of the memories I have of that 1992 team that really sticks with me: I tried to carry them, and in the end I couldn't. But dang it if they didn't carry me instead."

That statement speaks to the evolution of the Blue Jays. Once a club that always came up short in the big game or down the stretch, it now had enough moxie, talent, confidence and self-awareness to carry one of the best pitchers of the decade. There was a singularity of purpose that came from the shrewd acquisitions of players who knew how to win, or players of remarkable pedigree and currency without a championship to show for it. That the Blue Jays were able to blend these personalities—some of whom had been bitter rivals—into a cohesive whole is in large measure due to their manager. But Joe Carter also maintains that the Blue Jays had by then developed a culture of self-policing that helped expedite the process.

"Why would there be issues?" Carter asked. "There's two things about these acquisitions. In the case of Jack, you were getting one of the best big-game pitchers out there. That meant he was pitching for you; it also meant you never had to face him. It was like getting two guys, in some ways."

That maturity and sense of self was revealed again in 1993, when Cito Gaston sounded out a group of players, including Carter, about adding old foe Rickey Henderson at the trade deadline. Carter remembers the reaction of the group as being "you're kidding us, right?

"We all looked at each other, and one of us said, 'You crazy, Cito? Get him here as quickly as you can,'" Carter said. "We all knew about Rickey. Yeah, he was thought of as a bit of a hot dog. But he could help us win."

The New York Yankees would later use the same approach during the Joe Torre years, when the team won four World Series. "Joe Torre would talk about that when he was managing the Yankees to all those titles," Buck Martinez said. "You have to bring that one guy in—in their case, a Wade Boggs or a Roger Clemens—that not only fulfills a need but brings in new blood so that everybody gets to remember how special it is to win a title."

The Blue Jays ran out another big acquisition in Game 2 in

29-year-old right-hander David Cone. Cone was 4–3 (2.55 ERA) with a WHIP of 1.283 and would re-sign as a free agent with his hometown Kansas City Royals after a post-season in which he started four games and had control problems. But as had been the case with Candy Maldonado in 1991, Gaston believed the deal added an intangible to the club (the 1992 Blue Jays came into the season still reeling from 1991's post-season debacle against the Twins).

"People always ask me which pitcher I was the most comfortable with, and it would have to be Cone," Gaston said. "David Cone on the mound with a lead was probably the most comfortable situation I've found myself in. It's a funny thing, but in 1991 I thought we needed another hitter to win. Thought it would be Maldonado. In 1992, I thought we'd need another pitcher and every now and then I'd think of Cone. Cone . . . it just seemed as if he wasn't really doing anything with the Mets. I never mentioned it to Pat or Paul, but it might have been one of those wishful thinking things."

In fact, Gaston said Cone made him more comfortable than any pitcher he'd ever managed until Roy Halladay. Cone led the majors with 261 strikeouts (214 in the National League, 47 with the Blue Jays), and while he didn't get the win in Game 2–pinch-hitter Ed Sprague's two-run homer off Braves closer Jeff Reardon capped a Toronto comeback–he did become the third pitcher since 1979 to get a hit in a World Series game, singling in Pat Borders as part of a two-hit game.

Sprague's homer would resonate throughout the Series. He would later tell reporters that veteran teammate Rance Mulliniks told him to look for a low fastball from Reardon, and that's precisely the pitch he sent over the wall in left field. It was the first pinch-hit homer to take a team from behind into the lead in a World Series game since Kirk Gibson hobbled around the bases in Game 1 of the 1988 Series after taking Dennis Eckersley deep. Gaston had also seen Sprague collect a pinch-hit single off of Eckersley with two out in a 4–3 loss in Game 1 of the ALCS—another right-hander on right-hander matchup, as was his at bat with Reardon. "Sprague all the way," is how Gaston described his decision.

Much as Winfield's bunt in Game 3 would be out of character for the Blue Jays (Gaston's team had just 26 sacrifice bunts in 162 regular-season games, tied with the New York Yankees for fewest in the AL, and Winfield had just one bunt during the regular season), so too was a decision to pinch-hit Derek Bell for Manny Lee in front of Sprague during Game 2. Sprague, after all, was pinch-hitting for pitcher Duane Ward. Bell, on the other hand, was pinch-hitting for a regular (a switch-hitter, at that), and Gaston used pinch-hitters all of 55 times during the season, the second-fewest in the AL ahead of only the Milwaukee Brewers (52).

SECOND-GUESSING GASTON

A reluctance to pinch-hit was just part of the reason Gaston's detractors spent the entirety of his managerial career decrying him for being too "laissez-faire," yet Gaston proved to have a deft hand in his World Series close-up. This was the Series in which Gaston responded to a question about "half-managing"–a reference to the fact that many people believed he ran his talented team on cruise control–by throwing out the phrase "half-reporting." Gaston wouldn't shed the feeling that he wasn't receiving his due even after the 1993 Series. It was in spring training a year later, when a reporter from Montreal asked him about Expos manager Felipe Alou's ability to shepherd the financially strapped team into a position of contention, that Gaston responded by saying, somewhat icily, that while he was impressed by

Alou's success, particularly as a man of colour, it was he who had the two World Series rings.

Throughout his career with the Blue Jays, Gaston was second-guessed to the point where he came to believe that race played a role, that he wasn't getting the slack or the credit that would normally come the way of a white manager. He had been Cox's hitting coach and was a close friend, and must have known that most observers were giving the managerial edge to 'Coxie,' but in the 1992 series it was Gaston's moves that seemed as prescient as Cox's seemed out of step. Game 3 offered a classic example: Winfield dropped a clean sacrifice to advance Roberto Alomar to third and Joe Carter to second ahead of Candy Maldonado's game-winning single. In comparison? Cox, who fumed in Game 4 when Game 1 hero Damon Berryhill popped up an attempted bunt with Brian Hunter on first and Ron Gant on third, kept left-handed hitters Deion Sanders and Sid Bream in the dugout in the eighth inning with the Braves losing 2–1 and runners in scoring position and two out, letting right-hander Jeff Blauser face Blue Jays righty Duane Ward. Blauser hit a ball directly to John Olerud, who was shading two feet off the first-base line. Cox would say later, with a sense of helplessness, that he didn't know why Olerud was there; truth is, one of Gaston's central philosophies was to guard the lines in late innings. It was no surprise to anybody who had watched the Blue Jays, who were now up 3–1 and on the verge of capturing their first World Series, at home no less.

But those old doubts remained. In addition to the whole flag flip, Game 2 saw umpire Mike Reilly's botched call on a play at the plate, when Alomar appeared to have scored on a wild pitch by John Smoltz. In Game 3, it was especially easy to wonder whether the baseball gods had it in for the Blue Jays when umpire Bob Davidson cost the team a triple play: Devon White crashed into the wall to catch David Justice's liner to centre, then fired the ball back to the infield. Gruber tagged Deion Sanders on the heel as he chased him back toward second base, but Davidson called Sanders safe. Terry Pendleton had already been called out for passing Sanders, but it was clearly a triple play, and to Davidson's credit, he later acknowledged the error.

White's catch, in the fourth inning of a game in which neither team had threatened to score, immediately recalled Willie Mays' famous over-the-shoulder grab off Vic Wertz in the 1954 World Series. As White described the play later, he had been shading the left-handed hitting Justice to the right. He had to take his eye off the ball, establish the warning track and then time his jump. "Then I have to get the ball back in so Sanders doesn't have time to tag," he said. White admitted he'd seen replays of Mays' catch, but tried to downplay his effort slightly before acknowledging he had, in fact, sneaked more than one look at the replay of his own catch on the SkyDome's Jumbotron scoreboard. "Couldn't take my eyes off it," he said.

Later, a Gruber error on a liner off the bat of Otis Nixon in the eighth inning set in motion a chain of events that would see the Braves take a 2–1 lead. But Gruber atoned for his mistake, leading off the bottom of the eighth by slugging a game-tying homer off Steve Avery, and suddenly the baseball gods seemed to be favouring the Canadian team—but not before playing around with some irony in Game 5, when Lonnie Smith slugged a grand slam off of Jack Morris in a 7–2 win, one year after his own costly base-running error contributed to a 1–0 Braves loss to Morris and the Minnesota Twins in Game 7 of that season's World Series.

The Braves signalled their intentions early, when Terry Pendleton doubled in the first run of the game, giving Atlanta its first extra-base hit in the series from their third, fourth or fifth hitters. Justice, their cleanup hitter, homered in the fourth for his first hit, and then Smith effectively ended the game. Gaston came out to the mound to remove Morris to a chorus of boos, and was faced with post-game questions about whether his trademark loyalty had in fact cost the Blue Jays one of the biggest games in franchise history.

But in Game 6, back in Atlanta, it was another set of Gaston's personnel decisions that made the difference. With the designated hitter not in play in the National League park, Cito decided he needed Carter's right-handed bat in the lineup against left-hander Steve Avery. That meant Carter was at first while John Olerud sat, and Candy Maldonado and Dave Winfield were manning the outfield corners.

It was Winfield's two-run double with two out in the 11th that promised to deliver the first World Series to a team based outside of the US. With veteran left-hander Charlie Leibrandt on the mound instead of the shaky Reardon, the righty-swinging Winfield pulled a 3–2 pitch down the left-field line, just as Gaston predicted aloud in the Blue Jays dugout. Remember how Cox had been surprised, in Game 4, to see Olerud guarding the line? Gaston knew that type of thinking was foreign to Cox and Jimy Williams, the Braves' third-base coach and the man Gaston had replaced as Blue Jays manager. He had an idea where Winfield's first post-season extra-base hit, at the age of 41, was going to go—telling the dugout before the swing that Winfield would find some love down the line.

The Blue Jays finally had a chance to put the game away in the bottom of the 11th, when Gaston brought in Mike Timlin, who turned around the switch-hitting Otis Nixon. Nixon, who had been rescued from a life of booze and drugs in part because of the confidence the Montreal Expos had shown in him in the late '80s, was a much weaker hitter from the left side of the plate, by some 80 percentage points. But he was a few steps closer to first base, which in Joe Carter's mind raised the very real possibility of a bunt, something he relayed to Timlin (while he was simultaneously trying to erase memories of Bill Buckner's famous error in Game 6 of the 1986 World Series). Nixon's bunt was fielded cleanly by Timlin–Nixon would say later that six inches more and he would have beaten it out–and Major League Baseball awoke the next morning with a Canadian World Series champion.

Joe Carter's loping, leaping run around the bases after homering to win Game 6 of the 1993 World Series gave the franchise its primary Kodak moment. But the sight of Carter–thrusting both arms in the air and jumping as he ran toward Timlin following that final out of 1992's Game 6–is for many Blue Jays fans almost its equal.

Barring the success of the Toronto Argonauts, it had been a lean period for Toronto sports. The Maple Leafs hadn't won a Stanley Cup since 1967, and the Blue Jays had flirted with a title for so long that they had earned their "Blow Jays" moniker. The city was primed for a parade.

Meanwhile, "Stand Pat" (as Gillick had once been known) disappeared for good when he had traded for Roberto Alomar and Joe Carter and filled in the gaps with other pieces, and he would aggressively turn over the roster in time for a title defence in 1993, after being criticized so often just a couple of seasons earlier for being reluctant to make moves. "When we got Candy Maldonado," Cito Gaston remembers, "I walked up to Beeston and said, 'Now, we'll win.'" With the acquistion of Alomar and Carter, the game of baseball changed in Toronto and, ultimately, in Canada, forever. But as high as the standard seemed following the 1992 Series, Toronto hadn't seen anything yet. The 1992 World Series ended with Joe Carter touching first base ahead of Otis Nixon. Carter's bat—not his glove—would end the 1993 season as well, in a manner none of us will ever forget.

TOUCH 'EM ALL

WINNING THE 1992 WORLD SERIES WAS, IN THE words of Roberto Alomar, "like when you graduate from college. That's what I felt like. I felt like I had graduated from the game of baseball."

So what, then, would it be like to win the 1993 World Series? To win back-to-back championships? It hadn't happened all that often in baseball since the 1960s. The Oakland Athletics won three consecutive World Series from 1972 to 1974, the Cincinnati Reds won in 1975–76 and the New York Yankees won back-to-back in 1961–62 and 1977–78, before winning three straight a long twenty years later, from 1998 to 2000. Sometimes, economics played a role. When the Florida Marlins won their first World Series in 1997, the club was stripped bare the next season because of salary concerns, leaving one of its players, Moises Alou, to muse about how not being able to rehash the merry times at spring training took some of the lustre out of being world champions.

But when Pat Gillick and the Blue Jays brain trust began the process of overhauling the 1992 world champions, the focus was partly on economics—Gillick wanted to keep the payroll at $48 million—and partly on replicating the dynamics that had brought the team its first world title. Dave Winfield, Tom Henke, David Cone, Kelly Gruber, Jimmy Key and Candy Maldonado all left the fold. Gillick didn't waste time, telling several of the players between the final out of Game 6 and the World Series parade. "Face to face," he said. "Like we did everything."

Joe Carter was re-signed to a contract of four years and $25 million, of which just three years were guaranteed. Dave Stewart was signed and so too was Paul Molitor, who agreed to a three-year, $13 million deal.

"It's hard to keep the same incentive level of play over two years," said Gillick. "Sure, salary reasons were behind some of the decisions. But part of it was we needed to change the mix too. Ideally, what you want to find are guys who know how to win, but just haven't had the chance to get there. A guy like Molitor."

Cito Gaston went into spring training with a dozen changes to the roster, and a sense very early on that he had a different team than the one in 1992. "We had just about everything on that '92 team," said Gaston. Added Duane Ward, who would have 45 saves in 1993 after the departure of Tom Henke, "That 1992 team was the type of team that you just knew would withstand any type of lull, that even if you lost a couple of games in a row it was going to end."

WELCOME TO THE WAMCO ERA

The 1993 team, in comparison, was an offensive machine. It was WAMCO: White, Alomar, Molitor, Carter and Olerud at the top of the lineup—with Olerud, Molitor and Alomar finishing one, two, three in the batting race after Alomar pipped Kenny Lofton on the final day of the regular season. "We just flat outscored people," said Gaston.

Pat Hentgen, who spent 1992 in a bullpen that included David Wells, moved into the starting rotation in 1993, and at the age of 24 went 19–9 with an ERA of 3.87. He remembered the team as being very confident offensively. "People talk about teams passing the baton, believing that if they don't do it the next guy will," Hentgen said. "That's what that team did. Us Blue Jays pitchers would feel sorry for the opposition."

So it was in many ways a new team that showed up in Dunedin, Florida, for spring training. Morris and Stewart were more often than not pitching on guile as much as stuff, yet while the Blue Jays averaged the second-most runs in the American League and tied for the league lead in team batting, they didn't pitch all that poorly either. Although they were 10th in WHIP they were fifth in earned run average.

Yet as the season went on, Alomar saw some similarities with the 1992 Blue Jays. They were found in the guts of the team.

"Both of the teams had one thing in mind: winning," said Alomar. "We didn't have many egos. If somebody didn't play hard every day, somebody would let you know. If you weren't in the dugout cheering your teammates, somebody would let you know. Both of those teams were the same in the dugout. We'd be watching for little things to help us win. If we could steal pitches, we would. We'd look for anything to help us win.

"When I played for the Baltimore Orioles, I played with one of the smartest guys in the game: Cal Ripken. It was all baseball, and that's what it was like with the Blue Jays. We'd stay late. We'd talk baseball. It was a really united group."

Molitor was a different cat than Winfield, but just as Winfield's cocksure nature was exactly what the Blue Jays needed to finally vanquish their post-season ghosts in 1992, Molitor's steadiness was form-fitted to a group that by now had all the identity it needed. It had become a professional club, a group of hitters who talked baseball and self-policed. In the clubhouse, Molitor was very much, in Alomar's words, "the guy to follow." And woe to any pitcher in the bullpen who was caught flicking sunflower seeds or cutting up around Duane Ward, who would immediately get in his face and ask him who was up, who was on deck and what pitches the hitter liked.

The favoured Blue Jays, who'd finished 95–67 and seven games in front of the New York Yankees to win their fifth American League East title (their fourth in five years) beat the Chicago White Sox in six games in the ALCS to advance to the World Series, and Gaston's critics were again left to mull over how his calm, trusting approach contrasted with that of the opposing manager. Gaston—who as manager of the AL All-Star team for the Midsummer Classic in Baltimore had four Blue Jays (Alomar, Molitor, Carter and Olerud) in the first five spots of his batting order and took seven Jays with him—used the same nine players in every inning of every game. White Sox manager Gene Lamont, meanwhile, was blindsided by grumbling from George Bell and Bo Jackson, who were upset by their manager's use of their talents.

The Blue Jays again had the highest payroll in the majors in 1993, and were considered to be the measuring stick for franchises (the mere thought must shock the new generation of Blue Jays fans), while the National League champion Phillies, bless them, were a scruffy, boozing, tobacco-chewing group of grinders. They led their league with 665 walks and 877 runs despite the fact home run leaders Darren Daulton and Pete Incaviglia hit just 24 each. Juan Guzman, the Blue Jays' starter in Game 1 of the World Series, said they looked like truck drivers.

Philadelphia's Terry Mulholland described himself and his teammates as being "kind of like that old, chewed-up piece of gum that's laying on the ground. Nobody notices it until they step on it. Then they try to pull us off the sole of their shoes, and before they know it, we're all over that shoe, and now you've got a ruined pair of wingtips."

The Phillies pulled off the same worst-to-first trick in the National League East that the 1991 Atlanta Braves managed in the NL West. Among the teams that pressed the Phillies to the end were Felipe Alou's Montreal Expos, who finished three games back, signalling the force they'd be in 1994. The Phillies were personified by centre fielder Lenny "Nails" Dykstra, beer-bellied first baseman John Kruk—famously quoted as telling a female fan that "I ain't an athlete, lady, I'm a ballplayer"—and closer Mitch

"Wild Thing" Williams, who went 2–0 in the Phillies' six-game win over the Braves in the NL Championship Series, with both decisions coming in blown saves. His response to the worry of Phillies fans was to tell his critics that they could go "piss up a rope."

A MESSY START

A series that would be best remembered for Joe Carter's walk-off home run began with a promised pitching gem that turned into a mess. Game 1 of the 1993 Fall Classic was something less than advertised. Instead of a matchup between staff aces Curt Schilling of the Phillies and Guzman of the Blue Jays, the 8–5 Blue Jays win was a 21-hit affair at the SkyDome in which the home team committed three of the game's four errors. The Phillies mashed right-handed pitching during the regular season and in Guzman, Dave Stewart, Pat Hentgen and Todd Stottlemyre they would see four right-handed starters. The Blue Jays, conversely, had slightly more difficulty with left-handed pitchers, and the Phillies had both Mulholland and veteran Danny Jackson.

But Game 1 came down to the Blue Jays' better bullpen (Al Leiter—who said he pretended it was a spring training game against a familiar foe, since the clubs trained within minutes of each other—tossed 2⅔ innings of sterling relief) and Gold Glove defence by Alomar. He used every inch of his frame to snag a liner off the bat of Dykstra and then knocked down a bouncer from Mariano Duncan with two out, two on and the score tied 4–4 in the sixth inning that prevented Kevin Stocker from scoring. Kruk struck out with the bases loaded to end the threat and John Olerud homered off Schilling in the bottom of the sixth to give the Blue Jays a lead they'd never relinquish.

The Phillies left 11 men on base, despite holding the lead on three separate occasions. But they left Toronto with a split of the first two games, following a 6–4 win in Game 2 in which Jim Eisenreich–who'd retired from the game between 1984–87 due to disabling Tourette Syndrome, but was viewed as just another quirky guy in a quirky clubhouse–slammed a three-run homer off Stewart. It was an oddly unprofessional outing from the Blue Jays, which saw future Hall of Famer and stolen base king Rickey Henderson thrown out stealing second in the first inning and Alomar getting caught off second with the tying run at home plate in the eighth. Vintage Gaston style was on display after the game, when he simply shrugged and said that Alomar, whom he referred to as a low-maintenance ballplayer, normally didn't do that. No muss. No fuss.

Gaston faced a familiar dilemma with the series heading to Veterans Stadium for Games 3, 4 and 5. The designated hitter would not be in effect, as was the case the year before in Atlanta when Gaston put Dave Winfield in the outfield and Joe Carter at first base–and had things work out swimmingly. This time, the quandary was what to do about Molitor, whom general manager Pat Gillick referred to as the best offensive player in the American League in the previous 15 years. Gaston had already told reporters that the only way Molitor would ever play in the outfield would be if everybody else had died. Since that hadn't happened, Olerud would be the odd man out once again, his American League–leading .363 batting average shunted aside in favour of Molitor, whose right-handed bat figured to play even better against Danny Jackson, the Phillies' lefty starter. Molitor's .332 average wasn't all that bad either–second in the league, in fact, to Olerud.

Molitor, who would go on to win the Most Valuable Player Award in the series, tripled in a pair of first-inning runs and homered during the third in a 10–3 Blue Jays win, handling with aplomb the defensive responsibilities incumbent on a first baseman.

Gaston told everybody that come Game 4, with the right-hander Tommy Greene back on the mound, Olerud would be at first base once again. Conventional wisdom would have Molitor on the bench, since Gaston seemed to want to stay with his regular third baseman, Ed Sprague, and Molitor was three years and a wrecked shoulder past his previous stint at third. But Gaston called Molitor into his office before Game 4 to suss out his thoughts about playing the hot corner, and when the lineup card went up, Molitor was in the position he had played for a grand total of two games since starting 112 games at third for the 1989 Milwaukee Brewers. Although Molitor had taken ground balls at third, true professional that he was, he did not press the issue until Gaston gave him the opening. Molitor would tell reporters that his message to Gaston was simple: don't make your decision based on concerns about my health or putting me in a position where you're asking me to do too much.

Game 4 was a four-hour-and-fourteen-minute affair, won 15–14 by the Blue Jays with the teams combining for 32 hits. The Phillies twice saw five-run leads evaporate, including during a six-run Blue Jays eighth inning in which Molitor smoked a double down the third-base line that his counterpart, Dave Hollins, couldn't handle. That brought in a run, making the score 14–10. One pitch later, Tony Fernandez—the shortstop who had been traded to San Diego as part of the Carter/Alomar deal and who hit .306 after the Blue Jays reacquired him in June from the New York Mets—singled in the 11th run on the first pitch from closer Mitch Williams. Cue the comeback, with Blue Jays closer Duane Ward retiring all four men he faced during the eighth to restore some order and pick up the save. Phillies reliever Larry Andersen later said it was "like taking a patient off life-support."

SCHILLING RISING

It was a well-pitched, 2–0 win for the Phillies in Game 5 that sent the series back to Toronto for Game 6, with the Blue Jays leading 3–2 and looking to celebrate a World Series win on Canadian soil. In Game 5, Schilling, also the Game 1 starter for the Phillies, shut out the Blue Jays in a complete-game five-hitter, marking only the second time in either the regular season or the playoffs that the Blue Jays had been blanked (Fernando Valenzuela, then with the Baltimore Orioles, held them to six hits in a 6–0 Orioles win on June 30). Schilling was aided by three double plays and helped his own cause when he knocked down a ball hit hard back up the box by Rickey Henderson, catching pinch-runner Willie Canate in a run-down between third and home plate. Juan Guzman, who started for the Blue Jays, lost for the first time since June 20, although he was hardly a push-over–allowing only five hits over seven innings.

As it turned out, the victory had longer-term implications for Schilling than for anyone else. Although the Blue Jays would go on to win the Series, Schilling used his performance in Game 5 as a springboard to a reputation as one of the best clutch pitchers of his generation. Indeed, you could make the argument that Schilling inherited Jack Morris's crown as a dominant post-season performer, going 10–1 (2.12) in the playoffs through the rest of his career, sharing Most Valuable Player honours with teammate Randy Johnson when the Arizona Diamondbacks beat the New York Yankees in the 2001 World Series, and then going on to pitch one of the most memorable games in baseball history for Boston. Schilling won Game 6 of the 2004 AL Championship Series against the New York Yankees with blood seeping through his sock, the result of an as-yet-unhealed scar from surgery to stabilize the tendon sheath in his right ankle. The Red Sox also won Game 7, becoming the first team in baseball history to come back from a 3–0 deficit to win a best-of-seven series. Schilling also pitched in the Red Sox's World Series win over the St. Louis Cardinals—again with blood seeping through his sock—as the Red Sox won their first World Series in 86 years.

CUE CARTER

In Toronto, meanwhile, the city announced plans for a parade to honour the Blue Jays only to see the team lose Game 5 and head back home for Game 6. To some this seemed like an unnecessary jinx, but in the end the gods smiled on the city and its team.

Things started well enough, with Molitor's run-scoring triple, an Alomar single and a Carter sacrifice fly staking the Blue Jays to a 3–0 lead. Molitor homered to make the score 5–1 in the fifth, but the Phillies scored five runs in the seventh inning to go up 6–5, three of those runs coming on Lenny Dykstra's homer off Dave Stewart, who had spent the day before his start honouring a commitment to Toronto's Harbour Light Centre by serving Thanksgiving dinner to the homeless.

Cue Mitch Williams—and Carter.

After a scoreless eighth, the Phillies brought on the "Wild Thing," as Williams was known, and the Phillies closer walked Rickey Henderson to open the inning. That put Williams in a predicament, as Henderson was on the way to becoming the most accomplished base-stealer of all time. Williams elected to use a "slide-step" delivery, which quickened his time to the plate but also shaved some velocity from his fastball. Williams would later say he'd never used the slide-step before—odd, considering the fact that the National League was considered more of a base-stealing league than the American League—and with one out he seemed to show signs of his inexperience, yielding a single to Molitor. That brought Carter to the plate, and with the count 2–2 he lined a game-winning homer into the auxiliary press box in SkyDome's left field. It was the second World Series–winning homer in baseball history—Bill Mazeroski broke open a 9–9 tie with a ninth-inning homer off the New York Yankees' Ralph Terry to win the 1960 World Series for the Pittsburgh Pirates—but the first struck by a player whose team was losing at the time.

In contrast to the animosity that permeated Roberto Alomar's homer off Oakland's Dennis Eckersley in the 1992 ALCS, the sequence of events surrounding Carter's homer was purely baseball business. It started with the presence of Henderson on second base. Henderson didn't hit much after the Blue Jays acquired him in a trade with the Athletics for pitching prospect Steve Karsay and Jose Herrera, putting up an OPS of .675 while hitting .215 with four homers, three doubles, 12 RBIs and 22 stolen bases in 44 games; he was merely a contributor during the Blue Jays' run through the post-season. But with Henderson on second and one out, the Phillies and Williams were concerned that he might steal third, which would have enabled a sacrifice fly from Carter to bring him in. Carter already had three sacrifice flies in the series.

Phillies manager Jim Fregosi was on solid ground in putting Williams out on the mound, despite his meltdown in Game 4. Williams was his closer; he had 43 saves and allowed all of three homers during the regular season. Wildness isn't always manifested in baseball in a quantitative manner; it's not as much the number of wild pitches a pitcher throws as it is the location of the pitches. Williams had thrown a nasty 2–1 slider that Carter swung at hopelessly for strike two. But there was nothing foul about his next swing.

"What I remember most about the swing is that I didn't hook it foul," Carter said. "It's what I think of every time I see it on TV— 99.99% of the time, I hook that pitch foul into the third-base dugout, and had I not been looking for a breaking ball, that's probably what would have happened."

Williams had thrown a breaking ball on the previous pitch, and as Carter stepped back into the box, he instinctively said to himself, "Look for the slider, again." It was something Bobby Bonds, his hitting coach with the Cleveland Indians, had told him during a conversation around the batting cage. "Bobby would say, 'Look for the slider. If you're thinking off-speed pitch, it's easier to react to the fastball than it is the other way around.' I've always had that philosophy. It stayed with me."

And it paid off handsomely for Carter, his teammates, a franchise and a country. Years later, Carter would ask Williams why he hadn't thrown him another breaking pitch. "I told him, 'Man, you saw my swing on that pitch before. Why didn't you go back to it?' He told me that in his mind, he wanted to get me out with a fastball high and away. He said, 'I didn't even remember your swing on the 2–1 pitch. All I remember is that I had two strikes with you . . . and I was going to go with the game plan. I was going to go with the scouting report.'"

Carter paused. "I've always believed a scouting report was there to give you an idea what to do in a situation if you don't have an idea. People change, even during the course of the game. That's why when people say it's a game of adjustments; it really is just that."

Williams had become something of a cartoon character throughout the Series, his wildness a point of reference in a good-natured clubhouse. Curt Schilling showed up in the interview room at Veterans Stadium before Game 6 wearing a button that read "I survived watching Mitch pitch in the 1993 World Series," and Williams himself regaled reporters with stories, including the time in 1987 when the Texas Rangers suggested he see a hypnotist. "I saw him three times, then he went to see a psychiatrist," Williams said. Given tapes to help him hypnotize himself, Williams said he used them as an excuse to grab a nap, but then eventually gave in and used the tapes for three months.

Carter and Williams had been acquaintances in the way of opposing players during their career—a nod of encouragement or quick "hey" as they went about their daily business when their teams faced each other. Now, in Carter's words, they have "kind of become tied at the hip." They haven't yet started doing joint autograph sessions or things of that nature—Mookie Wilson of the New York Mets and Bill Buckner of the Boston Red Sox have started to cash in on their roles in Buckner's infamous 1986 World Series Game 6 fielding error—but they do attend events together. Carter went on to broadcast after his career ended—he'd work on Blue Jays telecasts when Jim Fregosi was managing the Blue Jays, which was a bit of a trip—and Williams attended Carter's annual charity golf tournament in Toronto in 2012. "We did a thing for ESPN, a bowling thing, in 1998," Carter said, laughing. "Mitch had a bowling alley some place around Philly. Maybe it's one of those things where we feel that the longer we wait, the more the demand will be."

During that 2012 trip to take part in Carter's event, Williams found himself on the putting green before going out on the course. He looked up to see Carter, Joe Carter Sr. (the player's father) and Jordan, Joe Jr.'s son.

Without missing a beat, Williams looked at his old adversary, shook his head, and said, "Great. Now everybody in Toronto looks like Joe Carter."

THE NEST
EMPTIES

THIS MUCH WE KNOW ABOUT THE TWO SEASONS IN which Roger Clemens pitched with the Toronto Blue Jays: statistically, they provided some of the most dominant pitching in the history of Major League Baseball. Clemens won pitching's version of the Triple Crown in both 1997 and 1998 (wins, strikeouts and earned runs) en route to winning back-to-back Cy Young awards as the most outstanding pitcher in the American League.

During those two seasons, a young pitcher named Roy Halladay moved quietly through the clubhouse during spring training. The former first-round draft pick was first called up to the majors in late 1998, and would eventually turn into the standard against which all future Blue Jays pitchers would be judged, but back then he was just a big kid from Colorado with a good fastball and not much of an idea. Clemens was always larger than life, and Halladay would soon turn into the same type of pitcher and personality, someone around whom others walked as if on eggshells. Interestingly, it wasn't Clemens who caught Halladay's eye back then, but another right-handed pitcher: Pat Hentgen.

"Roger is a different breed," Halladay said on June 9, 2003, as he sat in the visitors' clubhouse in Cincinnati watching on television as Clemens, in the uniform of the New York Yankees, continued pursuing 300 career wins in an interleague game against the Chicago Cubs. "For me, Hentgen was the guy who taught me what it means to go out and do your job each time out," Halladay said. "With Roger, you don't see a lot of the stuff he does and the work he puts in because it's never really around the field. He likes to do a lot of the stuff away from the field, and I'm the type of person who likes to do their work here [in the clubhouse]. I like being around the guys."

DARK DAYS

The acquisition of Clemens by the Blue Jays was a last-gasp ploy to revive the flickering fires of a franchise that had fallen out of public favour in a dramatic hurry. "We were surprised how quickly it turned," said Paul Beeston. After the 1993 World Series win came the interruption of the 1994 players strike, and then a very long dry spell. The Blue Jays wouldn't finish above third place in the American League East until 2006. They would run through managers, see attendance tumble into the bottom third of the major league table, and go through two ownership changes. Clemens was merely the first of many attempts to stop the bleeding. It failed. Despite Clemens' performance, the Blue Jays spiralled into last place in the American League East in 1997 and finished 26 games back in 1998. Neither was Clemens a boon to attendance: the average crowd at the SkyDome in 1997 was 31,967—a slight uptick from 1996's average of 31,600—while in 1998 that average fell to 30,300, marking the last time the Blue Jays would average more than 30,000 fans per game.

Beeston negotiated the contract with Clemens' agents, Randal and Alan Hendricks, and signed Clemens to a four-year, $31.1 million deal after the 1996 season, by which time Clemens had tired of a tense, angst-ridden relationship with the Boston Red Sox and general manager Dan Duquette. Clemens was also promised an out clause that allowed him to request a trade after any season and gave him no-trade protection. It made sense in some ways that the Blue Jays felt they had a shot; the Hendricks brothers had a good relationship with the team, representing both George Bell and Al Leiter, and the Blue Jays still had enough of a family feel for Beeston to give Clemens both the hard and soft sell—painting the organization as a place where Clemens and his kids could be comfortable.

This was the end of the Blue Jays' benevolent original ownership group that had had its roots in the Canadian brewing and banking industry. A Belgian-based brewery would take over and run the team, and a strange sort of rot started to set in around the franchise, which was now drawing only 2.5 million fans per season, down from more than four million in the team's heyday.

Major League Baseball's steroid era tainted all of the game's 30 teams. When former senator George Mitchell, who had once served as Senate Majority Leader, released the findings of a 21-month investigation into the use of anabolic steroids and human growth hormone (HGH) in Major League Baseball (*Report to the Commissioner of Baseball of an Independent Investigation Into the Illegal Use of Steroids and Other Performance Enhancing Substances by Players in Major League Baseball*) no fewer than 89 different players were named as having used performance enhancing drugs (PEDs). The 490-page report deserves to be taken for what it was. A long-time friend of baseball's power brokers and head of a so-called Blue Ribbon Panel that reported on the game's economics in 2000, Mitchell was also a director of the Boston Red Sox during the time he compiled the report. Yet it was hardly a whitewash, and gave commissioner Bud Selig a blueprint for co-operation with the Major League Baseball Players Association as the sport took nascent steps toward drug testing.

Two of the names mentioned most often in the Mitchell Report were Clemens and Brian McNamee, a personal trainer to Clemens and New York Yankees teammates Andy Pettitte and Chuck Knoblauch. McNamee would figure prominently in the four-year legal odyssey that ultimately saw Clemens found not guilty, on June 18, 2012, of lying to Congress about his use of steroids and human growth hormone. The US Justice Department based much of its case on testimony from McNamee (in August 2012, McNamee filed a defamation suit against Clemens in a federal court in New York), and that brought the Blue Jays right into the middle of the scandal. The two men had met in Toronto when a former assistant general manager of the Blue Jays, Tim McCleary, hired McNamee to be a bullpen catcher and conditioning coach. Like McNamee, a former New York City police officer, McCleary was an alumnus of St. John's University and a native of Queens, New York. McCleary worked as a spokesman for the American League in the early 1990s before joining the Yankees, and he was the conduit through which McNamee entered the game's bloodstream, working as a bullpen catcher with the Yankees before joining the Blue Jays in 1998.

Baseball—players, owners, GMs, fans and media—for the most part turned a blind eye to the use of PEDs in the game. That players were getting much bigger was obvious: in a 2002 *Sports Illustrated* cover story on Ken Caminiti, published a little more than two years before he would die of a drug overdose, the former slugger claimed he'd used steroids in 1996 when he won the National League's Most Valuable Player Award with the San Diego Padres. Mark McGwire and Sammy Sosa were credited with helping baseball regain a place of prominence on the professional sports landscape when they waged a head-to-head battle for the 1998 home run title and pursuit of Roger Maris's single-season home run record: McGwire won with 70 homers (a figure that stood until Barry Bonds ripped 73 three years later), and it was only during an appearance in front of a congressional subcommittee in 2005 that the significance of a mid-summer admission in 1998 that he'd used androstenedione—a protein supplement that produced testosterone—became apparent. Also in 2005, Jose Canseco's book *Juiced: Wild Times, Rampant 'Roids, Smash Hits and How Baseball Got Big* detailed the use of PEDs by himself and other players through the '90s. Among Canseco's stops during that time? Toronto.

In an interview with Toronto's Southam News in August 1998, McNamee discussed androstenedione, saying, "They're all testosterone precursors. I don't recommend it, but guys take it. I take it. I think it works." As author Tom Maloney related in the article, Canseco overheard the interview and piped up, "C'mon, they're steroids."

People around the Blue Jays saw the same thing everybody else saw: players were working out like fiends, not just getting bigger biceps, hitting more homers farther and throwing more pitches faster, but also seeing cap sizes increase—a sign of bone growth spurred by HGH use. Canseco's book detailed the taking of substances in clubhouse washrooms, but as anybody who's spent any time in a clubhouse can tell you, there is no shortage of places off-limits to prying eyes. Absent a testing program, hard evidence was difficult to come by.

"McNamee was the kind of guy who wasn't afraid to get into a player's face, who'd say, 'If you've already run a mile, good. Let's go for two more miles,'" Gord Ash, then the Blue Jays' general manager, said. "We never had any player complaints about him like we'd had with some of our other [strength and conditioning people] who came before him. It was clear he was developing a very personal relationship with Roger, but that seemed natural because Roger liked to work and [McNamee] liked to push people."

Perhaps if Clemens had been a closer things might have been different for the team. When many of the central characters look back at the Blue Jays' descent after 1993, the health of closer Duane Ward is often the first item mentioned. Ward, who saved 45 games in the 1993 World Series season and had 12 saves, a 1.95 earned run average and 1.135 WHIP in 1992, came up lame in 1994 and the Blue Jays never recovered. "We got off to a pretty good start," said Gaston. "I tried everybody under the sun out of the bullpen, including Todd [Stottlemyre]. Todd is not afraid to do anything, but he couldn't close out games for us. We just didn't have a closer. Ward had done that for us for a long time.

"You know what? I guess that's when I started to think that things were changing, because the thing is, it just didn't seem like we tried to get anybody. I don't know that, but it seems like it. In 1985, we had Bill Caudill here, and when he didn't work out we went out and got Henke. This time, nothing happened."

In some ways, the downfall was to be expected. By 1995, Roberto Alomar was a year away from free agency, as was Devon White, and John Olerud wasn't hitting. Pat Gillick had left. When Gord Ash traded David Cone to the New York Yankees on July 28, the signal was unmistakable. The Blue Jays were 36–47 and on their way to a 56–88 finish. Alomar was so upset with the trade that he sat out a game, which along with sitting out the final weekend of the regular season, ostensibly because of a bad back (and, perhaps, to protect a .300 average), created a fissure between Alomar and the team that took years to mend.

"That for me was the turning point," said Buck Martinez, who had left his catching duties behind and was then serving as the club broadcaster. "I walked into the clubhouse and was pissed. I asked him, 'What are you doing?' He said, 'I think we can win this thing, and we traded Cone, and I don't know why we did it.' I told him that it wasn't an Alomar move, that it wasn't how his father would want him to represent the name. Things just started to unravel after that."

But it was Ward's injury that many close to the team believe exacerbated the downfall. Ward was, in the words of Joe Carter, probably the most valuable player of the back-to-back World Series teams. Used mostly as Tom Henke's set-up man in 1992 before getting the closer's job in 1993, he was 9–7 in those two seasons with an earned run average of 2.03, striking out 200 and walking 64 in 173 innings pitched. In the Blue Jays' two World Series appearances, he allowed one earned run in eight innings, going 3–0 with two saves while striking out 13 and walking just one.

"Lots of closers have one pitch," said Carter. "It becomes their signature. Wardo could throw 95 or 96 miles per hour with a curveball that everybody kept calling a splitter. I remember having a long discussion with Bo Jackson about it one time. He wouldn't believe me.

"Automatic. Duane Ward was automatic," Carter continued. "And when he got hurt—it was like the pieces started falling apart."

All these years later, nobody seems to know how it happened. Ward believes he remembers when the shoulder injury occurred: in a close game against the New York Yankees in 1993, Ward got up to "do his thing" and suddenly found that he couldn't throw the ball. Three cortisone shots and a week off later, he was back to gut out the remainder of the season with what turned out to be a two-inch tear in his shoulder. When December rolled around, Ward told the Blue Jays he was having trouble lifting his arm.

"The last pitch Wardo threw was 93 miles per hour," Gillick said. "I know, because I still have it on videotape."

Pat Hentgen cannot talk enough about the impact of Ward's injury on the franchise. "He was the horse. He had become our foundation," Hentgen said. "I don't think we realized even when we were winning how much he solidified the bullpen, and how important he was in maintaining everybody else's roles."

Ward said it still gives him an odd feeling when he hears people talk about his acquisition and departure as being franchise-altering moments. But he appreciates it, and he wonders to this day if he shouldn't have handled the injury differently. Thing is, Ward had known Dr. James Andrews, the consulting specialist, since he was an 18-year-old draft pick for Atlanta and Andrews was the Braves' team doctor. Andrews counselled against surgery, telling Ward that even from his first checkup, his shoulder had always been clean. "He told me that he didn't want to go in there," said Ward. "So I couldn't really rehabilitate or anything. Looking back now, I wish we'd had the surgery sooner. Done it immediately after the Series, maybe."

Ward's reluctance was representative of the fact that for many of the returning Blue Jays, 1994 looked like another World Series possibility. "We all thought we were going to do it again," said Hentgen.

THE LAST STRAW

It has become an article of faith that the 1994 player's strike killed baseball in Montreal. That is true only if you believe that a successful or even exciting conclusion to the season would have smoked out the political and corporate champion that the team never had in the days following Charles Bronfman's sale to Claude Brochu, that the goodwill would have led to the brush fire becoming something larger and, ultimately, to the building of a new stadium that was necessary for the franchise's long-term survival.

But Paul Beeston believes the impact on the Toronto marketplace was at least as significant because it changed the discussion surrounding the Blue Jays. Those daily storylines that are the very fabric of baseball dialogue were suddenly absent. This hitter's slump or that pitcher's in-season refinement were no longer in the public consciousness—and never mind the result from the previous night's game. At the core of baseball's resonance with its fans is the day-to-day nature of the game. Baseball doesn't do off-days; a slump is a slump and a streak is a streak. It explains why Cal Ripken Jr.'s breaking of Lou Gehrig's consecutive-games streak struck a chord with so many baseball fans. It reinforced the day-to-day reality of the game, the idea that, for all the big money and fame, the really good ones still had to punch the clock every day.

Howard Starkman, the Blue Jays' long-time public relations director, believes another overlooked aspect of the labour stoppage is the fact that the Blue Jays approached the strike differently than most teams. When baseball elected to move on by using replacement players—going so far as to start 1995's spring training with replacements before future Supreme Court Justice Sonia Sotomayor, then a US District Court judge in New York, granted an injunction that allowed major league players to return—the Blue Jays did so haltingly. Gaston did not manage replacement players that spring, and with the threat of provincial anti-scab legislation making games in Ontario a dubious alternative, the Blue Jays planned on playing regular season games at their spring training site in Dunedin. Indeed, the entire Blue Jays organization treated the whole episode as distasteful, and those in the front office say Beeston felt it was beneath the team to even try to sell the concept of "replacement players" to loyal season ticketholders—who had given the team three consecutive seasons of attendance above four million.

"We didn't do any marketing," said Starkman. "When it got settled, we were way behind from a ticket point of view. We never caught up. Plus, Gord had to fool around with replacement players. There wasn't much work done on the main team."

The team needed it too, although management's initial inclination was to write off 1994 as an almost predestined flop due to age, injuries that wouldn't happen again, and the natural cynicism that can come with back-to-back World Series wins.

Beeston thinks that another sport's labour stoppage had an impact on Blue Jays attendance too. The NHL went through a 14-week lockout in 1994–95, throwing out the All-Star Game and causing the cancellation of 468 games. The lockout and its aftermath contributed to the moving of the Quebec Nordiques to Colorado and the Winnipeg Jets to Phoenix.

"I think a lot of people just said, 'Fuck the athletes,'" said Beeston. "'What is it with these guys? You've taken baseball and now hockey.' In this city, we got a double whammy, and to me that's when and where the fall started."

It was, Beeston said, a confluence of events. "Issue Number One? We had all that success, and after awhile people were, 'I will come later on.' The Atlanta Braves went through the same thing. The novelty of the SkyDome had worn off, and because of the size of the stadium, people suddenly realized smaller crowds meant they didn't have to buy tickets in advance. Toronto became a city where people would wait and see how the team was doing, how the weather was, who our opponents were. Suddenly, there were all these decision points that basically allowed people to wait. We lost our momentum, and then the players started to leave."

The comparison with Atlanta is apt, although the Braves' decline is likely more striking because they kept going to the post-season year after year, unlike the Blue Jays—who wouldn't get a sniff after 1993. The Braves went to the playoffs for 14 consecutive seasons (from 1991 to 2005) and played in four World Series during that time (including their loss to the Blue Jays), winning one. During that run, they moved from Atlanta–Fulton County Stadium to Turner Field, which was built for the 1996 Olympics. They drew 3,884,720 in 1993, but by the end of that post-season run average attendance was down to 2,521,167. Attendance slumped for the playoffs too: in 2002, when the Braves opened a playoff series against the San Francisco Giants, they did so in front of a crowd of 41,903 in the 54,357-seat Turner Field. In the 2005 National League Division Series against the Houston Astros, the final year of that 14-year run, a crowd of just 40,590 looked on.

Joe Carter said that the Blue Jays showed up in spring training in 1994 talking about a "three-peat." Carter had earned passage as Canada's house guest for the rest of his life, but when he went home to Kansas in the off-season a couple of days after homering off Mitch Williams and found that his neighbours had cut a number 29 (his uniform number) into his front lawn and stuffed his garage full of blue and white balloons, he laughed and prepared for another winter being away from his teammates. That was what made keeping the core of the team together so special. "You go home after the parade and all of a sudden it's, this needs sweeping and the leaves need raking," he said. "But you know that when spring training starts, you're all there as champions."

But there was a flip side to the presence of all those Blue Jays veterans. As it became more and more obvious that a serious labour disruption was on the horizon, players who were actively involved in the Major League Baseball Players Association—like Carter and Paul Molitor—had their attention divided. "Paul and I were on some of the committees, and I think for a lot of players in the game it was a time where we lost focus," Carter said. "Especially the veterans. We knew the guys before us had put their butts on the line in these things, and we knew it was time for us to do the same thing for the guys behind us. That's the way it is in baseball."

"Whatever happened," Carter added, "the truth is we lost our edge."

Another truth is that the Blue Jays never recaptured it. The desert beckoned. Those post-season aspirations? Little more than a mirage.

"We thought when we got David Cone [for the second time] in 1995 that it was a message we were interested in winning," said Beeston. "Then we went out and got Roger Clemens. He did his part, but we just didn't win. Instead, we just kind of drifted down."

Hindsight suggests that the jury-rigged spring training that came after the end of the strike, coupled with the fact that the 1994 season wasn't played to its conclusion, prevented management and ownership from getting an accurate read on the team. But even with that, the fall was shocking. In 1995, the Blue Jays finished 56–88 (.389), tied with the Minnesota Twins for the worst record in baseball. The organization averaged 39,357 fans per game, almost 10,000 fewer per game than during the strike-interrupted season. In 1996, the average fell to 31,600. By then, the core of the team was gone—and Gillick joined the Baltimore Orioles as their GM in 1995. That began an uncanny, canary-in-a-coal-mine run that would see Gillick pull the chute on several teams just before they went into a downward spiral. The Blue Jays, Orioles and Seattle Mariners didn't return to the playoffs after Gillick walked away. Ash called it Gillick's "sense of the clock," the same one, no doubt, that helped Gillick make decisions about personnel matters.

OFF-FIELD WOES

Events not related to sports also conspired against the Blue Jays. In early 1993, the controlling company of John Labatt Limited, Brascan, sold the company to the Belgium-based Interbrew SA, the makers of Stella Artois. There was a restiveness around Labatt leading up to the sale, with an ill-fated purchase of a Mexican brewery and reports of interest in purchasing Madison Square Garden creating tension between shareholders, the majority of whom believed it was time to focus on the company's roots; namely, the brewing and selling of beer. Beeston, a mainstay of Toronto's Tory-blue business community, was aware of the machinations—including a play for Labatt by Gerry Schwartz and his investment company, Onex. "I received a call from Gerry one day, saying, 'We're going to buy this and I want you to know the management team—all of them—are safe as far as their jobs go.'"

But Interbrew's offer was $400,000 more than Onex's, and that meant that Beeston had a new point man to deal with: Allan Chapin, a lawyer from New York who was on Interbrew's board of directors and who would be chairman of the Blue Jays. Beeston's first phone call with Chapin was far different than the one with Schwartz. "The team was up for sale," Beeston said. "I knew that the first time I spoke to him."

Professional sports teams are bought and sold all the time, of course, but there was a comfort level with the Blue Jays' owners that would be hard to replicate today. Yes, the Blue Jays were owned by corporate Canada during their glory days, but those corporations had faces: Don McDougall, president of Labatt and a native of Prince Edward Island who never forgot the lessons he learned on the ground as a beer salesman; Peter N. E. Hardy; Peter Widdrington (also from Labatt); and Howard Webster, the son of a wealthy Montreal family.

It was apparent that the new owners were not cut from the same cloth, and two years after the club was purchased by Interbrew, with Beeston working as MLB's chief operating officer—moving into baseball's head office on Park Avenue in New York City while still maintaining an office at the SkyDome—Sam Pollock, one of the architects of the Montreal Canadiens dynasty, took over as president of the Blue Jays. But the word throughout baseball and in the Toronto business community was clear: the road to buying the Blue Jays didn't necessarily start in Pollock's office, or even in Chapin's. It started in New York City, with Beeston. Beeston, who would still often come into his Toronto office on Monday morning, fly to New York until Thursday, and return for the weekend, had in fact kept his eyes open for buyers during the two seasons he spent under Interbrew's ownership, which had been given a six-month grace period by the office of the baseball commissioner to sell the team. That agreement turned into a six-year rolling agreement, and Beeston admits that he tried and failed to put together an ownership group on his own, while keeping a watchful eye on sneak attacks and bids by groups like the Mirvish family of Toronto and Murray Frum, backed by money from California investors. Interbrew instead pulled the team off the market, with Chapin saying that the company wanted instead to focus on winning. But many saw Beeston and his growing influence within the commissioner's office as one of the reasons the deal never came off, and it is a sentiment Beeston does nothing to downplay. Chapin had been quietly maneuvering behind Beeston's back, talking to other major league owners. "The California guys thought they could come in the back way and buy the team," said Beeston. "And Chapin was stupid enough to think that if you got some owners onside, that's all it would take."

One person who was well aware of Beeston's role as de facto steward of the franchise during those years is Phil Lind, vice-chairman of Rogers Communications. Lind, along with corporate counsel Albert Gnat, played a significant role in directing non-sports fan Ted Rogers toward the purchase of the team.

"Beeston was very influential in this thing," said Lind. "Paul was a friend of mine for awhile. Our wives may have known each other originally, but Paul was everybody's friend. I'd run into him and I'd say, 'It's curious, but I meet three or four different groups wandering around town that keep telling me they have the Blue Jays.' Paul said they hadn't, and when we broached the subject that Rogers might buy them, I had the impression the way was pretty clear."

As the ownership of Interbrew wore on and attendance fell, stories began to surface that the commissioner's office was concerned about the future of the team. It was an understandable sentiment: after all, the Expos were living a hand-to-mouth existence under Claude Brochu and a group of Quebec businessmen with a benign interest in the game. Truly, it was a group that put a new spin on the phrase "limited partnership," and the team proved to be easy pickings for Jeffrey Loria, a New York art dealer who had previously lost the Baltimore Orioles in an auction court battle with Peter Angelos. Loria purchased controlling interest in the Expos for a song—US$12 million, roughly—and immediately set about buying out his partners by exercising a clause that gave him first crack at their stake if they failed to respond to cash calls. Loria, of course, parlayed ownership of the Expos into a World Series with the Miami Marlins and a new ballpark in south Florida.

But there were differences between the Expos and the Blue Jays. The SkyDome was a Taj Mahal compared to Olympic Stadium, and at its worst Blue Jays attendance was still twice that of Montreal. Furthermore, the Blue Jays had Beeston while the Expos had no political champion in their own city or province, never mind the commissioner's office.

"Look," Beeston said. "There's nothing worse for any league than having a team that is perpetually for sale. The thing is, the Blue Jays were always for sale, so the only real concern for [baseball commissioner/then head of the executive council] Bud Selig was who was going to buy it. The team was only going to a group that I wanted it to go to. I know that sounds arrogant, but it's absolutely true. They could have come up with the wealthiest guy in the world, and if I told Bud this guy would be bad for the team or bad for the city, the sale wasn't going to happen."

Beeston chuckled when asked if Loria ever attempted to buy the Blue Jays. "He was never in there," Beeston said. "He was busy finessing the Expos. He may well have figured out that out here, he'd have to pay real money."

Besides, Beeston already knew whom he wanted to own the team. What he didn't know was that those owners would eventually re-hire him as president and chief executive officer of both the Blue Jays and Rogers Centre, first on an interim basis and then full time, overseeing another Canadian-born general manager who seemed poised to lead the organization back to its glory days.

6

THE VILLAGE
IDIOT

TED ROGERS SELDOM WENT TO WATCH HIS BASEBALL
team play, even after the SkyDome was renamed Rogers Centre. By then in his 70s, Rogers would show up for the home opener and catch a few innings from his seat in the front row, to the right of the Blue Jays dugout. Then, between innings, he'd walk slowly onto the field, past the front of the dugout, and take an elevator to the owner's suite, oblivious to the fact he had just been on the field. In 2002, a crowd of 47,469 had shown up to see the home opener, a 7–2 win over the Minnesota Twins, and Rogers took a detour to the press box, where he greeted columnist Dave Perkins of the *Toronto Star* with the words, "Hello, I'm the village idiot."

Well, not exactly. Edward Rogers Jr.–Ted Rogers–was Canada's version of American cable magnate Ted Turner, right down to the quirkiness. Prone to wearing jogging shoes with his suits in his final years, Rogers described himself in his autobiography, aptly titled *Relentless*, as "an over-achiever from strong stock." Rogers' forefathers were Loyalist Quakers. He owed his career in communications to his father, who invented the alternating current radio tube at the age of 24 and who passed away when the younger Rogers was just five. Ted Rogers developed a reputation as something of a maverick, riding wild and free during the nascent days of telecommunications and broadcast services in Canada. He considered himself an outsider; despite the fact that he attended Upper Canada College and became active in the Progressive Conservative Party, he was hardly a typical Toronto Tory, casting his lot instead with the populism of Saskatchewan's John G. Diefenbaker as Rogers set about making his bones within the party.

Ted Rogers was part of a successful bid to bring CFTO-TV into existence as the first privately owned television station in Toronto. But it was in radio where Rogers made his mark, leading a group that purchased CHFI-FM for $85,000 in 1960 and eventually adding an AM station as well. Seven years later, Rogers delved into the world of cable television, a move that would put him and his family on a financial tightrope on several occasions—in *Relentless*, he revealed that at the end of August 1982, Rogers Cablesystems Limited's long-term debt was $566.7 million. In fact, the company didn't become a revenue generator until Michael Milken, the father of the "junk bond" (who was sentenced to 10 years in a federal penitentiary for racketeering and securities fraud), helped the company out with one of his high-yield bank issues.

Rogers favoured the bold move. He made another one in the early 1980s, when he used his own money to get into wireless communications when the company's board of directors wouldn't support the idea. (He eventually sold the shares back to the public company.)

Clearly, Ted Rogers was a man not afraid to take risks. What he wasn't was a baseball fan, or, for that matter, a sports fan at all. True, he did sit on the board of directors of the Toronto Maple Leafs when Steve Stavros ran the team, and was linked to a $1 billion bid to buy the Leafs just before he purchased the Blue Jays. But that was pretty much the extent of it. For that reason, his and his company's engagement with the team was often questioned in the early years of his ownership, especially when significant financial losses were reported in the first year.

"Ted—well, Ted really had no idea what the game was about," Paul Beeston said, chuckling. "How many innings there were in a game, who the players were, how many strikes or balls . . . none of that stuff."

Indeed, the stories of Ted Rogers' forays to the stadium are legion, all of them spun with an endearing quality. Phil Lind, currently vice-chairman of Rogers Communications, can barely contain himself as he talks about Rogers looking at Tony Viner, formerly president and chief executive officer of Rogers Media, and wondering why a player who had just drawn a base on balls "isn't running, for god's sake." Or about the time Rogers stood up and cheered for a ninth-inning double because he saw so many in the crowd rising, only to have Lind grab his arm and say, "Ted, sit down, for god's sake. Sit down. Please. That's the wrong team." The game was against the Boston Red Sox, which meant that Rogers Centre had drawn its usual quantity of citizens from Red Sox Nation.

When it came to baseball, Ted Rogers, in the words of Lind, "didn't have a clue." But he loved the crowd. "He should have been a politician," Lind said, smiling. "He'd be there Opening Day, sitting in the 'In The Action' seats, and people would ask him to sign balls and sign things and there was nothing more exciting to him than the adoration. He was activated by it, so energized that you'd think at times he'd wished he'd bought four teams."

BUYING THE INTANGIBLE

Payroll is the prism through which the American League East is, out of necessity, viewed. Such is life when you are chasing the New York Yankees and Boston Red Sox. And until the Blue Jays ponied up in the winter of 2012 in the 12-player trade with the Florida Marlins, the acquisition and signing of R. A. Dickey, and Melky Cabrera's free-agent deal, the connection between payroll and ownership was a difficult one for fans to make. How does a team with the wealthiest owner in baseball, in one of the biggest cities in North America—a club that is a product for the owner's series of national sports channels—have a payroll that is mid-market at best? It does not make for a warm and fuzzy relationship with the fans, as the Blue Jays learned in the 2011 off-season when they were pilloried for a stillborn attempt to sign free-agent Japanese pitcher Yu Darvish, and when general manager Alex Anthopoulos made what to him was a logical connection between attendance, revenue generation and payroll. At times, it appears as if there is no trust between the team's owners and its fans.

Were he still alive, that sentiment might puzzle Ted Rogers. Although there was a business reason for buying the team—live sports has become a broadcast beachhead for advertisers looking for ways around a PVR world—Phil Lind thinks there was something less quantitative behind the purchase. He believes that buying the Blue Jays "put us in people's hearts in a way we hadn't been before.

"I don't know if this is a rationalization or what, but keeping the team in Toronto was a factor for him," said Lind. "Ted believed in Toronto. He saw keeping the Blue Jays as a viable team as something that was very important.

"Our board was not in favour of the deal. I mean, when the question was asked at our board meeting—do we buy the team?— there may have been one or maybe two hands raised in favour of it. Certainly mine was up, but I don't know if there were too many others. Ted always felt that there was an intangible thing we could get from buying the Blue Jays, something that could be established between himself and southern Ontario and maybe even all of Canada. And that's probably why the board never bought it, because it wasn't tangible. You couldn't say, 'Look, this thing is worth another $10 million in sales,' because that just isn't there. But there is a personality to a sports team that makes it different."

It was in fact a business setback that paved the way for Rogers' acquisition of the Blue Jays, and it wasn't immediately clear that the company, often hammered by its critics for an affinity for debt-financing, had actually paid for the team in cash. The Blue Jays were purchased after Rogers made a play for Videotron, a

Quebec-based cable TV provider. On February 7, 2000, it was announced that the Toronto-based TV magnate had acquired the company for $5.6 billion in a friendly takeover. Project Macdonald-Cartier (as it was called within the company), appeared to have gone swimmingly until nationalist sentiment reared up in Quebec, with the Caisse de dépôt et placement du Québec–the investment arm of the Quebec civil service–setting up a partnership with Pierre Karl Peladeau's Quebecor and submitting a competing bid of $5.88 billion for Videotron.

Staring at a greater than anticipated loss in its most recent report, Rogers took the $240 million breakup fee and bought the Blue Jays. "Money," Lind said, "that just sort of arrived one day. New money."

At the time, Tony Viner had just become vice-president and chief executive officer of Rogers Media, having spent a decade as president and CEO of Rogers Broadcasting. Viner was the driving force behind the conversion of AM rock 'n' roll station CFTR–the call letters were in honour of Ted Rogers Sr.–to an all-news format in 1993. The new station, 680 News, would become one of the biggest revenue-generating stations in Canada, and one of the bigger AM stations in North America. Ted Rogers wanted Viner's opinion on buying the Blue Jays, so Viner reminded his boss about how the Molson family sometimes found that beer sales were impacted by the performance of or a crisis with the Montreal Canadiens, whom they owned.

"I said I wouldn't buy them," said Viner, who would eventually have the Blue Jays under his aegis when the team was moved under the umbrella of Rogers Media. "I told him, 'The problem is that people are paying you $400 and $500 a month in cable and wireless fees, and they're going to feel as if they have an even stronger affinity for the team. If they need a switch-hitting third baseman . . . they're going to rain on your parade to do it.' I just thought it was going to get too wrapped up in our corporate identity."

Rogers' response?

"Ted said, 'Tony, thanks very much. You're my media advisor and have been my media advisor for 20 years.' Then he bought the team the next day. Ted was a great believer in listening to advice. That didn't mean he'd take it. It turned out to be a fabulous decision. It became the anchor for Sportsnet."

It cost Rogers US$112 million to buy 80 percent of the Blue Jays from Interbrew. Rogers eventually bought out the 10 percent of the team that had been held by the Canadian Imperial Bank of Commerce, then purchased Interbrew's remaining shares. In 2005, the company capped off the purchase by landing the SkyDome itself for CAD$25 million, a stunningly low figure for a facility that cost more than CAD$560 million to build, and which had been privatized in 1994.

The skepticism within Rogers about owning a baseball team was understandable. For some, there were disturbing echoes of the arguments that had gone on around Labatt ahead of the team's sale to Interbrew: the notion that a brewery ought to focus first and foremost on brewing beer, not owning a baseball team. In fact, Ted Rogers himself had counselled against his company taking its eye off its core mission, chastened by experiences that resulted from his holding a large stake in Famous Players theatres through Canadian Cablesystems. In his autobiography, Rogers described his feelings on the day he sold his 49 percent stake in the theatre chain: "I mustn't have been thinking clearly. Movie theatres were not my main business, or something I was passionate about or truly understood."

Yet in addition to Lind's suggestion that Rogers viewed owning the baseball team as a means of putting a more personalized touch on his relationship with the marketplace, the deal made more sense financially than might have first appeared. Rogers himself would explain that he saw the team as a branding opportunity in what was the largest consumer market in the country. Furthermore, the growth in value of major league franchises—even smaller franchises—soon made it apparent to the company that they were going to recoup their initial investment in multiples. According to *Forbes* magazine, the average value of a Major League Baseball franchise was $605 million in 2012, an increase of 16 percent over the previous year. Whatever money Rogers lost could be made up by selling the team, if that ever became a necessity.

GROWING PAINS

The first year of ownership came as a shock to Rogers. The Blue Jays lost $52.9 million in 2001, offset slightly by a US$9.8 million injection of revenue-sharing money. Blue Jays president and chief executive officer Paul Godfrey told reporters the loss was "considerably more than anticipated," and laid the blame at the feet of the Canadian dollar, estimating that the exchange rate represented a $40 million hit for the team. The Blue Jays had lost money for the four years leading up to the sale, but the size of the 2001 loss created a stir among Bay Street analysts and at Rogers headquarters. The company said publicly that while it wasn't pursuing minority partners, it was open to being approached. And when the Blue Jays lost $15 million in the first quarter of 2002, Rogers chief financial officer Al Horn told analysts on a conference call that, "If it looks like it can't be fixed, for whatever reason, then we will look at other alternatives. But you can rest assured, an ongoing commitment of $50 million into the Blue Jays is not going to be the case."

The message was received. Viner credits Godfrey with doing "an excellent job of keeping everybody informed.

"Ted was never afraid to invest," Viner continued. "The analogy I often made was that I had a relatively successful rock 'n' roll station and I went in one day to Ted and said, 'I have a rock 'n' roll station which, I believe, is going to make about a million bucks this year. But I can turn it into a loss of $7 million next year. How do you like the plan so far?' Ted believed there was always going to be an initial 'burn' rate in whatever he did. He never believed he was going to have to sustain $55 million in losses per year just because of what happened in the first year. He was always buying distressed properties. Plus, you have to look at it in the context of wireless, which was really taking off at that point. So that loss became less and less impactful."

The role played by Phil Lind in convincing Rogers to purchase the team cannot be underplayed. Lind was a long-time friend of Paul Beeston, and while Lind had his eye on pursuing an NFL franchise for the city, the Blue Jays were a more immediate proposition. It was in 1997, after a failed attempt to purchase the club on the part of Toronto real estate developer Murray Frum, that Beeston and Lind started talking about the possibility of having Rogers purchase the team. The late Albert Gnat from the Toronto law firm of Lang Michener LLP also served as one of the point men in the transaction and was in frequent contact with Beeston, who had more or less assumed the role of de facto protector of the franchise.

"Really, my sole involvement was that I would feed Phil and Albert information," said Beeston. "It was Phil, I always felt, who was bound and determined to buy the team. Plus, I think he knew it would provide a good, steady diet of content for their television network."

Ted Rogers knew whom he trusted as the deal started to come together; he also knew whom he wanted to run his team: Godfrey, a powerful Toronto politico and part of the city's Tory establishment who had a hankering to become a sports administrator.

It was July 4, 2000–just four days after Godfrey, the publisher of the *Toronto Sun*, left the Sun Media newspaper chain following its purchase by Quebecor. He was intrigued by Rogers' proposition, but also wanted to know why Rogers was so keen to bring him in.

"I told Ted, 'I've never run a baseball team before,'" said Godfrey. "Ted said, 'I know that, but you never ran a newspaper before you ran one, either, and you never ran a city before you ran one, either.'"

The idea of running the Blue Jays had immediate appeal to Godfrey. Raised in a blue-collar, Jewish family near Toronto's Kensington Market, he had been involved in the civic pursuit of a major league franchise as far back as 1969, when as a city councillor in the Toronto suburb of North York he paid his own way to the winter meetings in Bal Harbour, Florida, to talk up Toronto as a baseball city. As chairman of Metropolitan Toronto from 1973–84, he took the lead in a $15 million overhaul of Exhibition Stadium that was essential to the city landing a franchise. While he had his hand in provincial politics as part of a group of largely conservative businessmen, Godfrey envisioned himself as something of a sportsman. Like Lind, he had always harboured ambitions of bringing an NFL franchise to Toronto–it was natural that Rogers would end up negotiating with Buffalo Bills owner Ralph Wilson to bring NFL games to Rogers Centre–and at least part of him must have believed that involvement with the Blue Jays amounted to a foot in the door with future synergies for a potential NFL play. Interestingly, it was when he was largely left out of the negotiations with the Bills on a series of exhibition games and regular-season games that Godfrey began to question his place within the organization.

Initially, though, Godfrey embraced his new role with zealousness and realized very quickly that Ted Rogers was not going to be a hands-on owner. In fact, Godfrey would say later that commissioner Bud Selig often seemed miffed that Rogers never bothered to attend owners meetings.

"I remember, we were on a private jet going to Milwaukee to meet Bud, and Ted said, 'If they ask a business question, I'll answer. But if they ask about baseball, you just jump right in.'"

FROM SKYDOME TO ROGERS CENTRE

Capturing the SkyDome from Sportsco International LP and putting the Rogers name on it was crucial to cementing the relationship, according to Godfrey. On the day the purchase of the building was announced, Godfrey told people with the team that naming rights to the facility would not be sold; it would be called the Rogers Centre because the building needed a significant amount of work and Rogers' pride in his family's name meant he wouldn't let it go to seed any further.

That made sense, because the family name was hugely important to Rogers: his television properties changed their name from Rogers Sportsnet to Sportsnet, for example, only after his death. Rogers frequently referred to the importance of the family name in no small part due to the fact that his father's businesses had been closed after his death. "After my father's death, we lost it for awhile," Rogers said. "But we have it back now, and I have worked extraordinarily hard to ensure that it stays there long after I'm gone."

Yet Viner said that Rogers' first inclination was to call the building The Rogers SkyDome. Viner talked him out of it, saying that people would only refer to it as SkyDome and that it made sense to call it the Rogers Centre. Rogers relented when Viner told him, "Ted, nobody calls the O'Keefe Centre the O'Keefe Centre any more," a reference to a Toronto arts theatre that changed its name to The Hummingbird Centre and is now called The Sony Centre. "Funny," added Viner, "but for a multi-billion-dollar company there was no market research or anything that went into the name."

The SkyDome had not aged well since opening its doors in 1989. It had become the focus of numerous legal battles while the baseball team—its primary tenant—existed under the terms of a byzantine lease. Built for $562.8 million, it was sold to Labatt for $151 million in 1994, then sold out of bankruptcy to a group comprising Chicago investors and local businessmen—including Blue Jays general manager Pat Gillick—for $80 million in 1999. The SkyDome hotel was parcelled off to a Vancouver investment group that hired Marriott to manage it. But by 2005 one of the Chicago partners, long-time sports executive Alan Cohen, had passed away, and the other Chicago partner, Harvey Walken, was in deteriorating health with a degenerative lung disease.

"We had to buy the building," Godfrey said. "It just made no sense to not have the team and the building. In fact, about a month after being named to the job by Ted, I had met with Sportsco, and they wanted $100 million for the building. We weren't going to do more than $50 million. The thing that tipped us off that we could do better was when the city let it out of the bag that they were three years behind in property taxes."

Walken was offered $50 million again in a meeting with Godfrey, and declined a second time. Three months later, Rogers told Godfrey to offer $15 million, an offer that reportedly enraged Walken. "He blew up and walked out," said Godfrey. Three weeks later, Walken's son-in-law called Godfrey and said, simply, "You have to do better." Godfrey said $50 million or even $40 million was not in the cards. "We settled on $25 million and when I called Ted he said, 'If we wait a couple of months I'll get it for nothing out of bankruptcy.' I said, 'Ted, you're getting the Dome for $25 million.' We really needed to do something; I mean, we were getting nasty letters from the commissioner's office about the state of the soap dishes in the umpires' changing room."

Owning the building removed a logistical impediment to making some long-needed improvements. The Blue Jays' lease was a convoluted thing—from a complex system of staggered payments to the team from the landlord for luxury suite and premium seat revenue, down to the Blue Jays getting control of the Jumbotron scoreboard for 30 seconds during breaks between innings. "We are two not-for-profit organizations eating from the same baseball pie," Silvio D'Addario, then the SkyDome's chief operating officer, explained to the *Globe and Mail* in September 2004, "and what happens is that, at the end of the day, we're both hungry for the crumbs that are left. But because of the nature of our agreement, it's less than 100 percent clear who gets what crumb."

In making the announcement, Ted Rogers himself said, "We feel freed up. For the first time we're going to be able to do some things, because we've been shackled before. If I had known what I know now, I wouldn't have bought the team alone. Now we have the building, so we can make a difference.

"You have to plant some seed," Rogers said, "not only harvest."

So what does Rogers harvest from the baseball team and its building, which is now the seventh-oldest facility in the majors? That is a question that has occupied the minds of observers and fans ever since Rogers bought the team and then put its operation under the Rogers Media umbrella. Certainly, the questions about whether or not the team will leave Toronto have ceased, as much due to the robust economics of Major League Baseball and the Canadian dollar as anything. But beyond the hard economic facts, there was little hand-wringing about the future of the team brought on by Rogers' death, his company's continued dance with the NFL or, most recently, its purchase (along with telecommunications rival Bell Media) of controlling interest in Maple Leaf Sports and Entertainment Limited. That was not always the case in the Interbrew years, or even during the early years of Rogers' ownership, when faint-hearted observers pegged the Blue Jays as a long-term contraction worry—even though it had been duly noted that Rogers paid cash for the team, which made them the least of Bud Selig's worries at a time when he was fretting about debt-to-equity ratios.

Franchise value has something to do with that—not the guestimated, water-cooler value offered by publications such as *Forbes*, but the value of franchises that has been reflected in recent sale prices. Never mind the big markets—the Los Angeles Dodgers were sold for $2 billion in 2012—it's the sale price for teams such as the Texas Rangers ($593 million), Houston Astros ($610 million) and, most recently, the San Diego Padres ($800 million) that reveal the growth in values.

That doesn't necessarily mean that the Blue Jays could fetch $1 billion for Rogers—although as a Rogers executive said this winter, "I'm sure Beeston thinks he could get a billion for the whole thing"—but it has made it easier to swallow whatever the Blue Jays' recent losses have been. And while baseball's most recent collective bargaining agreement has placed a new onus on teams that have been chronic recipients of revenue-sharing money, while also hammering franchises flirting with the game's luxury tax, the greater willingness to spend money shown this winter by teams such as the Kansas City Royals and, yes, the Blue Jays, has been fuelled by the fact that baseball has successfully negotiated US network television contracts worth a total of $1.5 billion annually over eight years. The money kicks in in 2014.

BETTING ON THE FUTURE

Beeston calls the Blue Jays' aggressive winter of 2013 the start of a "three-year bet." His pitch of the 12-player trade with the Miami Marlins to Rogers president and CEO Nadir Mohamed—delivered before Mohamed stepped on a plane to London—was that the payroll hit for 2013 would be covered by increased ticket sales. He also pledged to cover the long-term hit, and while Beeston wouldn't say so publicly, it's a guess that increased ticket prices and luxury suite fees, expiring and renegotiated corporate partnerships (that figure to be turned into higher revenue if the product is better), and a bigger Canadian television package when the current deal expires in 2014 will be the underpinnings of growth. If the Blue Jays draw three million fans this season, as Beeston is forecasting, it will mean an estimated $35 million more to the team's coffers.

Beeston is guarded about giving out hard numbers, but it is not out of the question that the Blue Jays could inch into the black this season. According to the organization, merchandise sales doubled after the team ditched the black-and-gray uniforms that Godfrey and his marketing team rolled out for the 2004 season. The move to that colour scheme coincided with a decision to drop the "Blue" from the team's name—a response, Godfrey said, to market surveys that showed the black-and-silvery-grey colour scheme resonated with a younger demographic at a time when the team had already altered its original logo and added a third jersey, with a cartoonish bird. The new Blue Jays jersey and logo, rolled out for 2012, featured the return of the Maple Leaf that had been taken off the black jerseys. Some in the commissioner's office didn't want the Maple Leaf to be given prominence because it was considered overtly political, but Beeston convinced the marketers that it was a key to the brand. He suggested that if they didn't like it, they could come up to Toronto on Opening Day and tell the folks why exactly the Maple Leaf was an issue.

"My goal has always been to get into the black and become a part of the big-market caucus once again," said Beeston, who never tires of reminding people that the club actually put more money into revenue sharing than any other team during its run in the early 1990s, and who, upon replacing Godfrey, told the commissioner's office that the Blue Jays no longer needed a $5 million annual currency equalization payment.

Beeston is clearly hoping that the financial restrictions he placed on the team when he took over in 2009 have resulted in a kind of "peace dividend" from ownership, that good stewardship is being rewarded in 2013 and beyond.

There are certainly issues he will face: Nadir Mohamed, the chief executive officer of Rogers with whom Beeston has developed an effective rapport, has stepped down and while the Rogers Centre has undergone a steady series of facelifts, it still retains the same issues of scope and feel that are inherent in multi-use venues at a time when the trend in baseball is small, quaint and quirky. Beeston, however, talks boldly about the facility, noting its downtown location, while also being clear that his vision for the building includes a natural grass field. Only Toronto and Tampa Bay still play on artificial turf, and concerns about the surface were cited as a reason that free agent Carlos Beltran elected not to sign with the Blue Jays for the 2012 season. Beeston must also ensure that the Blue Jays' priorities don't get lost in the shuffle, given the size of Rogers Communications and the competing priorities and philosophies that might arise within Rogers Media.

The exact nature of the relationship between Rogers' broadcast properties and the team will not likely ever be publicly known, according to Beeston. "You'll never find that out," he said, chuckling, while noting that teams, such as the Blue Jays, that are owned by broadcast interests are subject to repeated and unannounced audits by the commissioner's office for the purposes of revenue sharing. For outsiders, there is a whole left hand/right hand, Peter/Paul element to the relationship that usually rears up when discussion gets around to television rights. The Blue Jays, with their national reach, currently receive an estimated $35 million per year under the terms of their contract with Sportsnet at a time when the San Diego

Padres, for example, can talk about receiving $1.2 billion over 30 years from Fox. Indeed, regional sports networks have become an economic driver for major league teams, and while Beeston realizes the industry is much more regulated in Canada than in the US, he is also aware that it is an area of discrepancy that could inhibit the team's long-range plans. There are unique elements to the Blue Jays' marketplace—as strong as baseball is, it is not Canada's pastime in any of its major markets; it's a sport played in the summer, when TV viewership is down; there are four-and-a-half time zones, which means prime time in the east is drive home time in British Columbia; and there's a French-speaking province. Even if the team is successful and rate cards for Sportsnet telecasts go up, as they did this off-season, Beeston knows he will still need to use the bully pulpit of the Blue Jays presidency to ensure his voice is heard.

Because Canadian broadcast regulations are generally more restrictive than those in the US, the strength of the Blue Jays is reflected for Sportsnet not by subscriptions but by advertising rates, which depend on ratings. And based on market research and ratings from the past two seasons, a million viewers a night during a September pennant race does not seem far-fetched. The numbers showed that the Blue Jays' demographics started to skew younger in 2011, that the combination of a smart television advertising campaign based on players' faces and names—Jose Bautista, Brett Lawrie, J. P. Arencibia and Ricky Romero, in particular—as well as the new uniforms, made them, well, cool. Ratings showed the Blue Jays' viewership up between 5 and 22 percent across all demographic groups from 2011 to 2012, despite the disastrous September. National viewership breached the 700,000 plateau 21 times, led by the 1,2674,6000 viewers for the home opener on April 9, 2012. In 2011, only nine games had viewership of more than 700,000. Increases across adult demographics from 2010 to 2011 were within the 15- to 22-percent range, with pronounced growth in the number of female viewers. No wonder that Keith Pelley, president of Rogers Media, gets excited about the possibility of what he calls "meaningful games" in September. There was no Sportsnet when the Blue Jays won back-to-back World Series. And social media? Please.

But this isn't the first time that the Blue Jays seemed poised on the brink of big things. Like Alex Anthopoulos, J. P. Ricciardi had his shot at playing big market bingo too. When Ted Rogers purchased the team back in 2000, he famously promised not to "skimp on the light bulbs." By 2005, the club was closing in on breaking even (after sucking up $239.1 million in losses in four years) and was getting closer to Rogers' unstated goal of $10 million in losses. At the time, Rogers was comfortable telling reporters that they needed to view the team as part of a bigger whole. Besides, he said, it was time to deal with "the content, as well as the transmitters and wires."

Never mind the light bulbs; by 2005 the Blue Jays were clearly planning to shoot for some stars. But let's not get ahead of ourselves. The years between Rogers' purchase of the team and those relatively rosy days of 2005 would see some hard slogging, and more than a few challenges.

7

ONE LAST FLOURISH

THE SIGNS ARE ALL TOO FAMILIAR TO ANYBODY WHO has started to believe their future lies with another organization. Meetings are held without your input, stuff crosses your desk that catches you off guard—"Er, yeah, of course I knew that. How couldn't I?"—and decisions are made without your approval.

For Gord Ash, the first sign that Rogers Communications' ownership of the Toronto Blue Jays did not necessarily auger well for his own future came at the winter meetings in Dallas just after the 2000 season, three months or so after the team was sold to the Toronto-based company. The winter meetings had ceased to be what they once were—an annual gathering of general managers, scouts, personnel advisors and coaches in which proximity allowed clubs to actively pursue discussions and make trades that addressed their off-season issues—and at times became little more than a dog-and-pony show for free agents and their representatives. But there was still a critical mass created by so many decision- and opinion-makers being in one hotel.

It is typical for media at the winter meetings to be granted a daily scrum with the GM of the team they are covering. The rest of the time is devoted to scouring the hotel lobby or bar, picking up scuttlebutt and schmoozing and, occasionally, chasing down honest-to-goodness trade rumours with some substance.

On this particular day, the mood inside the Blue Jays suite was a little off-putting. Ash seemed quiet, a bit disengaged as he sat tapping away on a laptop computer. The usual fishing expedition hadn't even begun ("How many teams have you talked to this morning? Do you think you can address all your needs here? Do you have any more meetings set up today?") when reporters were told that the Blue Jays had re-signed shortstop Alex Gonzalez to a four-year, $21 million contract. The deal flew in the face of everything that had been said behind the scenes by scouts and by Ash himself, and it quickly became clear that the contract had been negotiated with Gonzalez's agents, Bob Gilhooley and Jim Bronner, by president and chief executive officer Paul Godfrey. The sides had been roughly $5 million per year apart when Ash issued what amounted to a take-it-or-leave-it proposition of $19 million, and the organization seemed set to move on to other options.

The contract hardly registered in the grand scheme of things: those were the winter meetings in which baseball lost its collective mind, with $739 million in contracts dispensed ahead of a winter that would see $1.04 billion doled out to 49 free agents—including $252 million over 10 years to Alex Rodriguez by the Texas Rangers, $160 million over eight years to Manny Ramirez by the Boston Red Sox and $121 million over eight years to pitcher Mike Hampton by the Colorado Rockies, the last of which is widely known as one of the worst free-agent contracts in baseball history. But Ash rightly believed that the Blue Jays had overpaid for Gonzalez, and as the season went on he saw more and more signs that he was being shuttled toward the door.

The Gonzalez deal stuck in his craw not just because the organization had some depth at the position in Felipe Lopez and Cesar Izturis—both of whom would go on to become major leaguers—but also because of the message it sent. Ash's scouts were unanimous in their opposition to re-signing Gonzalez, so it wasn't only Ash who was being effectively overruled.

"Clearly, that signing was in my mind a mistake, and it was a mistake for most of the room in terms of scouting opinions," said Ash. "I loved Alex, but I just thought that it was way too much money for what he could provide and how we could fill the position. One of the things we had at the time was a boatload of middle infielders, and I didn't think we needed to sign him regardless of the cost. That probably was the beginning of the end for me. Paul was determined to sign him; he thought it was an important public relations move.

"So, I said, 'Be my guest.'"

Until this winter, it had become a *cri de coeur* among Blue Jays fans that ownership of the team was unwilling to spend money in keeping with the size of the marketplace, that for all of current president and chief executive officer Paul Beeston's bold talk of viewing the franchise not as a small- or mid-market team but as a large-market club (one of the reasons Beeston asked the commissioner's office to stop currency equalization payments was that he felt it was an affront to the team's market), the spending on payroll did not match those intentions. But the Blue Jays spent money in those early years of Rogers' ownership and they'd do so again under J. P. Ricciardi. Thing is, it wasn't just a matter of spending money; it was a matter of how it was spent.

THE DELGADO DEAL

When the Blue Jays were winning their back-to-back World Series, they did so with the biggest payrolls in the game, but they had fallen into a kind of purgatory during Interbrew's ownership. The new owners, however, didn't waste any time trying to make an impression in Toronto. Following the time-honoured tradition of new ownerships in every city and every sport, they signed a player to a huge contract, in this case slugging first baseman Carlos Delgado.

The man charged with getting it done was Ash, who'd replaced Pat Gillick as GM prior to the 1995 season. Ash, a native of Toronto, had worked his way up from the Blue Jays' ticket department, spending a year in that capacity after his graduation from York University before advancing to operations supervisor and assistant director of stadium operations in 1980. Four years later, he was named administrator of baseball personnel, a largely bureaucratic position in the baseball operations department, and five years after that he was promoted to assistant GM.

On the eve of the 2000 World Series, less than a month after the announcement of Rogers' purchase of Interbrew's share in the team, the Blue Jays held another news conference to announce they'd made Delgado the highest-paid player in the history of the game. Getting his name on a four-year, $68 million contract helped set the parameters for baseball's off-season spending binge.

The deal enraged officials in commissioner Bud Selig's office, particularly the commissioner himself, who, in addition to pointless fretting about the growth of salaries, preferred clubs to refrain from making major announcements around the game's jewel event. More to the point, Selig and the other owners had not yet formally approved the sale from Interbrew to Rogers. Selig was noticeably irritated during an interview on the field at Yankee Stadium prior to Game 1 of the World Series. Out of the scrum came the suggestion that some owners must have raised their eyebrows at a deal of that size being given out by a new owner. "It raised more than my eyebrow," the commissioner responded. "Let's just say that it's an interesting situation."

Subsequent to the announcement of the contract, an October 31 vote to approve the sale of the team to Rogers was unexpectedly delayed. The sale eventually went through, but a message had been sent. At a time when Selig considered publicly fretting about payroll escalation to be part of his job, and when words such as "contraction" were regularly bandied around, one was expected to play ball with the commissioner's office.

Godfrey, of course, defended Delgado's contract by describing him as a franchise player. He claimed that the signing was "part of our attempt to regain our fans" at a time when attendance at the Rogers Centre had fallen to 2,163,464 from 4,057,947 in seven seasons. As part of the deal, Delgado was also given a no-trade clause. The previous winter, another core player, Shawn Green, had been traded to the Los Angeles Dodgers in a multi-player deal after telling the Blue Jays he would pursue free agency. It was immediately after that transaction that the Blue Jays signed Delgado to a three-year, $36 million contract extension that would allow him to demand a trade after the 2000 season. Locking him up further clearly carried a financial premium.

Ash, who is now assistant GM of the Milwaukee Brewers under GM Doug Melvin, saw the contract as good business all around, and chuckles at the suggestion that it didn't seem to take long to get Delgado's name on a contract once Rogers bought the team. "I hate to tell you how little time it took," he said. "Half an hour, maybe?"

He is also quick to point out that much of the groundwork for the deal had been done under the previous ownership group. He and Delgado's agent, David Sloane, had held a number of discussions. It was clear all along that Delgado, a hugely productive player, wanted to stay in Toronto—and that the Blue Jays wanted him.

"I thought the market was pretty clear," said Ash. "And I still think to this day that even though it was a heavy number per year, the beauty of the contract was it was short, compared to what was happening in the business at the time. I really thought it was a win for us. Yes, it was $17 million a year, but you know what? It was relatively short term, and the Blue Jays had always operated under the idea that shorter is better. What a lot of people never appreciated was that we were able to get a deal done in that environment that only covered four years. Not six, seven or eight. They just never gave it any thought at all while they were complaining about it."

Ash knew what the reaction would be from the commissioner's office, however. The chief operating officer for Major League Baseball was his old boss, Paul Beeston. But Ash had heard from other people in the industry that MLB was becoming concerned about an exodus of talent from the organization at a time when the team located a few hours northeast, the Expos, seemed to provide a daily cautionary tale.

"I can tell you that when we traded Shawn Green, which was kind of a forced deal, I had baseball insiders tell me I'd better sign

Delgado and better do it quickly and not worry about the cost," Ash said. "I just think it was pretty clear what was needed. You had to establish your core. We had a lot of defections through the '90s, and here was a guy who was a quality, productive player and a good representative of the organization."

REVOLVING MANAGERS

The 2000 Blue Jays had finished only four-and-a-half games back of the American League East champion New York Yankees, losing eight of their final 10 games and costing manager Jim Fregosi his job. Fregosi had been named to the job halfway through spring training in a strange set of circumstances: Tim Johnson, who'd led the Blue Jays to an 88-win season that stands as their best since 1993, was fired after a bizarre controversy stemming from lies about his service record in Vietnam that Johnson would use to motivate or entertain players. None of it seemed to faze Fregosi, who joked that he was a man of firsts, anyhow, since he was the only player ever traded for Hall of Famer Nolan Ryan.

The profanity-tossing, chain-smoking Fregosi believed he had the club positioned for the stretch drive in what was his second season. They were in first place in late June and leading the wild-card race as late as August—in a year where the New York Yankees would top the division with the lowest winning percentage of any postseason qualifier, then go on to beat the New York Mets in the World Series. It was also a season of turmoil that saw Fregosi's pitching coach, Rick Langford, fired in July and replaced by assistant GM Dave Stewart, whose relationship with Fregosi was tenuous. Fregosi was a hard-ass; a barrel-chested baseball lifer and six-time All-Star shortstop who'd led a ribald life as a member of a swashbuckling California Angels expansion team. He was livid over Langford's firing, telling reporters that he'd never had a coach fired out from underneath him before, and it was clear that he didn't trust Stewart, whom he saw as a conduit to the front office. Fregosi lived hard; he was involved in a barroom altercation in the early hours of June 12, 1999, when he and Blue Jays pitching coach Mel Queen went to Legends sports bar in the Holiday Inn near Philadelphia's Veterans Stadium following an interleague game and apparently became embroiled in an argument with fans.

The altercation, which at one point involved the Philadelphia Police's organized crime squad, apparently stemmed from statements Fregosi made in a four-year-old exchange with Philadelphia reporters. As manager of the Phillies, Fregosi had taken a shot at critics who called in to sports station WIP, saying they were a "bunch of guys in South Philly that fuck their sisters." Fregosi thought it was harmless banter, one of those self-regulated, off-the-record things that were said all the time in his pre-game media sessions. The difference this time was that a Philadelphia radio station ran with it.

But despite all this, Fregosi managed a good game, and in 2000 the Blue Jays had All-Star seasons from both Delgado and left-hander David Wells, who set a club record with 15 wins before the All-Star break (the Blue Jays were tied for the division lead at the break). Wells would become the second-oldest pitcher in baseball history to hit the 20-win mark for the first time, at the age of 37. Delgado finished the season with a club-record 137 runs batted in as the Blue Jays tied a major league record with four players hitting 30-plus homers in a season (Delgado and Tony Batista each had 41, Brad Fullmer clubbed 32 and Jose Cruz Jr. hit 31.) But in the end, it was an inability to milk successful seasons out of three young starting pitchers that was most costly. Chris Carpenter, 25, Kelvim Escobar, 24 and Roy Halladay, 23, were considered future cornerstones, but they were lit up all season long. Carpenter finished 10–12 with a 6.26 earned run average and a WHIP of 1.637; Escobar was 10–15 (5.35) with a WHIP of 1.506; and Halladay ended 4–7 (10.64) with a 2.202 WHIP.

The lingering image of the season could be found in the vistors' clubhouse at Jacobs Field in Cleveland after an 11–4 loss to the Indians in the final game of the season. Wells, who had been bothered by a recurrence of gout in one of his toes, lasted just $2\frac{1}{3}$ innings, and instead of staying around for post-game commentary, left his locker empty except for a jockstrap that hung limply off a hook.

It was that kind of season. Attendance dwindled with the Blue Jays' post-season chances, and it was apparent that the new ownership believed it needed a new face on the franchise. So while Ash was rewarded with a three-year contract extension, the ink on the deal was barely dry before the GM told Fregosi he would not be returning to manage the team.

A NOT-SO-FRESH START

Fregosi's replacement was Buck Martinez, the popular former Blue Jays catcher from the 1970s and '80s who had made a successful transition to the broadcast booth. Martinez worked as diligently at his new craft as he had behind the plate, and was omnipresent as a broadcaster, sitting in on the manager's pre-game sessions and staking out a regular spot around the cage during batting practice. He had been a candidate for the manager's vacancy when Johnson was hired, along with Davey Johnson and World Series hero Paul Molitor, who at the time was still playing for the Minnesota Twins. The Blue Jays asked again about Molitor's availability before hiring Martinez—Molitor had moved into a coaching role by that point—and were not given permission to talk to him.

"We had gone through the process a couple of times and had interviewed a bunch of guys by design because we had been in-house for so long that we wanted to see what was out there," said

Ash. "I did like Tim Johnson's baseball ability. I thought he ran a good game. The personality part was a little concerning to me, in retrospect. We couldn't find group consensus—Tim Wilken and Dave Stewart [assistant GMs] and Sam Pollock [president and CEO] were involved. But I liked the fact there was a prior connection to the club, that coming to a foreign country wouldn't be a big deal—we were still dealing with that, even at that point, from other baseball people—but it was obviously the wrong decision.

"As we looked to the next time, we wanted to find somebody who was a great communicator. I really felt that way and still feel that way, that the way the game has gone now, many managers' forte is their ability to manage the clubhouse. I thought because of his passion and communication skills, it would be one of Buck's strengths. I still believe in his ability to communicate and share his vision and sell players on the idea that, 'Hey, this is the way we want to do it.' I still don't know if it would work over the long term."

In keeping with the idea of a fresh start, Rogers Communications bumped the club's 2001 payroll up to $76,895,999 (from $46,363,332 in the final year of Interbrew ownership), and while a strong 16–9 April put together by a club with a young core suggested that the 25th anniversary season might indeed be something special, the Blue Jays ran into a 2–6 homestand in late June and early July that essentially buried the club. The team finished 80–82 in Martinez's first season, which was played out against a strange sense of foreboding.

It had started back in January, when Ash traded lefty David Wells to the Chicago White Sox in a six-player deal that saw the Blue Jays land left-handed pitcher Mike Sirotka. The deal seemed to make sense at the time, since the Blue Jays had a young nucleus of starting pitchers and Wells' value was not going to be any higher, coming as he was off the best year of his career. But Sirotka, who was 15–10 and averaged over 200 innings per season as a big league starter, never pitched a meaningful game for the Jays; less than a month after the trade, a complete tear was found in the labrum of his right shoulder. Ash filed notice with the commissioner's office, but White Sox's GM Kenny Williams—a former Toronto Blue Jays player—was adamant that the White Sox had been above board in the transaction. On April 13, a home game against the Kansas City Royals was cancelled when debris fell to the field at the SkyDome after a test run of the retractable roof (the roof would be functioning on August 3 that same year, thankfully, when home plate umpire Tim Welke requested it be closed due to a swarm of aphids), and two months later the Baltimore Orioles claimed hard-hitting infielder Tony Batista on waivers. It was a move that sent a disquieting message to Blue Jays fans when it was painted as something that would save the team roughly $13 million in salary over the next 2½ seasons—an odd about-face from increasing the payroll by 50 percent.

It was a hard team to fall in love with, those 2001 Blue Jays; they were relatively young and well paid, yet strangely amorphous. That held true even in the case of their marquee player, Delgado, who passed Joe Carter as the Blue Jays' all-time home run leader, yet never seemed to completely win over the fans.

Off the field, things were also coming to a head. The Blue Jays' landlords, Chicago-based Sportsco International LP, were in the new owner's crosshairs due to growing complaints about the upkeep at the facility and a strange sense of penuriousness that saw the big scoreboard kept off until just before game-time to save money. Meanwhile, Ted Rogers was about to find out the cost of owning a baseball team: with losses that approached $50 million, Rogers made it known they would consider partnerships.

The loss wasn't a total shock; Rogers, a publicly traded company, had given the street guidance that it would lose between $40 million and $60 million on the team, which had reversed a trend of three consecutive seasons of decreasing attendance, but just barely, with an increase of 75,317 to 1,895,236.

By the last month of the season, it seemed apparent that Ash was going to lose his position as vice-president and general manager, and the move was finally made with six days left in the regular season. Ash was not surprised, although he was disappointed. "Right up until a couple of days before I was let go we had talked about moving some people into different responsibilities. It was about 99 percent done, and it all fell apart after I left. That's what bothered me; we disrupted a lot of people's lives."

It was also not surprising that Ash took the high road on his way out. "Paul was very fair with me and did act as a sounding board, but at the same time his agenda was to drive attendance and keep the fans happy, and sometimes the decisions we make don't make the fans happy. You can't allow yourselves to fall into that trap, but we did do some of that and it worked against us."

Martinez was retained as manager even after Ash's replacement, former Oakland Athletics director of player personnel J. P. Ricciardi, came to power. But Martinez told confidants he believed the die was cast the day Ricciardi took over, and he was right. Martinez would be fired on June 3, 2002, after the Blue Jays' worst start in two decades saw them 20–33 and sporting an 8–20 home record that would send Godfrey and Ricciardi out of the GM's box with ashen faces. Upon taking over the job, Ricciardi had told people he thought the Blue Jays were a bit of a soft team, and one particularly galvanizing moment early in the 2002 season came when Carlos Delgado stopped running in the eighth inning of a loss to the Tampa Bay Rays after he thought Ben Grieve of the Rays had made a leaping catch of a Jose Cruz Jr. double.

It was a tough season all around for managers: Martinez was no less than the fifth manager fired since Opening Day, including Phil Garner (Detroit Tigers), Buddy Bell (Colorado Rockies), Tony Muser (Kansas City Royals) and Davey Lopes (Milwaukee Brewers). And he wouldn't be the last manager fired by J. P. Ricciardi. Far from it.

MONEYBALL
NORTH

J. P. RICCIARDI PLAYED A MINOR ROLE IN TORONTO

Blue Jays history long before the announcement, in November 2001, that he had replaced Gord Ash as the fourth general manager since the team's inception in 1976. In fact, it can even be argued that he played a role in Joe Carter's walk-off home run in the 1993 World Series.

Sort of.

Ricciardi, a native of Worcester, Massachusetts, was the Athletics' eastern supervisor of scouting in 1993, when the organization was looking to parlay veteran assets into pitchers and prospects for the future. One year after losing to the Blue Jays in the ALCS, the Athletics were on their way to a last-place finish in the American League West Division, a staggering 26 games behind the Chicago White Sox. Among the players they were making available, of course, was outfielder and future stolen-base king and Hall of Famer Rickey Henderson.

The Athletics reasoned that Henderson was a player who might be particularly attractive to teams in the American League East, especially the top three contenders: the Blue Jays, New York Yankees and Baltimore Orioles. As July rolled over into August, the Blue Jays found themselves tied atop the division despite a losing month, and had been talking trade with other teams; at one point, rumour had it they were looking to add hard-throwing left-hander Randy Johnson (then with the Seattle Mariners). Instead, GM Pat Gillick decided to address what he perceived to be the need for an established lead-off hitter. He wanted Henderson.

The scout assigned by the Athletics to "sit" on pitching prospects that might be acquired for Henderson was Ricciardi. The Blue Jays' top pitching prospect, Steve Karsay, ended up being the price, along with outfielder Jose Herrera (initially a "player to be named later"). Henderson, of course, was on second base when

Carter took Mitch Williams deep to secure the World Series trophy.

But in November 2001, no one was thinking about the Ricciardi-Carter connection. The Blue Jays had never really had to go outside the organization to find a GM before. Peter Bavasi held the position during the club's first season before he was fired and replaced by Pat Gillick, who had been hired as the organization's vice-president of player personnel. Gillick's remarkable run started in 1978 and ended in 1994 when the job was handed off to Gord Ash. But the in-house promotions ended there, and in choosing Ricciardi after a long search, Paul Godfrey couldn't possibly have gone any farther outside the organization.

Ricciardi's hometown newspaper, the *Worcester Telegram*, would refer to him as a "born scrapper from Grafton Hill." He was as different in personality from Ash as he was in physical stature. Ash, a large man, was raised within the Blue Jays system and understood the sensibilities of the organization. He also prided himself on returning phone calls and being available to any reporter regardless of how critical that reporter had been, moving comfortably on and off the record. Ricciardi, who had been an undersized infielder, feuded regularly with elements of the Toronto media and could be extremely caustic. He enjoyed a verbal thrust and parry, but he also played favourites; he was disliked by some segments of the Toronto media because it was believed he was more forthcoming with journalists from the US. Ricciardi came from a large, extended, Italian immigrant family—"my grandparents' names are inscribed on the walls of Ellis Island," he told a gathering in May 2001, when he and his father, Johnny Ricciardi, were inducted into the Worcester Chapter of the Sons of Italy Hall of Fame—and he was something of a local sports celebrity. The Ricciardi family was well known—he called it "kinda a cross between the Sopranos and *Everybody Loves Raymond*"—and working as an eastern scout dovetailed nicely with his lifestyle of choice. He was based in Worcester, could spend time with his wife, Diane, and his two young sons, coach varsity boys basketball at Holy Name High School during the off-season, and essentially call his shot during the baseball season.

New England is a hothouse for baseball, with the Red Sox a regional source of pride and angst, the Cape Cod League a summertime staple of player development, and a culture ripe with baseball dialogue. It is also fertile ground for players and executives, with a history of mentorship from the likes of Hall of Fame executive Roland Hemond, a native of Central Falls, Rhode Island, and the late Harry Dalton of West Springfield, Massachusetts, who came up through the Baltimore Orioles organization to become GM of the Milwaukee Brewers. Dalton would mentor the likes of John Schuerholz of the Atlanta Braves and Dan Duquette, the current Orioles GM who had also served in that capacity with the Red Sox and Montreal Expos. In 2012, Duquette was one of four alumni from schools affiliated with the New England Small Colleges Athletic Association to serve as a big league GM, joining Neal Huntington of the Pittsburgh Pirates, Jed Hoyer of the Chicago Cubs and Ben Cherington of the Red Sox.

Ricciardi's father had a stint as a minor leaguer with the Red Sox, so it was no surprise his son would fall naturally into the region's baseball culture. J. P. was a high school teammate of former major league catcher and manager Rich Gedman on a state championship team at St. Peter-Marian High School. He spent two years with the New York Mets as a minor leaguer, posting a career average of .200, but along the way he was teammates with two Mets first-round picks from vastly different backgrounds, both of whom would go on to play a major role in his professional career: Billy Beane, a gifted athlete who had forsaken a college scholarship to Stanford University, and John Gibbons, a plain-spoken high school catcher from Texas who would one day be hired by Ricciardi to manage the Blue Jays (then re-hired to manage the team before the 2013 season by Ricciardi's successor, Alex Anthopoulos).

Ricciardi coached and managed in the Yankees and Milwaukee Brewers minor league systems before joining the Athletics in 1985, earning promotion to special assistant to the general manager in 1994.

THE BILLY BEANE WAY

Blue Jays president and chief executive officer Paul Godfrey, like many baseball executives, was intrigued by the approach being used by Beane, the general manager of the Oakland Athletics. That approach also intrigued *New York Times* bestselling author Michael Lewis, who was in the process of writing *Moneyball*, a book that would turn into a bestseller and spawn a Hollywood movie that focused on how Beane and the underfunded Athletics used statistically enhanced baseball analysis to defy what they saw as the game's natural tendency to overvalue the mind's eye. What Godfrey needed was somebody who understood that in Ted Rogers' world, it was an absolute must that there be limited "sticker shock," a phrase that he and Ricciardi would use often in their discussions after Ricciardi took the job.

Godfrey aimed high at the start of his search. Of course, there was always the titillating possibility of a return by Gillick, who was GM of the Mariners at the time, but Godfrey couldn't afford to wait. So he called Beane, who immediately mentioned his Number Two: Paul DePodesta, a Harvard-educated number cruncher who was the co-star of *Moneyball*.

Godfrey concurred that DePodesta was a great candidate. He was, in fact, already the Blue Jays' second choice and he hadn't even been interviewed. "But you're our first choice," Godfrey said to Beane. Beane's response was thanks but no thanks. He was not ready to leave California, as much for personal as professional reasons. Godfrey therefore wasn't surprised a year later when Beane turned down the job of a lifetime—GM of the Red Sox—citing family matters. Beane was divorced from his wife, Tara, but still maintained contact with her and their daughter, Casey, both of whom lived in Newport Beach. "She calls, I drop everything," Godfrey remembers Beane saying.

DePodesta was a logical name for the Blue Jays, since he was widely considered to be the executor of Beane's hypothetical musings. It was DePodesta who sparked Beane's intellectual curiosity, which had been piqued during his time under Sandy Alderson. The former Marine and San Francisco lawyer with degrees from Dartmouth and Harvard was the Athletics' GM when Beane finally realized he was a failed prospect and gave up his playing career to join the organization's front office.

More than a decade before the publication of *Moneyball*, Alderson had quietly institutionalized what amounted to a philosophical underpinning based on the importance of on-base percentage, and put it into effect when hard economic times hit the organization. He had always been skeptical about the scouting of baseball players, failing to understand how people who practised what everybody agreed was an imperfect science could be so certain when they expressed their views. He also wondered openly about the power of the baseball manager, believing the manager ought to be an on-field extension of the front office, running the game and the team the way the front office wanted it run.

So DePodesta it was. From Godfrey's point of view—with a loss of $52.9 million after one year of Rogers ownership and an exchange rate that was killing a club that paid its uniformed personnel in US dollars while collecting revenue at home in Canadian dollars—the main thing was to get the program in place. If not Beane,

DePodesta—whose first job in sports had been as an intern with the Canadian Football League's Baltimore Stallions—would do.

In 2003, DePodesta would be invited by Credit Suisse Boston to give a speech to bankers and business executives, the result of his prominence as one of the protagonists in *Moneyball*, which by that point was seen as an intellectual treatise on market inefficiency. DePodesta was no less harsh on scouts in his speech as Lewis was in his book, but it was one particular statement that seemed to sum up the philosophy and why it was attractive to owners of baseball teams: "Ninety percent of the player population in baseball is replaceable by someone who makes less."

Not surprisingly, DePodesta interviewed well with the Blue Jays, but in the end he, too, turned down the job for personal reasons. He was about to get married, and the prospect of relocating his new family to Toronto three weeks before the wedding was simply not doable. DePodesta would remain with the Athletics until joining the Los Angeles Dodgers in February 2004, holding that job for two seasons, in which the Dodgers would experience their first playoff win in 16 years only to follow it with their worst record in 11 years.

But Godfrey was still not dissuaded from his dream of Moneyball North. He had looked elsewhere originally: truth is, the first choice all along had been Terry Ryan, GM of the Minnesota Twins, an organization that had made its mark through shrewd scouting and a cost-effective approach to team building. But the Twins did not give Godfrey permission to speak to Ryan. Dave Dombrowski—who had been GM of the Expos and Florida Marlins, winning a World Series with the latter—visited Toronto and was interested in the job; it was a short flight to his hometown of Chicago. But Detroit was closer. It was also looking for a GM, and Tigers owner Mike Ilitch offered Dombrowski an ownership stake in the team as well as its presidency. The Blue Jays were blown out of the water. John Hart, who was in the process of leaving the Indians for the Texas Rangers; Doug Melvin, who had been the Rangers GM and would go on to fill that capacity with the Milwaukee Brewers, with Gord Ash as one of his assistants; and Buck Showalter, the former Yankees and Rangers manager who would go on to manage the Arizona Diamondbacks, also interviewed for the job.

BILLY'S BASEBALL GUY

And so, as rejection followed rejection, Godfrey started to wonder about a name that kept coming up in his email box, and in chat rooms and on message boards. It is normal for potential GMs to float their names or interest to favoured reporters or publications, but J. P. Ricciardi's name seldom came out of the rumour mill. Indeed, following his promotion to special assistant with the Athletics, the only time Ricciardi remembered musing about a job that interested him was in 1997, when the Cleveland Indians offered him the post of director of scouting. Godfrey just remembers hearing and reading people talking about "Billy's baseball guy." He called Beane, who said he would talk to Ricciardi before giving approval, only because he didn't think Ricciardi necessarily wanted the job.

Beane's feelings were accurate. Ricciardi liked living in Worcester and wasn't looking to change jobs. But Beane told him it wouldn't hurt to listen to what the Blue Jays were offering, that if nothing else the experience of being interviewed would be good.

"I never really had ambitions to be a general manager," Ricciardi said. "But Billy made sense. I thought I'd go up there, jump on a plane and come home and kind of figure out what the whole process was about and then move forward with my life."

Ricciardi was offered and accepted the job within four hours.

Even before the first scout was fired (and he'd fire a lot of them) or the first player traded (he'd trade a lot of them), Ricciardi's hiring was cloaked in controversy, and although none of it was his own doing, it set a tone that would continue throughout his reign. By the time Ricciardi was fired as GM in 2009–by Paul Beeston, who had returned from the commissioner's office to replace Godfrey– he had fought an all-fronts war against public perception and the reality of working for a team owned by a publicly traded company. One of the first points of contention–that truly was not of his doing–involved Dave Stewart. The tough right-handed pitcher with the trademark menacing stare, a Cy Young Award–winner to boot, was one of the heroes of the Blue Jays' World Series winning teams, and stayed around the organization after his retirement, filling a variety of roles. Stewart was, according to most people, at best a long-shot candidate for the GM's job after Ash's departure, but that's not the way he viewed it, and on his way out he blistered the organization for what he saw as a slight based on the fact he was an African-American.

The truth was that as a pitching coach and front office executive, Stewart had had run-ins with players and run-ins with people who questioned his loyalty to Ash. In addition, some of his personnel recommendations–including signing Joey Hamilton, arguably one of the least popular citizens of any Blue Jays clubhouse–did not inspire confidence. But in fairness to Stewart, it had not been a particularly good run for commissioner Bud Selig's attempts to get visible minorities into front office positions. Selig had become more militant in recent years in pressing teams to give minority candidates consideration, but all Stewart saw was white guy after white guy getting the jobs. The Dodgers promoted Dan Evans from within, the Rangers hired John Hart from the Indians, who in turn promoted Mark Shapiro from within. And now Ricciardi was getting a job Stewart felt was his.

"They think the only people capable of doing these jobs are white people," Stewart told the Associated Press. "I'm not speaking for myself, I'm speaking for a lot of minority candidates who have not been given the opportunity. The man I work for here, Paul Godfrey, told me he would like me to take on his manager's job before he hired Buck Martinez. Why was it okay to hire me to manage his club but not okay for me to be his GM?" Stewart went so far as to bring Ricciardi into the argument, telling the *Toronto Star*, "The more qualified guy didn't get the job. I can swallow some crap, but I can't swallow this much."

Against this backdrop, the Blue Jays unveiled Ricciardi as their new GM on November 14, 2001, less than two months after Ricciardi turned 42 years of age. Godfrey—the same man who had signed off on Delgado's market-rattling contract and had defied Ash and his scouts in giving shortstop Alex Gonzalez a multi-year deal—spent much of Ricciardi's introductory news conference hammering home the onerous financial position created by exchange rate issues, while the new GM spoke at length about on-base percentage. Godfrey made it clear that the Blue Jays could not compete with the Yankees and Red Sox in terms of payroll and talked about the success enjoyed by the Athletics. If the book had been out—*Moneyball* wasn't published until 2003—the very phrase would have dominated the news conference. For now, it was enough that Godfrey called Ricciardi an individual "who worked for an organization for 15 years that has produced winners, has got the experience of winning, has a vision going forward and a philosophy that has been tried and true.

"The fact is," Godfrey continued, "he is an obvious disciple of Billy Beane and I think that anybody following baseball would know that Billy Beane's experience has worked very well, and they do it with a lot less dollars than a number of others."

So there it was. Despite the fact that Ricciardi would seldom be mentioned in *Moneyball*, he was nevertheless cast in with a group that spurred what amounted to a civil war within the game. Despite the fact Ricciardi is never quoted in the book using the same harsh or critical language about scouts and their abilities that Beane, DePodesta or the author himself used, he became part of the cost-cutting, scout-unemploying, laptop-loving clique. Despite the fact that Lewis himself stressed the night-and-day's difference between Ricciardi and DePodesta—the latter was an "intellectual," in Lewis's words, while Ricciardi was "somebody who has a real, natural ability to manage people and is comfortable communicating with people in confrontational situations . . . who has a lot of street savvy and is a little more in the mix with baseball people"—Ricciardi still found himself in the crosshairs.

MUCH ADO ABOUT NUMBERS

Statistical analysis was hardly groundbreaking territory for baseball. Branch Rickey espoused the virtues of on-base percentage— the importance of getting on base by a walk, hit or hit by pitch—because he believed rightly that in a game with no time clock it was a means of extending and expanding a pitcher's workload, increasing the likelihood of a mistake on which the hitters could capitalize. Earl Weaver managed the Baltimore Orioles during their golden days using the same philosophy, while one of his players who went on to manage—Davey Johnson—was using computer punch cards long before most teachers or high school students.

Where Beane's approach cut too close to the bone—where "moneyball" itself cut too close to the bone for many in the industry—was in its open questioning of the cost-effectiveness of the type of analysis done by scouts, the guys in the field with their stopwatches and radar guns. Understand this: nobody gets filthy rich as a scout, unless you consider accumulating Marriott points and frequent flyer miles as a means of accruing wealth. Those who become lifers have long enjoyed an exalted status at the grassroots of the game. Baseball is an industry that thrives on gossip and internal politics, and in the field scouts are often the conduit, sitting together in reserved seats during games, dining together in press box dining rooms. There is a world-weary sense to many of them; a natural outgrowth, perhaps, of doing a job where their analyses can be brutally exposed or taken for granted, leading to a feeling that their long hours are often under-appreciated.

Eddie Bane, who was the Los Angeles Angels of Anaheim's director of scouting from 2004 to 2010, once referred to moneyball as "a threat to our industry," and blamed it for creating an adversarial climate. Appearing as part of a round table in the January 2005 issue of *Baseball America*, Bane said, "Our guys, the so-called old-school guys, the thought is out there that we don't know how to handle a computer and we wouldn't know how to use the stuff. I'm very comfortable with a computer. Our people are very comfortable with a computer. We do have to drag some of our old-time guys through it, but the main adversarial thing is that some of our old-time guys are losing jobs that we didn't feel they should be losing. It was due to cutbacks. Maybe the cutbacks were due to money or whatever. But we correlate it to the fact that some of the computer stuff is causing that. And we resent it."

Keith Law was a special consultant for Blue Jays general manager J. P. Ricciardi from 2002 to 2006. He was Ricciardi's statistics guy, his version of Paul DePodesta ("Rainman," Ricciardi would call him). Law, who graduated with honours from Harvard with a major in sociology and economics before completing his Masters of Business Administration at Carnegie Mellon's Tepper School of

Business, struck up a relationship Ricciardi while writing for *Baseball Prospectus*, a publication that had become *de rigueur* for all the cool kids. He and Ricciardi would eventually have a well-publicized falling out, but for awhile he was among the GM's most trusted confidants. He believes the tension between the old and new schools is totally understandable.

"One of the things that happened to J. P. was that the longer he was GM, the balance shifted for him between how much he leaned on analytics and how much he leaned on his own eyes," Law said. "I mean, I would never accuse J. P. of ignoring or being against analytics. But it's a hard thing for people to wrap their head around. The human brain is not wired to ignore what it sees, and part of moneyball was understanding the fact that what your brain thinks it sees may not be an accurate picture. I mean, it's hard to believe a guy you see make three great plays is actually a shitty defender until you examine every play a guy makes in an entire calendar year. And the fact is, the guy sucks."

Ricciardi said that whatever change occurred in his approach had as much to do with the ownership of the team as with any great philosophical shift on his part. "I don't think there was a lot of honesty as far as what they wanted," Ricciardi said. "They kind of said they wanted to follow what went on in Oakland, but I don't think they had any idea how to go about it. They were looking for a plan and the problem was the plan I came in with . . . I just don't think they understood how it would come about. I told them at the beginning it would be painful, that if you can't spend money there's only one way to do it and that's to rebuild through scouting and the draft and it's going to be a lot different doing it in a division with the New York Yankees and Boston Red Sox."

THE "SCOUT THING"

Ricciardi was about to discover that working for a club that has to answer to shareholders presented a unique set of political challenges and demanded a quickness of foot. His legacy is pretty much cemented, but as he moved on to a new job as a special assistant with Sandy Alderson, now the New York Mets' GM, the "scout thing," as he calls it, still rankles him. To this day, Ricciardi takes offence at the suggestion that he does not value the work of scouts or scouting. It is true that he fired upward of 20 scouts from the Blue Jays when he took over from Ash, and that his moves sent a shudder throughout the industry (since the Blue Jays were considered one of the best scouting organizations in the game). But he made it clear that the decision was taken due to wholesale cost-cutting throughout baseball operations as well as the usual "rationalization" that occurs whenever a new man steps into the position.

Tim Collins is one of the reasons the scout issue still bothers him.

J. P. Ricciardi was in his fifth season as general manager of the Toronto Blue Jays when he and his sons, Dante and Mariano, drove out one summer's night to watch an American Legion game in their hometown of Worcester. Ricciardi's kids would run around and play near the field; a few of Ricciardi's friends would be there too. East Side Post 201 had always been a going concern in Worcester baseball—Ricciardi himself had played for them as a youngster—and there was a pitcher scheduled to throw in the game that his buddies said Ricciardi needed to see.

Instead, he saw Tim Collins—about 150 pounds' worth of 17-year-old, a left-handed pitcher capable of only the mid-80s on the radar gun. But also 150 pounds of "can't be hit." "I was near the bullpen and heard this ball exploding into the catcher's glove,"

Ricciardi said. "I turned and looked and said to one of the guys, 'That sound is coming out of that little shit?'" Collins had gone undrafted out of Worcester Tech and was a couple of weeks away from attending the Community College of Rhode Island. That night, he was pretty much doing what he did all summer long, striking out people with an 82- or 83-miles-per-hour fastball and wondering about a career in construction. But Ricciardi liked what he saw, liked it enough to set up a bullpen session in front of his own scouts. Collins was signed for $10,000. He was traded to the Atlanta Braves by Ricciardi's successor, Alex Anthopoulos (in the move that brought shortstop Yunel Escobar to the Blue Jays), and then traded again to the Kansas City Royals. He has appeared in 140 games and has a 3.49 earned run average.

Ricciardi likes to tell the story because even a couple of seasons after being fired from his position as GM of the Blue Jays, he still hears about "that scout thing." Despite the fact that one of his closest confidants with the Blue Jays was life-long baseball manager/coach/scout Bobby Mattick–who used to tell Ricciardi's critics within the fraternity that they just didn't get the guy– Ricciardi still can't escape the notion that he is anti-scout. In truth, he was a hybrid, somebody who would use numbers to get a read on a player but then use his eyes to render judgment. A further truth? He was likely miscast as the GM of a team owned by a big company. "I've always been an evaluator and a field guy and that's never changed," Ricciardi said. "I've been in scouting my whole life, and it was really frustrating from my end in the sense that this is who I am and this is what I'm all about but no one seemed to notice it. It was like I was some geeky guy who came out of some front office and I was never that.

"I signed Timmy when I was GM of the Blue Jays. You don't just walk into a ballpark and sign a player if you don't have a background in scouting and player development."

Even his successor, Anthopoulos, says of Ricciardi, "Put J. P. on a field with three players there and ask him who of the three will play, and he'll be right almost all of the time." The 2012 Blue Jays were still very much a team compiled on Ricciardi's watch. Closer Casey Janssen was a Ricciardi draft pick, as was catcher J. P. Arencibia and starter Ricky Romero. Right fielder Jose Bautista was a Ricciardi trade acquisition from the Pittsburgh Pirates, and Blue Jays Player of the Year Edwin Encarnacion was another. Over 50 players were put into the major leagues by Ricciardi and his Blue Jays scouts and coaches—many, like Collins, have moved on—but against the big-spending New York Yankees and Boston Red Sox it was never enough.

Tony LaCava, who was hired by Ricciardi in 2002 and rose to the ranks of special advisor to Anthopoulos—turning down at least two GM's jobs, in Pittsburgh and Baltimore, in the process—remembers Ricciardi first as a competitor, as a guy capable of seeing a tall shortstop named Tanyon Sturtze and telling one of his scouting buddies, "I'm going to sign that kid as a pitcher" before calling in his report from a bar across the street.

"J. P.'s a very good baseball man—really more of a baseball guy than he is a statistical guy," said LaCava, who joined the Blue Jays after a brief stint with the Cleveland Indians following his departure from the Montreal Expos, where he served as director of player development. "When looking at the evidence, he would always seem to go to use his baseball scouting background to make the decision at the end of the day.

"He was a very good scout," added LaCava. "He was competitive. I knew when he was on a guy or in the park, you felt like you better have your A game. I remember the first time I met him, in '91 [when LaCava was scouting for the then California Angels], he asked me what area I had. I told him that I lived in Pittsburgh and was going to do Pennsylvania, New York and New England, which is a crazy, big area. He goes, 'Good luck!' Like that. Just, 'good luck with that!' I said, 'Well, okay.' I looked at that as a challenge. I started working my butt off and both of us were all over the place. He started working his way up the ladder with the Oakland Athletics and we'd talk about opportunities every now and then. It was just that nothing worked, until Toronto."

Though all the talk when Godfrey hired Ricciardi was about how the Blue Jays were going to become an extension of the Oakland Athletics, it turned out not to be the case. Not entirely, and, in Ricciardi's case, intentionally so. In the words of Keith Law, Ricciardi saw moneyball as a "way to enhance scouting, not as a replacement for it."

"He never bought into the more philosophical benefits of moneyball," Law said.

"It was a way of attacking the market. Instead, for J. P., it was a way to make sure we were scouting more effectively, to make sure we were going to see the right players. There was a difference between J. P. and, say, Paul [DePodesta]. If you sat down and spoke to each of them for 20 minutes, you'd come away thinking that Paul has a more analytical mind and that J. P. is more impetuous."

Being lumped in with the moneyball fraternity would naturally bring Ricciardi into conflict with people who remembered the Blue Jays for their profligate scouting system, but the fact is that Ricciardi did clean house in a whirlwind that struck some people as a little too zestful. He fired several long-tenured scouts and put himself in confrontation with, among others, Tim Wilken. The organization's hugely regarded director of scouting must have swallowed hard as he saw the carnage of Ricciardi's overhaul—not to mention taking note of Ricciardi's willingness to exercise the prerogative of any new GM and bring in his own people, especially people with whom he had personal ties. Ricciardi's next focus would be the roster.

ROSTER MOVES

The Blue Jays' 2002 payroll of $76,864,993 was in fact only a modest decrease from the payroll in Gord Ash's final year as GM ($76,895,999), but more than a third of it, $30.4 million, was eaten up by Delgado and Raul Mondesi, the erratic outfielder Ash had acquired from the Los Angeles Dodgers in the trade for Shawn Green. By the end of Ricciardi's first season, Mondesi had been sold off to the New York Yankees for left-hander Scott Wiggins. The deal was put together by Godfrey and Yankees owner George Steinbrenner, and announced by Ricciardi in the back of the press box at Boston's Fenway Park while the Blue Jays were in the middle of losing 4–0 to the Yankees' archrival Red Sox, en route to a 78–84 season. The Blue Jays agreed to pick up $6 million of the $13 million due to Mondesi in 2003, saving the remainder of his 2002 salary, which on a pro-rated basis came to about $5.5 million.

It was one of the most bizarre days of Ricciardi's first season in charge of the team. First, it came in Boston—near his home— and was a trade designed to help out the hated Yankees, which is why Ricciardi joked about how "my house is probably getting egged right now." Second, it had been preceded by reports in *Baseball Weekly* that the Red Sox wanted Ricciardi to be their GM, reports that would net Ricciardi a quick contract extension from the Blue Jays.

Ricciardi had signed a three-year contract when he agreed to become the Blue Jays' GM after the 2001 season, but that deal was torn up and replaced on October 8, 2002, by a five-year contract. The announcement was made a week after Paul Godfrey denied the Red Sox's request to talk to Ricciardi, ending a four-month narrative that seemed to point to Ricciardi leaving Toronto.

"Here's what I know about the whole situation," Ricciardi said. "The year before I took the job with the Blue Jays I got a call saying we'd like you to come to Boston. It wasn't going to be for the general manager's job, and I just told them, 'Look, I have a contract [with the Oakland Athletics] right now. So we can wait until the contract is up. They talked to me again when the Blue Jays' contract came up but by then I had already decided, why not go with Toronto? It's not like these jobs come around every day.

"So Paul called me and was kind of feeling me out about what I'd like to do," Ricciardi said (about the renewed interest from the Red Sox). "I said, 'Paul, if you're asking me if I want to go to work for a team that I grew up with? If you're asking me whether I want to work for a team that's 45 minutes from my house? You're asking me if I want to go to a team that has way more resources than the Blue Jays and that is absolutely going to go out and win? You're asking me that question?'

"He said, 'Yeah, I am,'" Ricciardi said, continuing. "I told him the answer is 'no.' I've given you my word. While it is appealing to me, I can't do that.'" Godfrey's next question was the obvious one: Did he want a contract extension? Ricciardi's response: "I'd be fine with that."

"That whole out clause was kind of a grey area to begin with," Ricciardi said. "But, yeah, I probably walked away from winning world championships. Thing is, though, I couldn't walk out on the Blue Jays."

The Mondesi deal was vintage Ricciardi. He had spent the first eight months of his tenure shedding expensive relievers (Billy Koch, Paul Quantrill, Dan Plesac and Pedro Borbon Jr. were all thrown overboard) as well as shortstop Alex Gonzalez and designated hitter Brad Fullmer. "We didn't get the brass ring in this deal, but we did get the second free ride around," Ricciardi said after

Mondesi was traded. "We're obviously rebuilding, and this helps keep the process going. It gets us out of a lot of money. We need to get past the point where we're strapped financially with guys who aren't going to be here when we turn the corner."

And that was a signal for reporters to descend, after the game, on the locker of the Blue Jays' highest paid player: Carlos Delgado.

STRANGE DAYS

DELGADO'S RELATIONSHIP WITH THE BLUE JAYS
and their fans was complicated even before Ricciardi's arrival. The General Manager made little secret of the fact that he felt hamstrung by the four-year, $68 million contract that Delgado was given before the sale of the team to Rogers Communications had been formally approved. Yet the contract was entirely defensible, when viewed in the context of the Shawn Green trade. Delgado is to post–World Series Blue Jays position players what Roy Halladay is to pitchers. Signed as a catcher by the Jays as a 16-year-old out of Aguadilla, Puerto Rico, in 1988, just before Puerto Rican players were made eligible for the amateur draft, Delgado was in the bullpen as an extra player during the Blue Jays' 1993 World Series win, receiving a ring even though he was not on the active roster. Delgado was big for a catcher, so he seemed destined for a position switch. The transition began in 1994, when he played left field in spring training before going down to the minor leagues where he was again asked to catch. But the seed was sown, and the full-time move to first base came in 1995 at Triple-A Syracuse.

"I was having a bit of an issue with my knees," Delgado said, "and Cito spoke to me about moving to first base. I said, 'You know, I've never played first base, but I'll give it a try.' It didn't take me long to realize it was the type of move that would stretch out my career." It certainly did that: Delgado had a couple of 162-game seasons, and could generally be counted on to play about 150 games. "If I was a catcher," Delgado said, "that never would have happened."

Delgado's makeup, in scout parlance, was off the charts when the Blue Jays signed him. He was a bright kid–well grounded and intuitive, able to think on his feet–and the move to first base reinforced in his mind the importance of adaptability. "Don't get me wrong, I'm very passionate about some things in my life, but I also understand there are other things that you can't have 100 percent control over," Delgado said. "I learned that you have to adjust along the way. I learned how to pick my fights, I guess, so that instead of being stubborn about something, I would try to find a way to make it better."

The truth is that there were teams who would have killed for a player of Delgado's temperament and sensibilities. He embraced life in Toronto, becoming an ambassador for the team and city. A sensitive, intelligent individual with a finely crafted worldview, he would sometimes ride his bicycle from his Yorkville condominium to the SkyDome. By the end of his Blue Jays career, Delgado led the club in home runs, runs batted in, walks, OPS, slugging percentage, extra-base hits, total bases and walks. He was a two-time All-Star and placed second in American League Most Valuable Player voting in 2003, losing to Alex Rodriguez (then of the Texas Rangers) despite posting a 1.019 OPS for the season and collecting 27 more RBIs than Rodriguez in the same number of games.

But Delgado, like Halladay, also became the personification of a team that was never able to take the ultimate step forward and gain a post-season berth. There were seasons where he believes the team was close—the 2000 campaign comes to mind—but ultimately it was the combination of a difficult division and the fact that the Blue Jays, in Delgado's words, "always seemed to be one or two pitchers away from putting it together." Vernon Wells, the fifth pick overall in the 1997 draft who was a Blue Jays regular from 2002 to 2010, said the team kept "running into the same situation several times." They'd play well in the first half, run into major injuries, and get caught by the superior strength of the Yankees and Red Sox. "Names, pedigree, money," Wells said, matter-of-factly. "That was the difference."

"In that division," added Delgado, "it wasn't like you were playing the Bad News Bears."

Managerial instability didn't help either. From the time of Cito Gaston's firing at the end of 1997, Delgado played for four different managers in seven years before departing as a free agent.

"It would have been nice to have one person stick around longer to bring a little more consistency," said Delgado. "Probably, it would have brought a lot more civility and identity too. It just seemed as if for a couple of years we didn't have our sights set on where we needed to be. I think stability could have brought that; if a manager is there for awhile, he has a better understanding of how best to use you to get the best performance for the team.

"What I'm saying," Delgado continued, "is that whenever you make a mistake, you have to regroup and go to a Plan B. Sometimes . . . it seemed we did not have a Plan B, or did not have money for a Plan B or didn't want to spend the money on a Plan B."

THE TIPPING POINT

Delgado had become isolated as a big-money player with the dealing of Mondesi in 2002, when he was in the second year of a four-year contract. Ricciardi had already started talking quietly to favoured members of the media about how Delgado's contract was an albatross, but Delgado didn't need to hear anything on or off the record to know where he stood.

"This is a business," said Delgado, who for the most part wore with dignity the bull's eye that had been painted on his back. "Today you're here, tomorrow you don't know where you'll be. And tomorrow became today for Mondy.

"This is a situation that hasn't come my way. I don't want to start any kind of rumours because it's not out there yet. If somebody comes my way and says people want to talk about it, we have to listen. If somebody comes up to me—and that somebody in this case is J. P.—and talks about it, then we have to worry about it."

Ricciardi's relationship with Delgado proved to be problematic for both men. Delgado read everything written about him, and had a pretty good idea of the origins of the notion that his contract was dragging down the franchise. Ricciardi was not able to deal with Delgado in that first season, a situation that became even more of an issue in 2003, when Rogers dropped payroll to $51,269,000, a figure that was 21st out of baseball's 32 teams and a staggering $101 million lower than the Yankees and more than $48 million behind the Red Sox. One year later, the payroll fell even further, to $50,017,000—still 21st and a little more than a million short of the 1995 Blue Jays payroll which, in that season, had been tops in the majors.

Keith Law is right when he calls the 2004 season a "tipping point." Manager Carlos Tosca had seemed a creative choice to replace Buck Martinez, and for awhile there was a quiet glow of competence around the team. Tosca was only the sixth manager in major league history to have never played the game at a professional level, but he'd been a well-respected minor league manager and knew his way around a lineup card. Tosca was in fact destined to become the Blue Jays' manager the day he was signed as third-base coach by Ricciardi at the 2001 winter meetings in Boston. Tosca replaced Terry Bevington, who had been fired from Buck Martinez's staff after the 2001 season along with hitting coach Cito Gaston. Tosca had spent three years with the Arizona Diamondbacks as bench coach to Buck Showalter, who was familiar to Ricciardi from their days together in the New York Yankees organization. Tosca also knew Jack Gillis (Ricciardi's former college coach at St. Leo's and the Blue Jays' scouting cross-checker) as well as Dick Scott, the Blue Jays' director of player personnel who joined the organization from the Diamondbacks. That was how Ricciardi did things; he valued loyalty and familiarity, which is why he also had his minor league roommate, John Gibbons, brought on as bullpen coordinator.

A native of Cuba who was fond of red wine and cigars, Tosca guided the team to a 58–51 record in 2002. The 2003 Blue Jays went 86–76 and finished 15 games out of first place and nine back of the wild card in a season in which much went well. Roy Halladay set a club record with 22 wins. Carlos Delgado had a monster OPS of 1.019 while belting 42 homers and 145 runs batted in. Vernon Wells set a team record with 215 hits, beating Tony Fernandez's 17-year-old record of 213. The Blue Jays had a 21–8 May and were one game out on June 23 when, after beating the Baltimore Orioles 13–4, they went into a 4–13 spiral.

Tosca was not given a contract extension, and when the 2004 Blue Jays laboured through a 7–15 April—starting 0–8 at home—and were six games out within the first two weeks of the season, Ricciardi started to make his concerns about Tosca known. After a game in late April where Tosca left starting pitcher Miguel Batista in too long (resulting in a blown three-run lead to the Minnesota Twins and leading to revelations that Tosca and putative closer Terry Adams had communication issues), Ricciardi, who said in an interview on May 1 that he found the team "hard to watch," openly second-guessed his manager on his weekly call-in show on the team's flagship station, Sportsnet 590 The Fan.

Ricciardi, remember, grew up in Red Sox Nation, where baseball was very much part of the daily bread of newspapers, radio and TV. He was a regular at Peter Gammons' *Hot Stove, Cool Music* gabfest in the off-season in Boston, and understood that if he put himself out there publicly he could avoid having his thoughts parsed through a media filter. The problem with Ricciardi's irregularly scheduled sessions in Toronto, hosted by Mike Wilner, was that Ricciardi was a little too glib and off-the-cuff. The result was radio gold: it was on one of these shows that we learned that slugger Adam Dunn didn't really like baseball, and that even though Carlos Delgado didn't think he needed a title to make his career a success, he was still a really good guy. It was also through these shows that Carlos Tosca must have developed the sense that his days managing the Blue Jays were dwindling.

In July, Ricciardi again agreed with a caller who took Tosca to task for wasting pinch-hitter Frank Catalanotto in a game against the Oakland Athletics. The end came after a 6–0 loss to the New York Yankees on August 7, when Ricciardi said he thought the club was "mailing it in." Tosca handled his post-game media responsibilities before being fired by Godfrey and Ricciardi, the latter of whom would later say the sluggish starts were particularly discouraging. A news conference was held at Yankee Stadium to make the formal announcement, and John Gibbons was handed the manager's reins on an interim basis, going 20–30 the rest of the way. The Blue Jays finished a whopping 33½ games out of first.

Wells, Catalanotto and Halladay all suffered injuries (Halladay missed much of the season with a sore shoulder). Pat Hentgen, in many ways the patron saint of all Blue Jays pitchers, heard a player with the Kansas City Royals describe his stuff as being "Double-A, at best" and retired in July with a 2–9 (6.95) record. What else could be said about a season that saw Tom Cheek, the club's beloved broadcaster, see a streak of 4,306 regular-season games end when he attended the funeral of his father, only to be diagnosed with a brain tumour after noticeably stumbling over his words a few days after his return? Cheek, who was inducted into the Baseball Hall of Fame as the winner of the 2013 Ford C. Frick Award for broadcast excellence, passed away in 2005.

As if things weren't bleak enough, the organization—and Ricciardi personally—had much of its soul ripped out when long-time scout Bobby Mattick, who had worked for the Blue Jays since their inception in 1976, died on December 16 at the age of 89. While the title "senior advisor" is thrown around often in the game, few have fit it in the manner of Mattick. Ricciardi's relationship with Mattick gave the lie to the idea that Ricciardi was a numbers wienie with no scouting bonafides. Friends of Mattick say that he had resolved to leave the organization early in Ricciardi's tenure, but that after a spring training visit in the GM's office a strong bond was kindled, one that often saw Mattick defend Ricciardi to his detractors.

THE END

That 2004 season was a painful parting for Delgado. Ricciardi had long believed that the first baseman's no-trade clause was an impediment to doing business with a restricted payroll—and Delgado had indeed used it to block any potential trade for four seasons. One year after narrowly missing the MVP, Delgado was limited to 128 games and hit just .269 while still managing 32 home runs. Delgado strained an intercostal muscle in his side in May just as he appeared to be getting his swing back. He would miss 33 games, and when he came back after the All-Star Break it was with the shadow of the July 31 trade deadline hanging over him.

The season resumed in Arlington, Texas, with a game against the Rangers, and while the Blue Jays and Delgado worked out in sweltering heat at what was then called Ameriquest Field, Ricciardi said that he was going to fly to Arlington and approach Delgado about waiving the clause. "If I don't ask Carlos about it, I won't know for sure if he wants to go or doesn't want to go. If he says he wants to explore some options . . . well, at this point it's just a matter of me going up to him. We'll talk."

"Let's not get ahead of ourselves," Delgado said warily during the team's workout the day before the resumption of the season.

The next day, in full view, Ricciardi approached Delgado behind the batting cage, within eyesight but out of earshot of the media and many of his teammates. The body language was clear. "I told them I would not be waiving my no-trade clause, and he [Ricciardi] said: 'That's your right, no problem.'" Delgado paused. "Then, I went out and hit.

"A lot went into this . . . moving, at this time . . ." Delgado said, his voice trailing off.

Ricciardi was succinct. "The book's closed," he said.

Delgado now says that he was aware that the Los Angeles Dodgers and Red Sox were enquiring about his availability, but he doesn't believe there was an actual trade in place that waiving his no-trade clause would have facilitated. That is true; Ricciardi will tell you that discussions with the two teams never progressed to the point where he asked about players in return, although he thinks both teams had an idea of what would have been appropriate.

With an eye on payroll, the Blue Jays were concerned that if they offered Delgado salary arbitration—a necessity under the game's collective agreement to qualify for compensation in the event Delgado signed with another club—he might actually accept it. In that case, the club would in the very least have been faced with the possibility of negotiating a one-year contract with Delgado or going to arbitration, where an independent arbitrator would have surely looked at Delgado's 2004 numbers—he hit

32 home runs and drove in 99 despite a .269 batting average—and handed him a deal that would have continued to hamstring the organization.

Predictably, the Blue Jays let Delgado walk at the end of the season without offering him arbitration. "I felt like I wasn't wanted," Delgado said. "But I also knew it was business, and that it was okay. It was," he said, "time to move on."

There was, however, a strangeness to the departure. While most of the city's media and many of the team's fans agreed that each side needed a change of scenery, even some of Delgado's critics felt Ricciardi hadn't handled it properly.

"I didn't know much about the moneyball thing," Delgado said. "I wanted to give myself and him a fair chance to start a relationship; I didn't want to just think this guy didn't like me because I had a big contract.

"Sometimes he did things . . . well, we had a difference of opinion," Delgado said, laughing. "But that's baseball. The thing is, it would have been nice if I was healthy. Then, I might have considered it [a trade]. It would have been nice, too, if he had talked it over with me—just me and him—before other people found out. That way people wouldn't have been, ah, exposed and taking a lot of heat."

In the end, Delgado would sign a four-year, $52 million free-agent contract with the Florida Marlins in January 2005. He would play five more seasons, the final four with the New York Mets, who acquired him in a trade for three minor leaguers and $7 million in cash. He remains one of the Blue Jays' career leaders in several offensive categories and will see his name go up on the Blue Jays Level of Excellence during the summer of 2013. In some ways, that will close the circle.

"The way it turned out, it was that I was too comfortable in Toronto, that I didn't want to go to a contender. Blah blah blah.

But, you know, I was hurt. What can I say? It's like having someone trade you while you're on the disabled list. I didn't think I could help anybody. Anyhow, a few years later with the Mets, I got to play on a contender on the biggest stage, and I proved my point in my own quiet manner."

There have been times, post-1993, that the Blue Jays' back-to-back World Series have felt like a millstone around the team's neck. Delgado certainly understands that history is sometimes a burden, even when it's successful history. It was no different when he was eventually traded from the Marlins to the Mets, where he finished out his career in 2009.

"You win, and it brings you fame and glory," Delgado said. "The Blue Jays had some great players before 1992 and 1993—you think of Dave Stieb and George Bell—but there's something about the World Series that makes it forever. I saw this when I was with the Mets. I mean, Jesus Christ, all you'd hear was about 1986. Everything you did was compared to '86. 'It was better in '86 . . . it was better in '86 . . . it was better in '86.'"

Unfortunately for the Jays and their fans, 1993 was fading further and further into the past. But just two months after Delgado signed with the Florida Marlins, Ricciardi received a promise that revived long-dormant aspirations.

10

THE BIG
PLUNGE

IT WAS A PHONE CALL J. P. RICCIARDI NEVER
imagined receiving. When the Blue Jays' general manager picked
up the phone on that day in early 2005, Paul Godfrey asked if he
was sitting down.

"Ted Rogers is going to announce a three-year payroll commitment worth $210 million," Godfrey explained. "What you don't
spend one season will carry over to the next."

Both men remember Ricciardi's immediate response.

"Shit, Paul," Ricciardi said. "I couldn't spend $70 million this
season if I tried."

Although the call, and the money, appeared to come out of the
blue, a story surfaced to explain things. Rogers had apparently
spent some time with Terry McGuirk, the former chief executive
officer of Turner Broadcasting (1996–2001) and president of the
Atlanta Braves. During the course of discussion, McGuirk asked
Rogers about his baseball club, and gently chided his older friend
for not spending more money on payroll. Those who know Ted
Rogers would later smile and say it was one time when Rogers not
only listened to advice but acted on it.

Tony Viner remembers the meeting that followed the phone call
this way. "What happened was that J. P. and Paul went up to Ted's
office, along with me, and Ted said, 'Now, we're clearly not spending enough money. I've chatted with a friend of mine and we're
clearly not spending enough money.' I remember J. P. laughing
after we'd left. J. P. said, 'You need two things: money and players
available, and the problem is, the players are gone.'

"Ted wouldn't have understood that," said Viner. "But by the
same token . . . nobody wants to turn down money. The only
thing we concluded was that if a deal came along that made sense
for whatever reason, they had Ted's agreement to step up. Ted was
interesting that way. He really did understand a higher payroll

didn't mean you were going to win, but if you didn't have a higher payroll you weren't going to be anywhere."

Keith Law had a different reaction. "The first thing we were asked was, 'So, what can we do with this?' And the first thing I remember thinking is, 'Well, that's it, the development plan is done.'" Law would leave the Blue Jays in 2006 and move on to a scouting analyst and baseball insider's role with ESPN, where he became one of Ricciardi's harshest critics, to the point where the relationship between the two became toxic. "The mandate was clear. We were supposed to make the big league club better right now and I think all of us took that to mean that it didn't matter if what we did hurt the long-term development of the club."

Law believes the money turned into a weapon in Ricciardi's hands. "It's one thing to do that and another thing to do that and tell the guy to fire it, and that's what happened because my understanding is J. P. couldn't go back to Rogers and say, 'I don't need this money.' People around the office were pretty excited, because it felt like we were no longer going to be financial also-rans. But the flip side is those of us who were more interested in development and the financial side of development—well, we knew right up front that that plan was going away."

The commitment was too late to be utilized in time for the 2005 season, since the crop had already been picked over, but coupled with the clearing of Carlos Delgado's contract off the books, it left Ricciardi with a rare opportunity: for the first time in his tenure as GM, he could make at least something resembling a financial run at the likes of the New York Yankees and Boston Red Sox, who were spending $208,306,817 and $123,505,125 in payroll in 2005, compared to the Blue Jays' Opening Day figure of $45,719,500.

The money made Ricciardi think differently about some of his decisions. This much is certain: if that phone call had come a bit earlier, the Delgado issue could have gone another way. Even if the decision not to try to re-sign him stood, the Blue Jays certainly would have felt comfortable enough financially to offer him salary arbitration, which would have given the organization the compensatory draft picks it decided to forgo by not doing so. "We probably would have been more inclined to keep him if we knew we had the money," said Ricciardi. "In hindsight, we would have leaned to wanting to keep him. But we definitely would have made him an offer to keep the picks."

WARNING SIGNS

Despite entering the 2005 season with Corey Koskie as their highest-profile signing, the Blue Jays finished just two games under .500 (80–82) and played .500 baseball until late August. This after Koskie fractured his thumb when he slid headfirst into second base in a game against the Minnesota Twins on May 19— an injury that caused him to miss 58 games and damaged his stroke to the point where his career was effectively over—and ace Roy Halladay sustained a fractured leg on a lined shot back up the box off the bat of the Texas Rangers' Kevin Mench on July 8. Meanwhile, Aaron Hill, an infielder from Louisiana State University who was Ricciardi's first choice in 2003 (13th overall), was promoted. He began his major league career with a bit of a flourish, and helped take the sting out of Koskie's injury. But nobody could replace Halladay, who was 12–4 with an earned run average of 2.41 at the time of the injury. Ricciardi has said that he'll go to his grave believing the club would have captured the AL Wild Card berth with a healthy Halladay. Instead, the Boston Red Sox took the slot for the third season in a row, with their 95 wins pretty much the standard number for an AL Wild Card winner in the mid-2000s.

That the Blue Jays hung around at all was a testament to their bullpen. In addition to Halladay's fracture, their Number Two starter, Ted Lilly, missed a month and laboured with a shoulder injury that needed constant monitoring. It was a patchwork group coming out of spring training, one of quantity if not quality, but by the end of the season the Blue Jays bullpen was statistically the best in the game. Gibbons had shown himself to be an adept handler of relief pitching—which is how most baseball people judge a manager. That, plus a substantial chunk of money left over from Ted Rogers' $210 million payroll commitment, hinted of a rosy future.

Yet despite the team's performance, there were, for many, warning signs that Ricciardi was deviating from some of the basic tenets of moneyball. Scott Schoeneweis, a lefty who became one of the stalwarts of that Blue Jays bullpen, signed a two-year, $5.2 million contract that seemed modest based on the market. But for moneyball adherents it flew in the face of the notion that relievers are a dime a dozen, and a dime is just about the right price to pay for one. *Baseball Prospectus* laid down the gauntlet in its 2005 season preview when it sniffed, "This past winter they [the Blue Jays] seemed to run as fast and as far from that mindset as possible, making moves than can charitably be considered questionable, and which likely set the team back a few years in their development."

Ricciardi would go from being a flavour of the month among the game's statistics set to something of a pariah. Though *Baseball Prospectus* had once lauded him for being one of the game's bright young things, he found himself and his tactics skewered in the introductory section of the Blue Jays portion of the guide: "A team has to do more than pay lip service to running their team in an informed fashion. If it doesn't, that team deserves the same amount of criticism we're so eager to heap on the usual punching bags."

By the end of his tenure, Ricciardi's feelings about *Baseball Prospectus* had done a one-eighty. The same man who once admonished a visitor to his office in Dunedin for carrying a copy of the club-issued media guide by tossing him a copy of *Baseball Prospectus* and saying, "This is what you should be reading," began to regularly rail against the publication's editorial stance. *Baseball Prospectus* would become an epithet around the Blue Jays offices. Ricciardi—hated by scouts and their fellow old-timey baseball supporters, and suddenly denigrated by the game's laptop superstars—couldn't keep anybody happy.

HALF MEASURES

For Keith Law, Rogers' payroll commitment only served to exacerbate the worst in a trend that he believed began with the signing of Koskie. Koskie's three-year, $17 million contract looked modest enough in a winter in which teams spent poorly (Carl Pavano signed a four-year, $39.5 million deal with the Yankees and was so ineffective that one New York newspaper started referring to him as "American Idle"; Edgar Renteria inked a four-year, $40 million contract with the Red Sox, and Pedro Martinez signed a four-year, $53 million deal with the New York Mets). But Law worried about the lost draft pick that resulted from the Koskie signing, not to mention that his 2004 batting average with the Minnesota Twins was a career low, or that he'd played in the second-fewest number of games to that point in his career. Koskie ended up playing 97 games due to injuries, hitting .249 with 11 home runs and 36 runs batted in. He was traded to the

Milwaukee Brewers, eventually retiring with post-concussion syndrome.

Law believes the Koskie signing was a reaction to a 2004 season in which the Blue Jays finished last in the AL East with a 67–94 record, 33½ games out of first place. The Blue Jays had 12 players go on the disabled list in 2004, losing 747 man-games to injury.

"We weren't that well constructed to begin with, and then seven guys we were counting on came up with significant injuries," said Law. "We never recovered and I think it caused upper management, J. P. and up, to question whether we were on the right path. After that, our focus was on just trying to acquire established major league players."

Law says that led to "a lot of half measures," of which Koskie was merely the first. "He was a Canadian we could sign even though he was not very good, and injury prone and probably declining," said Law. "It was, 'Well, this is the best we can do in the major league market,' rather than turning back and saying that we needed to improve our scouting and player development plan, or maybe make adjustments faster to how we used the talent market, particularly the draft."

Compounding the issue for Law was the fact that Ricciardi's emphasis on drafting college players over higher-ceilinged high school players had backfired. On this tactic, at least, Ricciardi seemed to be on solid moneyball ground, since one of the underpinnings of moneyball was that college players were more cost-effective. They were older than some 18-year-old high schooler and had already undergone the first few years of development on somebody else's dime. The trade-off was simple: the talent level might not be as high, but the player could get to the majors faster.

"My completely retrospective view on what we tried to do, especially the first two to three seasons, is that we were too late," said Law. "The idea was sound, but by that point we had fallen too far behind Oakland to be really effective. The inefficiencies we thought we were capturing? Too many teams were chasing them by that point. Two years earlier, we might have had a chance. If it was only Oakland and one, maybe two other clubs that were chasing those inefficiencies, I think we would have been far more successful."

The Blue Jays were left to settle for "small successes all over the place," said Law, without enough critical mass to allow the team to be "relevant at the big league level." Simply put, by the time Ricciardi was able to put into practice whatever his vision of moneyball was, other teams were doing it too. "The publication of *Moneyball* didn't help," Law said with a chuckle. "Because in my opinion, it spread the ideas faster than they would have otherwise spread. Ideas in any industry don't stay in one place for a very long time, particularly in a business as mobile as the baseball industry."

Ricciardi took only five high school players in the first 20 rounds of his first draft, picked two more in the first 20 rounds of 2003— the 18th and 19th rounds, to be exact—and selected one each with his top 20 picks in the next two drafts. It wasn't until 2006 that the Blue Jays would make a high schooler their top pick, when outfielder Travis Snider from Jackson, Washington, went 14th overall.

Snider was the only one of the high school players to make the major leagues, and was eventually traded in 2012 to the Pittsburgh Pirates. Ricciardi's first draft, which was led by North Carolina shortstop Russ Adams, was actually greeted with critical acclaim by *Baseball America*, the bible of scouting and player development, which suggested that the Blue Jays had the best draft of any team that year.

But Law said that a change had occurred by the time he arrived. The Cleveland Indians, Boston Red Sox, St. Louis

Cardinals, San Diego Padres and, of course, the Oakland Athletics were all taking a statistics-based approach to drafting. Law remembers sitting in the Blue Jays draft room in 2005, looking at the board, and saying to director of scouting Tony LaCava, another of Ricciardi's assistants, "Tony, we're in the third round and there's nobody left on our board with a chance of being an everyday guy."

Law says simply, "We were chasing an inefficiency that had largely closed."

Yet it's not all on Ricciardi. Paul Godfrey had convinced commissioner Bud Selig that the Blue Jays needed help in the form of a currency equalization payment, something close to US$5 million per season. There was a quid pro quo to everything that Selig did, however, and Godfrey was well aware of it. It explained why Godfrey went along with the commissioner's office when it came to "slotting," the process by which the commissioner's office suggests the level of bonus payments doled out to draft picks, particularly in the first round. Ricciardi couldn't be adventurous even if he'd wanted. Coupled with that fact was Ricciardi's inclination to stay out of the international free-agent market, because he did not like the risk-reward balance of gambling hundreds of thousands of dollars on signing 16- or 17-year-old players from places not covered by the draft, such as the Dominican Republic and Venezuela.

The Blue Jays had seen mostly limited results in Latin America under Gord Ash, signing the likes of Josephang Bernhardt and Diegomar Markwell. But the manner in which renowned Dominican Republic scout Epy Guerrero helped build the Blue Jays in the team's initial days had made international scouting a crucial part of the team's DNA. One year, Law remembers, the Blue Jays had an international budget of $900,000, "and we were using some of the money to sign the 30th round pick in the

June draft. I mean, we weren't even spending the little amount we had."

The Athletics did business that way too. But those close to Ricciardi believed he had also soured on the international market because it was a foray overseas that turned into one of the biggest flops of his time with the Athletics. It was Ricciardi who pushed Billy Beane in 1995 to select Ariel Prieto, a Cuban pitcher who had made himself eligible for the draft, over a two-sport star from the University of Tennessee, Todd Helton. Helton has spent his entire career with the Colorado Rockies and finished the 2012 season with 2,420 hits. Prieto appeared in 70 games and was out of the majors after 2001. Ricciardi made another call on a player who would end up being a core piece of the Rockies' future in shortstop Troy Tulowitzki, who went seventh overall in 2005 after Ricciardi passed on him and selected Cal State Fullerton pitcher Ricky Romero with the sixth selection overall. Romero hasn't turned out half-bad, despite his sub-par 2012. But Tulowitzki, from Cal Long Beach, has become one of the game's dominant shortstops, and just two years after the draft was providing the type of run-scoring offence that the player Ricciardi determined would be his everyday shortstop—his first-ever first-round pick Russ Adams—never came close to being.

THROWING OUT THE BOOK

But Ricciardi was hardly worried about draft picks after the 2005 season, when he torched whatever moneyball bona fides he had left. In fact, Ricciardi tore the moneyball guide to shreds when he made a left-handed pitcher with wacky, short-arming mechanics—B. J. Ryan—the highest-paid closer in the history of the game and signed him to a five-year, $47 million contract that surpassed in total value the contract that the Yankees had given to Mariano Rivera (who was only considered the greatest closer of all time and was already burnishing his Hall of Fame resumé). Ryan's contract, signed on November 29, 2005, was back-loaded, with $30 million due in the final three years, at $10 million per season, and the signing was trumpeted to much fanfare at the downtown Toronto offices of Rogers Communications, the so-called "Rogers Campus" that was the headquarters of one of Canada's largest companies. The announcement was big enough that owner Ted Rogers showed up: Rogers seldom made an appearance for events connected with his baseball team, and when he did there were times when his executive assistant, Jan Innes, would write the name of a particular player on his hand. Rogers told Ryan, "You make more money than I do."

Manager John Gibbons and Ricciardi both believed a power arm was a necessity to compete with the Yankees and Red Sox. Ricciardi didn't need Gibbons to tell him what every manager knows: it is easier to manage a game knowing who will have the ball in the ninth inning with a one-run lead. But, geez . . . is that knowledge worth $47 million? What about the risk of injuries?

"If I was worried about injuries I'd have everybody signed to one-year contracts," Ricciardi responded, adding that he was doing what the Blue Jays had done in their World Series years. He was signing free agents, just as Pat Gillick had signed the likes of Paul Molitor and Jack Morris. The difference this time was that there was a premium attached to coming to Toronto. Where Molitor and the likes joined the Blue Jays with an eye toward winning an elusive title or, as was the case of Morris, getting one more shot at glory, Ryan and the players that would follow him were doing it simply for the money and the length of contract. That's why Alex Anthopoulos's 2012 signing of R. A. Dickey to a contract extension was so notable: for the first time in years, a player had elected to sign on with the Blue Jays chiefly because the club had a chance to win.

Ryan's signing was a gamble, but at the time any concerns about the length and amount of investment took a back seat to the fact that the Blue Jays had outbid clubs for a wanted commodity. Ryan saved 36 games for the Baltimore Orioles in 2005, when they finished below the Blue Jays in the American League East in what was his first season as a closer. Until then, he'd had only six saves in six major league seasons and had been viewed mostly as a lefty specialist—somebody who could be called on to get out a left-handed batter. The Orioles handed him the closer's role with fingers crossed when Jorge Julio strained his forearm in spring training, and Ryan was dominating: his bulky 6-foot-4 frame and short-armed delivery adding deception to a devastating slider and fastball and resulting in 12.80 strikeouts per nine innings, leading all AL relievers. Conventional wisdom suggests pitchers that experience a sudden change in role or workload often experience arm troubles, but the Blue Jays viewed Ryan's $70\frac{1}{3}$ innings of work without alarm. In fact, the total innings were less than he'd pitched in 2004 as Julio's set-up man. All they saw was somebody who could strike out batters in the ninth inning, when ground-ball outs aren't necessarily the cure-all they can be earlier in the game.

Not for the first time in his tenure as Blue Jays president and CEO, Paul Godfrey received a call from the office of the baseball commissioner wondering what the hell he was doing (this time, it was commissioner Bud Selig's chief labour negotiator, Rob Manfred). Both Ricciardi and Godfrey defended the signing as being market savvy, knowing that the other prime closer on the market, Billy Wagner, was on the verge of agreeing to a four-year, $43 million contract with the Mets. Ricciardi wouldn't say so publicly, but he had effectively come to the conclusion that it was going to take an extra year on a contract to get free agents to sign with Toronto instead of someplace else, and everybody in the baseball world knew that the Mets, Detroit Tigers and Cleveland Indians had all made a play for Ryan. If it took an extra year to get Ryan, Ricciardi was okay with it.

He'd show that again a week later at the winter meetings in Dallas, Texas.

Throughout history, the meetings had been the site of several major transactions—to be expected given that most teams brought in their high-ranking executives, scouts, managers and coaches and split them up to visit other clubs, sussing out each other's needs and offers. Some of the Blue Jays' biggest deals—including Gord Ash's trade of Shawn Green to the Los Angeles Dodgers and the single biggest transaction in club history, Pat Gillick's acquisition of Roberto Alomar and Joe Carter—transpired at the winter meetings.

But Ricciardi went to Dallas to deal—not to acquire. First, he traded outfield prospect Gabe Gross, pitcher David Bush and prospect Zach Jackson to the Milwaukee Brewers for slugging first baseman Lyle Overbay. He also laid the groundwork for a deal that would be announced 20 days later: the acquisition of power-hitting third baseman Troy Glaus from the Arizona Diamondbacks for Miguel Batista and Orlando Hudson, the spectacular second baseman with the megawatt smile whose relationship with the GM had been red-flagged ever since he was quoted in an article using the word "pimping" to describe Ricciardi's style. It was harmless and greeted with little more than a roll of the eyes by the GM, but those within the Toronto media who suspected the worst of Ricciardi believed he had it out for Hudson from that point on.

With actual time in that particular off-season to spend the money that his owner had committed a year earlier, Ricciardi focused on both hitting and pitching. He made a run at a free-agent outfielder named Brian Giles, a 32-year-old left-handed hitter with a hefty post-season pedigree who elected to re-sign with the San Diego Padres for $3 million less in guaranteed money over three years instead of taking Ricciardi's three-year, $33 million offer. Ricciardi and his front office team owned the Dallas meetings. He called that team his "rats," and they scurried from club suite to club suite while he hunkered down to try and put to bed what would be the signature move of the off-season: signing right-handed pitcher A. J. Burnett.

THE PROBLEM CHILD

Flush with the success of signing Ryan and still flush with Ted Rogers' money, Ricciardi resolved to sign the biggest name and biggest gamble on the season's free-agent market. And that he did, getting Burnett's signature on a five-year, $55 million contract that included an out clause after the third year that helped put the Blue Jays over the top in a bidding war with the St. Louis Cardinals. If Burnett ended up exercising the clause, he would leave $24 million on the table, and on the day his contract was announced nobody could even fathom that type of decision. Burnett, of course, *would* end up exercising the clause—signing a five-year, $82.5 million contract with the New York Yankees after the 2008 season.

"William DeWitt [the Cardinals' president] came up to me at the owners' meetings in Arizona shortly after the deal and said—and I remember the words exactly—'So, you signed the problem child,'" Paul Godfrey said. "'Don't you guys know you overpaid by $15 million? We capped our offer at $40 million. We knew he was going to Toronto.' That's what DeWitt said."

DeWitt might not have been far off in terms of his financial assessment, but it was known that his team dearly wanted Burnett, whose jaw-dropping, raw power pitches have long hinted at stellar potential, yet whose career is best encapsulated by his one and only no-hitter with the Florida Marlins. Burnett beat the San Diego Padres 3–0 on May 12, 2001, in a game in which he walked nine, threw just 65 of 129 pitches for strikes and hit the Padres' Damian Jackson with a pitch that broke his right thumb. At one point, he threw nine consecutive balls. "Million dollar arm and ten-cent brain," was a favourite saying of former major league manager Buck Rodgers, and it seemed to fit Burnett. He was Nuke LaLoosh.

The Blue Jays had set the table for Burnett's signing the previous year when they hired Brad Arnsberg to be their Triple-A pitching coach at Syracuse. They also spoke to the Florida Marlins about acquiring Burnett at the trade deadline in 2005, but balked when the Marlins said they'd have to take on the 2½ years and $21.25 million left on the contract of third baseman Mike Lowell, who would end up being packaged along with Josh Beckett to the Boston Red Sox for Hanley Ramirez and Anibal Sanchez. (Beckett and Lowell, of course, went on to win the 2007 World Series with the Red Sox, and Lowell was named the Series' Most Valuable Player.)

Arnsberg was something of a pitching Svengali, a big, muscular Texan and former bonus baby pitcher who shredded his arm early in his career and moved into coaching. Arnsberg was a Type-A personality who could out-lift players in the weight room and treated his pitchers as if they were teammates. He and Burnett became close while Arnsberg was the pitching coach with the Marlins, where Arnsberg had been put in charge of the gilt-edged arms of Burnett and Beckett.

The Marlins won the World Series in 2003 with a payroll ranked

21st in the majors. Beckett was a beast against the New York Yankees in that series, winning the MVP award after going 1–1 with a 1.10 earned run average in two games. But Arnsberg was not part of the celebration. He'd been fired earlier in the season along with manager Jeff Torborg, resulting in a messy scene in which he and Marlins GM Larry Beinfest shouted at each other outside Arnsberg's residence. Yet while the Marlins were spraying champagne around the visitors' clubhouse at Yankee Stadium, Beckett stole away briefly and called Arnsberg on the telephone.

Burnett had no role in that World Series either. His season ended on April 11, when he underwent Tommy John surgery—the 11th Marlins pitcher to go under the knife in a span of 2½ years. Arnsberg, who would become the Blue Jays' pitching coach after the 2004 season and talk to Burnett on a regular basis during the free-agent courtship, said later that he and Torborg were "railroaded" by the Marlins and that the injuries had nothing to do with his methods. Pointing to his own career and the way it ended, he wondered how anybody thought he could have anything but his pitchers' best interests at heart, saying "everybody did anything and everything they could to break down the numbers" and make him seem the guilty party.

Burnett's relationship with the Marlins had been tortured; he'd had a brief salary holdout, a pointless endeavour for a player who at the time was still arbitration eligible and had no leverage, and he was dismissed in the final week of the 2005 season after publicly questioning the makeup of the team.

But then, that was A. J. He broke his foot stepping into a gutter while bowling. He was a fan of Goth singer Marilyn Manson and entered the game to "The Beautiful People," although, just for yucks, decided one day in Toronto that he wanted to change it up to New Kids on the Block's "Hangin' Tough." He arrived in the majors armed with a blazing fastball, a pierced nipple and tattoos galore, and the Blue Jays ended up living the full A. J. experience. He is a staple of baseball bloopers videos thanks to once firing a warm-up pitch with the Marlins that shattered the window of a pickup truck driving behind home plate and carrying the team's mascot, Billy the Marlin. He missed a month of that no-hit season when he broke his foot on a treadmill, and later missed a chunk of spring training with the Blue Jays in 2008 when he caught his right index finger on the door of a Range Rover—then decided not to tell the club about it until he showed up in Dunedin. Burnett also showed very early an ability to keep reporters on edge, which is a healthy trait given the monotony of the long season. He once angrily approached one of the reporters gathered around the entrance to the Blue Jays' spring training clubhouse, waiting for players to finish drills. Pulling the targeted reporter aside, Burnett proceeded to say he'd read the article detailing his TKO and found it funny. "Next time, though, get the damned colour of the car right," he added with a smile before walking away.

The five-year contract given to Burnett was the first deal of that length handed to a starting pitcher since the Texas Rangers signed Chan Ho Park to a $65 million contract in 2001, and for an organization that in its glory years had a policy of not giving out more than three-year contracts to pitchers it was a bold statement of intent.

Ricciardi agreed it was a leap of faith, but said that Roy Halladay had been hurt for two of the four years of his contract and that this was essentially the cost of doing business. "In the past, all we've really done is dabble in free agency," he said.

In fact, the Blue Jays had been chastened by their inability to land big-name free agents. Before the 2005 season, they'd courted free agent Matt Clement only to lose him to the Boston Red Sox and a three-year, $25 million contract. That deal would end up being considered the worst of Theo Epstein's tenure as Red Sox

GM, but Ricciardi came away vowing he'd be more aggressive given the chance. That was why Ryan was given the fifth year on his contract; it was why Burnett was given five years and the out clause (a suggestion made in the 11th hour as Ricciardi and Paul Godfrey finalized the deal with Burnett's agent, Darek Braunecker). The Blue Jays also threw in the financial equivalent of a number of limousine rides from the Burnett family home in Maryland to Toronto because Burnett's wife, Karen, was scared of flying.

The Blue Jays had put a full-court press on Burnett, and had Roy Halladay and Pat Hentgen push the team's case during an in-person visit to Rogers Centre by Burnett and his wife. Hentgen had retired and become an advisor to Ricciardi, and it was a shrewd move to have him involved. He had pitched in both St. Louis and Toronto, and the Cardinals were the Blue Jays' chief bidding opponent.

"Hentgen," Braunecker said as he stood smiling while Burnett was introduced at a news conference in Dallas, "now that was smart."

Braunecker, who also counts pitcher Cliff Lee among his clients, said that it is impossible to underestimate Arnsberg's role in getting Burnett to sign with the Blue Jays. "Let's put it this way: A. J.'s interest in Toronto really started and ended, initially at least, with Brad being there," Braunecker said. "But the Blue Jays were very aggressive. J. P. . . . well, J. P. can really sell. I mean, they pulled out all the stops. They flew us up to Toronto on a private jet and J. P. was with us. It was the first interaction he had with J. P. and when A. J. got off the plane he was sold on J. P. as well."

Burnett had hit the motherlode. Braunecker admits now that he was intent on setting new boundaries for pitchers at a time when teams had started to extend players before they became free agents, as the Blue Jays had done in covering Roy Halladay's initial years of free agency.

"We kind of slow-played the negotiations, as much as anything," Braunecker said. "I wanted to try and differentiate the contract from other deals that had been in the books. That's how the out clause happened; I was sitting in my hotel room before going in to make the deal and just kind of came up with it.

"There hadn't been many five-year deals done since September 11 because of insurance issues. Maybe one. My objective was first to re-establish the five-year market for starting pitchers. But at the same time, we had some concerns that J. P. only had two years remaining on his contract at the time. Same with the coaching staff. I told J. P. that, sure, A. J. liked Toronto, but his interest was because of the staff that was there, especially Arnsberg and Gibbons. I wanted him to have the ability to leave."

Braunecker met with the Cardinals before his final meeting with the Blue Jays, and while he says the Cardinals would not commit to a fifth year, Braunecker did get then Cardinals general manager Walt Jocketty to give his client a two-year out clause. With that in his back pocket, Braunecker pressed the issue with Ricciardi, summing up his argument in a manner that Ricciardi could not dispute: given the size of the contract that Ryan had signed and the one being proposed for Burnett, Braunecker told him, "You and I both know that if you don't win in a couple of years, they're going to turn the whole thing over.

"For us," Braunecker said, "that opt-out was the critical thing."

As for the limousine rides for Karen Burnett? Braunecker said simply that it was another way to build value and uniqueness into the deal, although it was true that Burnett's wife did not like flying. Back when the Blue Jays were young, the personal touch shown by the likes of Paul Beeston and Peter Hardy, and the attention to detail when it came to the players' families became a hallmark of the organization. Ricciardi, too, pitched the value of family in an attempt to overcome some of the disadvantages of the marketplace: the perceived issue of taxation (although the tax hit on athletes in Ontario is much less onerous than in many states, particularly since signing bonuses are taxed at a very favourable rate); the fact that Canada was still a foreign country and as such required the nuisance of passage through Canada Customs; the strangeness of the place. Those hurdles had long stood in the way of Blue Jays GMs, but they weren't as pronounced back in the days when the team was considered an annual threat for the post-season.

"I think it came from the fact J. P. himself had a young family, but it was clear right from the start that he recognized the value of having the wife and family comfortable," Braunecker said. "I wasn't surprised they were interested in A. J. What I was surprised about was how aggressive they were; they were way ahead of the curve."

A curve that, for all concerned, eventually led directly into a wall. But it was quite a ride.

"The money arrived, and the mandate changed," said Law. "That's when you start doing things like giving five-year contracts to closers. That's something the fans that are counting blown saves can point to. Then, you go out and sign an A. J. Burnett, and all the fans who were criticizing you for not spending money can say, 'Oh, hey, the Blue Jays are out there spending money now.' You're trying to make the club look better on paper, is what you're doing."

To finish off the spending spree, Ricciardi signed ace Roy Halladay to a three-year, $40 million contract extension in March 2006 that carried him through 2010. In fairness to Ricciardi, the increase in payroll had the desired impact: the Blue Jays put together their best three-year run since their back-to-back World Series wins, but as Ricciardi would note, it wasn't enough in the face of the Yankees and Red Sox's spending and dominance.

Including the 2000 season, the American League East has sent 22 teams to the post-season, nine of them wild card teams. Of those nine wild card teams from the East, only two had less than 94 wins.

"I was speaking to [ESPN commentator] Jayson Stark one day and I said, 'Do the math,'" Ricciardi said during the winter of 2013. "Look: we took our shot as an organization, and part of this job is timing. We took our shot when the Yankees and Red Sox were still dominant, and even our so-called big moves were just things that kept us stride for stride with those teams. They weren't the same as their big moves. That's why I credit Alex [Anthopoulos] for making the moves he's made this winter. I think the cycle's in his favour."

CLOSE, BUT NOT ENOUGH

The Blue Jays' 87–75 record in 2006 put them second in the AL East for the first time since that 1993 season. While they managed to move ahead of the Boston Red Sox, the team was still seven games back of the wild card Detroit Tigers. Even with an increase in payroll, the Blue Jays remained poor cousins to the Yankees and Red Sox, who generated immense amounts of revenue out of their ballparks—the Yankees would build a new Yankee Stadium—and their regional sports networks, the YES (Yankees Entertainment and Sports) Network and NESN (New England Sports Network).

The Blue Jays had five players chosen to the All-Star Game in 2006 (Ryan, Glaus, Halladay, Vernon Wells and Alex Rios), the most since the '93 team sent Roberto Alomar, Joe Carter, John Olerud, Paul Molitor, Pat Hentgen, Duane Ward and Devon White to the game in Baltimore. They also finished tied with the Cleveland Indians for the most extra-base hits in the AL, while finishing second in slugging percentage and third in batting average, despite losing Rios for the second half of the season with a staph infection. Yet there was a soft, white underbelly to the offence: they were seventh in runs scored. Compounding matters, Burnett missed the first two months of the season with a sore elbow while Gustavo Chacin, a left-hander counted upon after a solid rookie year, missed 2½ months with an elbow strain.

Despite all of the promise inherent in that three-year payroll commitment, and despite Ricciardi's aggressive use of the free-agent market, the Blue Jays never would advance to the playoffs. Ricciardi's former roommate would be fired as manager and the team would turn once again to an old hand. Cito Gaston never had gotten a proper send-off the first time around, despite a pair of World Series wins. Now he'd be in the dugout again, get that celebratory send-off with a reunion of the 1992 Blue Jays, and be in charge during the dying days of Ricciardi's tenure.

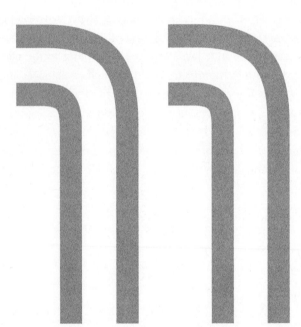

THE SHIP IS
SINKING

AS MUTINIES GO IT WAS HARDLY BLOODY. THE
Toronto Blue Jays were finishing off a dispiriting 2009 season
under Cito Gaston, wheezing their way to a 75–87 record and
heading into the final weekend series in Baltimore with an
unhappy clubhouse.

Aaron Hill. Lyle Overbay. Rod Barajas. Vernon Wells. This was
not a ranting, raving group—Hill, in fact, was about to be named
American League Comeback Player of the Year after returning
from a lengthy battle with post-concussion syndrome and had
made the All-Star team—but all of them suggested to reporters
during the team's final home stand that they had issues with the
manner in which Gaston communicated with them. "I think
everybody pretty much feels the same, for the most part," said
Hill, one of the players who had seen Gaston's predecessor John
Gibbons deal with the most serious clubhouse issues of Ricciardi's
tenure: an altercation with designated hitter/first baseman Shea
Hillenbrand after Hillenbrand, upset with the manner with which
Gibbons was using him, wrote 'the ship is sinking' and 'play for
yourself' on a white-board in the clubhouse.

Gaston would manage one final season before returning to the
senior advisor's role from which he had been plucked in 2008,
when Paul Godfrey and J. P. Ricciardi asked him to take over for
John Gibbons after an 8–7 loss to the Milwaukee Brewers—their
fifth consecutive and 11th in 14 games—which dropped the Blue
Jays' record to 35–39. All four players would be gone before the
start of the 2011 season, and Ricciardi himself would be fired by
the man who had replaced Godfrey, Paul Beeston, during a
clubhouse meeting with the insurrectionists before the series
against the Orioles.

It would be the end of a tumultuous eight years that had seen
Ricciardi exercise ownership's wishes and work with Godfrey to

cut down on losses in Rogers Communications' first few years of ownership while attempting to maintain relevance in the American League East. Ricciardi's record with the Blue Jays was 642–653 and the club had four third-place finishes, one second-place finish, a fifth-place finish and two fourths—including in his final season when the team finished 28 games out of the division lead. Ricciardi's firing was easy to predict when it became known that Beeston, then assistant (and soon-to-be) general manager Alex Anthopoulos and Tony Viner had made the trip to Baltimore. Gaston expressed more surprise than displeasure when he became aware of the issue, dodging questions while suggesting that the source of all the rumours was outside the clubhouse. That was taken to mean they were coming from somebody within the organization, or from players that had been traded or cut, specifically Scott Rolen and B. J. Ryan. It was also not true. Blue Jays players had approached at least three reporters around the team at different times in the final week of the 2009 season voicing similar concerns, but after the aforementioned meeting there was contrition, and players such as Hill and Overbay were back for the 2010 season, with Anthopoulos as their GM.

THE BEGINNING OF THE END?

It has come to be conventional wisdom that Ricciardi was done the day that Beeston replaced Godfrey, that the issues with Gaston at the end of 2009 were simply the last act of a play that had run its course. Yet Ricciardi had a year left on his contract, and the truth is both he and Beeston have said that there were discussions about giving him an extension in the summer, and that Beeston would likely have done so had Ricciardi agreed to one request: he had to move his family to Toronto. Ricciardi's young family had lasted one year in Toronto before returning to their home in Massachusetts, a move that seemed to raise the particularly parochial hackles of some in the local media who took it as an affront to the city.

Beeston jokes about not spending any time on the internet or having a BlackBerry, cellphone or iPhone—the latter claim is a white lie—but he is no Luddite. He is aware that the electronic world allows a person to work from home, wherever that home happens to be. But he nonetheless stands fast in wanting his GM to live in the city; it's as much a part of his principles as refusing to give out six-year contracts.

"I asked J. P. about it in July of that year, and there really was a chance we'd have given him an extension," Beeston said. "I knew he had moved his family up here in his first year, and . . . well, they lived in Oakville. I mean, I don't want to insult people who live in Oakville or Hamilton or anywhere else, but to get the feel of this city I believe you need to live in the city. I feel very strongly about this. I think it's important for the GM, the president, all of the key people to live in the city when they're involved in a sports franchise. I think it's critical.

"To me, operating a professional sports team is a public trust. You need to give back to the community. You need to get involved in things. Otherwise, I think people see you as an interloper."

Ricciardi had told his wife, Diane, after his seventh year that he was going to resign after the last year of his contract regardless of whether or not he was offered an extension. Ricciardi had several contacts in the game, and would have no difficulty returning to the fieldwork and scouting that had been his bread and butter before the Blue Jays hired him after the 2001 season. He'd also had feelers from ESPN, which was interested in seeing him do some studio work as an analyst. When he'd started the job, his sons, Dante and Mariano, were five and three years old. Now they were thirteen and eleven, and there was no way he was going to uproot them.

If there is any bitterness about the departure, Ricciardi keeps it well hidden. He still remains in contact with members of the front office and support staff and follows the progress of the players he's drafted and developed. Hindsight has given him time to put his years with the Blue Jays in context, and when he speaks it is not with a sense of anger as much as a sense of disappointment. Ricciardi says he still doesn't understand what was expected of him by ownership, and raises questions and concerns that are not much different from those being asked by an anxious fan base until the hectic winter of 2012. He believed he could put a playoff team on the field within five years, and whenever somebody asks him about where all his moneyball ideas went, he laughs and says, "I'd love to be able to do moneyball with money." For all the praise directed the way of Beane, the fact of the matter is that the last time the Oakland Athletics were a dominant force was from 1988 to 1992, when they won three American League pennants and a World Series with payrolls that were safely in the middle of the pack and, in 1991, when they had the highest payroll in the game.

"It's like anything else: a lot of times you get someplace, start working on something, and you begin to realize things are going to be different," Ricciardi said in the summer of 2012, his second season with the Mets under general manager Sandy Alderson.

"I knew my hands would be tied on a lot of things, but I think what made it worse was that I had one idea of what the team would be, Paul [Godfrey] had an idea of what the team would be, and ownership had an idea of what the team would be.

"I just don't know if we were ever on the same page, you know? I mean, you'd hear so many things. You'd hear that Rogers doesn't want to lose money; or that if the team is .500 and they aren't losing money they'll be happy with that. I just never felt like I had a definitive answer about what they wanted.

"I mean, I enjoyed my time there. I still have friends there. My wife still has friends there. I still consider Paul [Beeston] a friend. But you just sort of assume that somebody who has bought a team would have an idea about what they wanted to do with it.

"I just don't think they understood the business of baseball," Ricciardi said. "I don't think they were in it with both feet. Instead, they were dipping their toes in the water and that's not enough to beat the Yankees or Red Sox, because that's their whole business. Don't get me wrong: Rogers should be applauded for keeping the team in Toronto and wanting Canadian content. Nobody should ever take that away from them. But this is a tough business if you're not going to jump in with your whole body."

Tony Viner knew first hand that the key was presenting Ted Rogers and his board a plan. He wonders now if Ricciardi was ever really comfortable, especially toward the end of his tenure, with having to negotiate the various channels that came with an owner as large as Rogers. That would certainly tie in with the sometimes-impetuous approach Ricciardi could take to decisions.

"If you set out a plan and Ted and the board bought into it, money was never an issue," said Viner. "I can tell you that we would never go to J. P. or either of the Pauls and say, 'The payroll is $72 million, or $92 million or $107 million. Who's available? What have we got? How can we do it?' You're seeing it this winter [2012]: when the players are available, we've gone after them. Nobody's crazy; nobody's saying, 'We're a big company so we can spend money foolishly.' But by the same token, if these players are available and we can get them all, we'll do it.

"What we were lacking," Viner said, "was availability. What B. J. Ryan showed was when there was an opportunity we were willing to do something about it. Still, at the time I was responsible, nobody came to me and said, 'Look, if we can put these pieces together we can improve the team. We should do it and here's the plan.' If we were out-bid, it wasn't a decision by me. It was Paul [Godfrey] or J. P.

"I spoke to J. P. one time and said, 'Look, we need to go to the board and say, "the Billy Beane thing won't work."' But we need a plan that will work in the American League East, and that was sort of near the end of his tenure. We never really got there.

"That's really the only issue we had, which was, 'Give us a plan and show us how it's going to work if you deviate from it.' At Rogers, you always had a three-year plan. That's the way it was done. Three years, and you'd treat each year like the first year of the plan. I think, truly, J. P. perhaps felt that with a big company as opposed to an enthusiastic owner the task was too daunting, that it would be impossible to say, 'Look, what you really need is a payroll of $175 million because the Yankees are spending $210 million.' Ted absolutely wanted to win and would have done anything to be supportive of it."

BIG DEALS

Beeston's suggestion that Ricciardi might have received an extension even in that final year is, frankly, one of those things that can never be proven. Certainly, circumstances suggested that Ricciardi's tenure was coming to a close, although those that trace the beginning of the final act back to that day in Pittsburgh in 2008 when he was forced to fire his minor league roommate, John Gibbons, and replace him with Cito Gaston might be hasty. Gaston himself admits that Ricciardi had privately sounded him out during spring training in 2008 about whether he would ever entertain a manager's job. Gaston's response was the same as always: he would be interested, but he wasn't going to interview.

On the day after he fired Carlos Tosca in 2004, Ricciardi stood on the field at Yankee Stadium waiting for batting practice. He was asked for the personification of his perfect manager. It was a blue-sky question: Who would you choose if you could, all restrictions aside? Ricciardi thought for a second before answering: Lou Piniella, the long-time major league manager who would win three World Series and three Manager of the Year Awards with five different teams. But Lou Piniella was never going to come to Toronto. Even Gillick hadn't been able to swing it in the past. Gibbons, meanwhile, was Ricciardi's guy in more ways than one. Yes, the two had been teammates and roommates at Single-A Shelby of the South Atlantic League, and Ricciardi, like so many baseball people, equated familiarity with loyalty. But Keith Law also believes the two men shared identical philosophies about the running and calling of a game. "Gibby was, I think, the type of manager J. P. wanted to move toward when he took the job as GM."

They were an odd blend: the scrappy guy from Worcester, Massachusetts, and the slow-talking Texan who was actually born in Great Falls, Montana, and who played his first baseball game in Goose Bay, Labrador, while his father was in the service of the US Air Force (which led to one of Gibbons' best lines: "Labrador: now that's what you call a short season league"). Gibbons was drafted 24th in 1980 out of Douglas MacArthur High in San Antonio, Texas. Darryl Strawberry went first to the Mets in that draft; Billy Beane went 23rd, right in front of Gibbons. Gibbons was being fast-tracked to the Mets until his cheek was broken in a spring training collision with Joe Lefebvre. The Mets' answer was to acquire future Hall of Famer Gary Carter from the Montreal Expos—they do write themselves all over all things Canadian baseball, do they not?—and, after eight years, Gibbons decided to move into managing. He was without a job when Ricciardi asked him if he wanted to be a bullpen catcher, and he eventually became Carlos Tosca's first-base coach when Tosca replaced Buck Martinez as manager.

Historical revisionism is a by-product of any sports executive's firing, and while it is true that there were those inside the industry and inside the Blue Jays offices—hello there, Alex Anthopoulos and Keith Law—arguing *sotto voce* against the idea of giving B. J. Ryan a five-year contract, in fact the new aggressiveness was welcomed by the fan base. And just as that contract should be viewed in the context of the times, so too is it important to similarly view two other deals that would be held against Ricciardi long past the time he'd been fired.

In December 2006, the Blue Jays signed centre fielder Vernon Wells to a seven-year, $126 million contract extension (the sixth-largest contract in baseball history at the time), and in April 2008, Alex Rios agreed to a seven-year contract for $69,835,000. Wells was considered the heir apparent to Carlos Delgado— a homegrown, first-round draft pick (fifth overall) who was coming off an All-Star season in which he hit .303 with 32 home runs and 106 runs batted in and had an .899 OPS, all while winning a Gold Glove for defensive excellence. Rios was another homegrown outfielder, coming off an appearance in the 2007 All-Star Game and Home Run Derby, but also off a second-half slump. His 2008 season was less impressive—his OPS fell .054 points and he hit 15 homers—and his 2009 season was downright awful on and off the field. Rios was videotaped cursing at a heckling fan after he walked past a youngster seeking an autograph at a charity function in Toronto, and it was Rios's bone-headed play of a line drive by Prince Fielder that became lodged under some padding at Miller Park—Fielder would score on an inside-the-park home run as Rios dallied before picking up the ball—that low-lighted the 8–7 loss to the Brewers that proved Gibbons' undoing. Less than two months later, on August 10, Rios was allowed to join the Chicago White Sox on a waiver claim, with the White Sox picking up the remaining $60 million on his contract.

Wells' contract, however, needs to be viewed against the backdrop of three free-agent deals signed during the winter of 2006, when the Chicago Cubs inked Alfonso Soriano to an eight-year, $136 million deal, the Houston Astros signed Carlos Lee to a six-year, $100 million package and the Anaheim Angels committed five years and $50 million to Gary Matthews Jr. The Blue Jays and Wells had started talking before those deals were consummated, but both sides were left with the sense that the other was proceeding cautiously, with Paul Godfrey saying it was almost like neither of them wanted Wells' contract to set the market. Godfrey, by that point, had had enough of being reamed out by commissioner Bud Selig and chief labour lawyer Rob Manfred.

It was a bizarre negotiation, and while Ricciardi claims he never came close to trading Wells at the time, the deal almost fell apart when Wells' agents started wondering if they were under-valuing their client. Wells was, after all, only a year away from free agency, with rumours that teams such as his hometown Texas Rangers, the San Francisco Giants and Los Angeles Dodgers (all spurned by the likes of Soriano) might want to make a play. At one point, Ricciardi received a phone call from Wells while he was sitting in manager John Gibbons' office along with Alex Anthopoulos.

"Vernon called and said, 'Listen, I'm getting hit by the media here, what do you want me to tell them?'" said Ricciardi. "I told him that his agent was being difficult. I asked him what he wanted, and he said he wanted to stay in Toronto. So I told him we could probably work it out—you, me and Alex—but that if his agent got involved it would be tough. In the end, we worked it out. They basically got what they wanted."

But it wasn't just the market for free-agent outfielders that dictated the team sign Wells. The Blue Jays went into that off-season continuing their seemingly eternal search for starting pitching. A significant part of the plan was re-signing left-hander Ted Lilly, who went 15–13 and logged 181⅔ innings with 160 strikeouts. Lilly had featured in a celebrated run-in with Gibbons after refusing to hand over the ball on the mound in a game at the Rogers Centre, while in the middle of torching an eight-run lead; the two men needed to be separated when Gibbons charged into the runway leading to the clubhouse. The incident came just a month and two days after Gibbons and Hillenbrand came to blows. But Lilly and Gibbons had made up (they were jogging partners) and the Blue Jays believed they had not only a chance at re-signing him, but also of adding Gil Meche, who had thrown 186⅔ innings for the Seattle Mariners and, at the age of 28, would nicely round out a rotation built around Roy Halladay and A. J. Burnett.

Still, it was a difficult winter to fish in free-agent waters. Major League Baseball teams were in the process of spending more than $1 billion on free agents, highlighted by the San Francisco Giants signing left-hander Barry Zito to a seven-year contract that guaranteed him $126 million and included a staggering $37 million buyout. Who could blame them? Things were looking pretty good in the baseball world. Attendance had gone up in three consecutive seasons, revenue broke the $5 billion mark as returns continued to pile up—from network television deals and from baseball's burgeoning advanced media arm, MLB AM—and the preceding seven years had seen seven different

World Series champions. Yes, the game was wrestling with a steroid scandal, but that had little traction among fans, who made peace with the matter long before the chattering classes. So general managers went hunting, with the Chicago Cubs landing nine free agents (they eventually signed Lilly to a four-year, $40 million deal) and the Kansas City Royals—*the Kansas Frigging City Frigging Royals!*—snapping up Meche for five years and $55 million.

As Viner pointed out, the Blue Jays were left with money to spend and no arms of value to invest in. The Blue Jays didn't think they'd be able to sign Wells, but when Ted Rogers made his payroll commitment, Ricciardi said it was generally accepted that the three-year plan would grow exponentially each season and that the team could eventually expect a $100 million payroll. "Paul Godfrey told me there was a five-year plan," Ricciardi said. "I told him that was nice, but that we were still going to have to overpay for free agents to come here. I didn't care about whether they'd come here in the past; times were different. And Vernon was here, 28 and coming off a 200-hit season, a three-time All-Star, and that meant we'd have to overpay him to keep him off the market.

"If they had said they were going to pull the plug, we never would have signed Vernon. What we were thinking is: if we lose Vernon off a team we were trying to re-build, where would we go get a guy like this? We were looking at having Vernon for his four probably most productive years. We knew his deficiencies, that his on-base percentage would never be high and that he'd never be the star you'd hang your hat on. But in a bad year, we figured 25 homers and 80 RBIs. Hey, every organization in baseball has a contract that hangs over them."

RYAN AND RICCIARDI SAY GOODBYE

Ricciardi did have some solid, signature moves as a GM, getting mileage out of low-budget finds such as Frank Catalanotto and Gregg Zaun while also trading for Edwin Encarnacion and Jose Bautista—whose emergence as the first surprise slugger of what might be called the "post-steroid" generation is the root cause of the team's 2012 spending spree. But the Wells contract—as well as that of Rios and, to a certain degree, a two-year contract given to an aging Frank Thomas—are always held out as moves that backfired. Thomas, a future Hall of Famer, represented an $8 million hit when the Blue Jays released him in the second year of his contract, and the team also had to absorb $6 million of Corey Koskie's contract to move him to the Milwaukee Brewers in January 2006 for pitcher Brian Wolfe. Those costs paled in comparison, however, to B. J. Ryan's buyout. Most likely the beginning of the end for Ricciardi came the day in 2009 that Paul Beeston was forced to visit the Rogers Campus and tell chief executive officer Nadir Mohamed that he and Ricciardi wanted to release reliever Ryan, whom Gaston had tired of and who was owed $18 million from the five-year contract Ricciardi had given him.

Ryan had become a symbol of the Blue Jays' failed free-agent forays (although it is important to remember that the team did enjoy its best season post-Tim Johnson after Ricciardi spent money) because the incident brought into focus several aspects of Ricciardi's tenure that created flashpoints with the fan base and its conduit, the local media.

The major issue was the manner in which the injury that ultimately finished Ryan's career was handled. It must be said that Ryan came as advertised in 2006, recording 38 saves, striking out 10.70 batters per nine innings, posting a WHIP of 0.857 and holding opposing batters to a stingy .169 average. His save total was third in the American League, behind Francisco Rodriguez of the Los Angeles Angels of Anaheim and Bobby Jenks of the Chicago White Sox—and Ryan was one of five Blue Jays named to the AL All-Star Team. But something was amiss in spring training the next season: Ryan was touched for four hits and three earned runs by the Minnesota Twins on March 11, and was shut down with what the club said was a stiff back. "Just a little tightness," is how Ricciardi explained it to reporters.

In mid-April, the stiff back had become an elbow sprain, necessitating an examination by Dr. James Andrews. Less than a month later, Ryan underwent Tommy John tendon transplant surgery, ending his season. By then, Ricciardi had confessed on his radio show: the team had lied about Ryan's injury all spring. "It was his elbow that was bothering him. So we said it was his back so we could have a little more time. We didn't want the media to bother Ryan every day, asking him, 'How's your elbow? How are you feeling? Are you going to throw today? Are you feeling good?' There's a lot of things we don't tell the media, because the media doesn't need to know it and the fans don't need to know it.

"They're not lies," Ricciardi said, "if we know the truth."

Ryan rebounded in 2008 with 32 saves (albeit limited to 58 innings), but in 2009 he was hampered by a noticeable decrease in velocity and effectiveness, which left his bread-and-butter slider ineffective. Ryan was placed on the 15-day disabled list with tightness in his trapezius and was finally released on July 8 after 25 games—his WHIP was an awful 1.887 and he'd allowed five home runs in 20⅔ innings. There was a symbolism to Ryan's departure: it was even entered as a two-line item later in the month in Rogers Communications' annual report. So much for the avoidance of sticker shock that had been a hallmark of

Godfrey and Ricciardi's tenure (though Beeston had warned Rogers executives during spring training that the team had concerns about Ryan).

Ryan's release was red meat for Ricciardi's numerous media critics, many of whom suspected he was on his way out. Ricciardi enjoyed tangling with the media, but the tone and tenor of this debate was nasty enough that at times it required intervention from the team's media relations department and even president and CEO Paul Godfrey.

For Ricciardi, it was evidence of what he thought was the Toronto media's strange fixation with the position of GM, regardless of the sport; he felt as if the criticisms that were usually directed at players or coaches in other markets somehow ended up at the feet of the GM in Toronto. A key flashpoint stemmed from allegations that Ricciardi's policy of drafting college players was turning the Blue Jays into the "White Jays," as the *Toronto Star* claimed in May 2003, with mug shots of Blue Jays players plastered all over the front page of the country's largest-circulation English-language newspaper. The truth is it was the presentation of the article as much as its contents that seemed accusatory. Even first baseman Carlos Delgado, by then no great fan of the GM, called the package "probably the stupidest thing I've ever seen." Godfrey was outraged by the article and some in the organization went so far as to quietly start funnelling stories to the *Globe and Mail* and *Toronto Sun* in retaliation.

The end of Ricciardi's tenure meant the departure from Toronto of a GM rivalled as a lightning rod perhaps only by former Maple Leafs GM Brian Burke. Ricciardi was a polarizing figure, easily painted as arrogant and easily suspected as such by a fan base with an inborn hatred of all things Boston, a fan base easily offended and suspicious of other's arrogance. But Ricciardi's track record was hardly a total mess; indeed, his judgment on less-ballyhooed players was strong, and in Bautista he left the Blue Jays a decent parting gift. Hiring Alex Anthopoulos hasn't turned out that badly either.

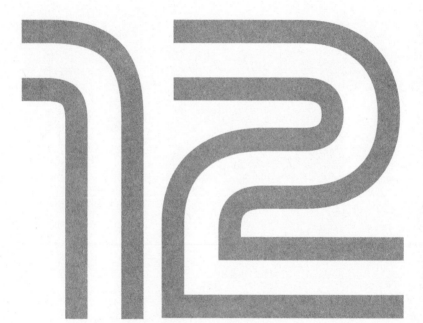

TOUCHE
LES TOUS(?)

ON THE NIGHT THAT JOE CARTER TOUCHED THEM all, the city of Montreal was doing what it normally does on a Saturday night. Crescent Street and boulevard Saint-Laurent were pulsating, restaurants in the Plateau were jammed and Madonna and her "Girlie Show" filled Stade Olympique. October was a safe time to book a concert at the facility; the Expos certainly weren't going to be using it.

It was a lovely night for a walk, and when Carter leapt high as his home run ball disappeared over the left-field wall, those who had stopped to see the end of the game through the windows of a pub or bar mostly shrugged. In the old-money Montreal enclave of Westmount, a teenage Alex Anthopoulos and some friends gathered at the home of Bryan Davis and watched the game before going out for the night. "I was 16, so . . . I don't know? Would we have been doing bars at that time?" Anthopoulos asked rhetorically over lunch in the shadows of Rogers Centre just days after making what president and CEO Paul Beeston called the biggest trade in franchise history. (Answer: of course you were doing bars. It's Montreal.)

"I can remember the Robbie Alomar home run [in 1992]. I was in the basement of a friend's in TMR [Town of Mount Royal]. Stefan Boudreault. We were playing a boardgame . . . geez, it might have been Monopoly, and watching the game on TV."

Anthopoulos paused, remembering Alomar's homer off Dennis Eckersley. "The Alomar homer was on a weekday. Carter was a weekend. I know we were getting ready to go out to a party or something. I mean, no way you'd play Monopoly with a buddy on a Saturday night. I'm not that much of a geek."

Anthopoulos was probably one hell of a Monopoly player, though, if the winter of 2012–13 is any indication. In the months of November and December, the GM fairly set up shop on Major

League Baseball's version of Park Avenue and the Boardwalk and littered the place with hotels. In pulling off his 12-player trade with the financially and spiritually distressed Miami Marlins—a move that landed starting pitchers Mark Buehrle and Josh Johnson, shortstop Jose Reyes and a potentially impactful utility player in Emilio Bonifacio—the signing of disgraced free-agent outfielder Melky Cabrera, and the follow-up acquisition of National League Cy Young Award–winner R. A. Dickey, it seemed as if Anthopoulos was trying to channel six years' worth of Pat Gillick's signature moves into one roll of the dice.

"Alex here is going to be a superstar," Ricciardi told a group of reporters gathered on the field one morning during spring training a few years earlier. He was right. Anthopoulos, who is as calculating as Ricciardi was impetuous, handled many of the nuts-and-bolts financial details of contracts during his time under Ricciardi and had become famous for his ability to tie up agents or other baseball officials on the telephone. Those within the organization say that Anthopoulos played the good lieutenant throughout Ricciardi's tenure, but also tried tactful methods of altering his boss's approach, such as preparing a detailed paper on the dangers of long-term contracts when he heard that the Blue Jays were about to sign B. J. Ryan. Anthopoulos never played the game professionally, but he was a product of grassroots, dirty-hands scouting and the type of odd-job sensibility that is important for someone who would otherwise be considered an outsider. He would turn out to be something of an old soul, in baseball terms, and immediately set about replenishing the scouting department while redoubling the team's efforts overseas.

But success hasn't come without a learning curve. Not that Anthopoulos minds. He's never been averse to legwork: as an assistant GM, he would attend the arbitration hearings of other teams and their players whenever possible. The sessions—during which lawyers for both the player and team try to persuade an arbitrator to decide between a salary offer and a salary request using largely statistically-based arguments—are open to any executive, and if they were held in Florida when the Blue Jays were in spring training, Anthopoulos would take advantage simply to get a greater sense of the process.

UP THROUGH THE RANKS

Anthopoulos joined the Blue Jays in 2003 as a scouting coordinator before being promoted to assistant GM. He became the GM following the 2009 season at the age of 32, and established himself quickly as someone who, in the words of Keith Law, was unafraid to speak up in what was "a tough front office in which to . . . say 'no.'" Law described Anthopoulos as having an almost Socratic mindset: he was questioning, analytical, and liked to sit around and debate players and trades. He also brought, in Law's words, "a nice balance between player evaluation and statistical measurement."

Anthopoulos's career in baseball was far from predetermined, and even at a time when it is no longer necessary for a major league GM to have played the game—or understand the complexities of hitting a curveball while nursing a wad of chewing tobacco in bubble gum—his path is that of an individualist.

Anthopoulos was a sports fan growing up in Montreal—"like everybody else is a sports fan, nothing special." Even then he was particularly taken by statistics, and never played baseball at anything remotely resembling a serious level. He attended undergraduate classes in economics at McMaster University in Hamilton, Ontario, and was working toward an engineering degree at McGill University when his father, John, passed away, ten days before Anthopoulos's 21st birthday.

"So there I am: working in a small company—we had eight employees—dealing with heating and insulation, which I have no interest in," Anthopoulos said. "I enrolled at Vanier College. I'm taking heating and ventilation classes at night, working all day, getting to class at 9 p.m., and the story of my life is pretty much all fans, grills and heating coils. Go home, get up at six the next morning to see contractors and look at blueprints. Go to school. Repeat."

That lasted two years, after which Anthopoulos worked as a bank teller. His first paycheque from a professional team came from the Montreal Expos, whose public relations director, P. J. Loyello, would go on to be vice-president of communications and broadcasting for the Marlins—and who had no idea what the future would hold for the kid he was paying $7 an hour to do photocopies for the home and visiting manager's offices.

"Someone told me one time that in baseball, you get paid in opportunity," Anthopoulos said. "And I was totally paid in opportunity my whole career. I made $38,500 my first year as AGM with the Blue Jays, but I didn't give a shit. I had a roommate; I had the bigger room because I was paying more of the rent; I was working in baseball. I realized one day that the money didn't matter if you weren't doing what you loved."

The Expos were in the process of exiting Montreal when Anthopoulos took his initial steps toward being a major league general manager, but opportunity abounded if a person was willing to look for it. Anthopoulos would watch batting practice at Olympic Stadium along with the scouts. (A word to the wise: if you are thinking of following Anthopoulos's career path, try to hook up with a team that has a stadium with a roof. Major league scouts frequent those facilities more than others because the guarantee of a game and BP makes them hugely cost-effective.) It was while watching Jeremy Giambi one day that he had an epiphany.

Giambi was one of the poster boys of Billy Beane's moneyball revolution, a doughy on-base percentage machine and notorious hard-liver, and Anthopoulos saw the same number everybody else did. "Great walks," he said. So Anthopoulos watched him swing during BP and, in his own words, "I'm just not feeling it. The numbers are so good, but I didn't like what my eyes were telling me. I guess that's the moment I realized it was about more than stats; the moment I realized you need to ask yourself why a guy's numbers are what they are."

Anthopoulos's education continued at one of the free-agent baseball academies in Fort Lauderdale, Florida, a facility that was owned and operated by Fred Ferreira, a long-time major league scout and the Expos' director of Latin American operations. Ferreira was the man who'd signed Bernie Williams and Roberto Kelly for the New York Yankees and signed Vladimir Guerrero for peanuts, and who is now executive director of international recruiting for the Baltimore Orioles. He was called the "Shark of the Caribbean" by former Expos manager Felipe Alou because of the manner in which he conducted business in the largely unregulated world of Latin-American scouting. When Major League Baseball decided to open spring training with replacement players in 1995, the Expos were more competitive than most teams, and Alou—no fan of the decision—stared at his collection of players one day and remarked, "We've got guys from Aruba and Europe. We might have illegal aliens. Or aliens." That, in a nutshell, was Fred Ferreira.

Anthopoulos wasn't paid a salary during his time with Ferreira. He lived in a hotel, helped with drills, picked up sandwiches for the players who breezed through the camp, and drove them to and from the airport. He was being paid in opportunity, to the point of being a millionaire. Ferreira let him go to the Dominican Republic with Arturo DeFreites, another well-known scout who worked for the Expos, and after 9/11 Anthopoulos travelled to Japan to help find players for the academy. "Fred would go to high-level meetings, the GM's meetings, and when he got back he'd dump these binders on me from the meetings," Anthopoulos said, chuckling. "I just soaked them up." When he was done with his day's work at the school, Anthopoulos would borrow a car, drive north to Jupiter, and watch Florida State League games.

Anthopoulos paid his way to scout school in Arizona (Major League Baseball provides classes in scouting), where he met Jon Lalonde, who would go on to be the Blue Jays' director of Canadian scouting. He asked for and received a video catalogue of everything the Central Scouting Bureau had going back to 1998, and to kill time would watch video of as many draft picks as possible—busts, superstars and middling guys. And in what is in some ways a quintessentially Canadian baseball story—given the way the game has flourished despite the exodus of one major league and several minor league franchises—Anthopoulos's career within the industry started to flourish even as his hometown team inched closer to a move.

It likely didn't seem that way one morning in Jupiter, after Anthopoulos spent an evening locked inside Roger Dean Stadium. Omar Minaya, who'd been appointed general manager of the Expos by commissioner Bud Selig after baseball assumed control of the franchise, had a month to put together a staff and get spring training running. Anthopoulos was literally waiting for Minaya outside the door at 5:30 one morning, volunteering to do odd jobs or anything else Minaya needed him to do. Minaya—very much flying by the seat of his pants and in need of necessities such as cellular telephones and photocopying machines—sent him off to run errands, and by the end of spring training Anthopoulos was the team's coordinator of scouting. It was in that capacity that he would develop a friendship with Dana Brown—a former teammate of Mo Vaughn's and Craig Biggio's at Seton Hall and a 35th round draft pick of the Philadelphia Phillies—who had met Minaya when the two were scouts. Minaya hired Brown to be his director of scouting; Brown in turn promoted Anthopoulos. Brown is now a special assistant to Anthopoulos with the Blue Jays: There is symmetry, isn't there? Minaya, the game's first Hispanic GM, hiring an African-American as his scouting director who in turn gave a Greek-Canadian kid his first break.

"Dana Brown was by far the one who encouraged me, of anybody," Anthopoulos said. "I'd call him after I watched those videos just to talk to him about them. What did he see? What was I seeing? I mean, I didn't mind what I was doing with the Expos even if we were so bare bones. But Dana kept telling me, 'Hey, you don't want to be an administrative guy. You have a feel for players. You just need to believe in yourself.'

"I think everybody, deep down, likes to believe that they can evaluate players," Anthopoulos continued. "I mean, I love to analyze things. That's just who I am, to a fault. And before I got down to Florida and worked with Fred, I thought I could pull out *The Bill James Handbook* and just pull up stats and be confident in telling you whether a player was any good. But when I got down to the field, I saw that nobody at Fred's school gave a shit about stats. You had guys from the Dominican Republic, Venezuela, and you had all kinds of swings and deliveries. For me, it was like finding a new toy; it really opened my eyes."

Since J. P. Ricciardi was typecast as a moneyball guy, thanks to his time with the Oakland Athletics, it was understandable that some would view Anthopoulos as being cut from the same cloth, even though Anthopoulos was never hired as a statistical analyst. Not that Anthopoulos is doctrinaire at any rate: he believes the debate that was spawned by *Moneyball* was ultimately productive for the game, although in an interview just before the release of the movie based on the book he said he thought that choosing one side over the other was akin to "operating with one eye closed." As for market inefficiencies? Anthopoulos shrugged. "Isn't everybody always trying to exploit market inefficiencies? Look, all teams have access to the same statistics. Not everybody has access to somebody's eyes or brains. I mean, you and I might have the same numbers in front of us but if I have the better evaluator? You can't compete with that.

"Really," Anthopoulos explained in a later interview, "the idea that a GM would be totally stats-based is wrong. You might find teams that are 80/20, or 70/30 or the other way around. But I think the idea that every young GM is a numbers guy is starting to change.

"The funny thing is," he added, "you really don't get a chance to sit down and talk shop with other GMs. There are guys with strong scouting backgrounds, like [Arizona Diamondbacks GM] Kevin Towers or [San Francisco Giants GM] Brian Sabean or [Milwaukee Brewers GM] Doug Melvin, but there's never really a window to talk about that type of stuff."

MAKING MOVES

One of Anthopoulos's first moves as GM was to double the size of one of the smallest scouting staffs in baseball. With the blessing of Paul Beeston, he moved boldly to go over slot for players in the amateur draft, a total departure from his predecessor, who had been instructed by Paul Godfrey to play along with the guidance provided by Bud Selig in part because the team was beholden to the commissioner's office for a currency equalization payment Godfrey believed was vital for showing the team's ownership that he was being a prudent manager.

Beyond rebuilding the scouting department, it is a fact that Anthopoulos spent the first two years of his tenure dismantling much of what Ricciardi had started. Beeston was doing the same off the field: the team's ticketing department was streamlined, and Beeston made it clear that he had viewed with suspicion some of the attendance figures that had been coming out of Rogers Centre. Even though, with baseball's revenue sharing program in place, it made more sense for teams to under-report than over-report attendance—especially if the team happened to be the recipient of revenue sharing, like the Blue Jays—Beeston decreed that the announced attendance would be paid attendance.

And so money was diverted to signing high-ceilinged draft picks, including the type of high schooler that Ricciardi had avoided until making Travis Snider a first-round pick in 2006. The Blue Jays also jumped into the international market, taking a run at Aroldis Chapman and winning a bidding war for another Cuban defector, Adeiny Hechavarria, who became part of that 12-player trade with the Marlins. Shaun Marcum was traded to the Milwaukee Brewers, despite his nominal ace status with the organization, in order to land Brett Lawrie (the tightly wound infielder was a former first-round pick by the Brewers who had come to be seen as a malcontent). But Anthopoulos's first task upon replacing Ricciardi was determining the fate of the best pitcher in club history, Roy Halladay. Nice trick, that.

Halladay had become a force of nature in his time with the Blue Jays: a six-time All-Star and the American League Cy Young Award winner in 2003. He was 148–76 in his Blue Jays career with a WHIP of 1.198. The 17th player chosen in the 1995 draft out of Arvada West High School in Arvada, Colorado, Halladay was a true product of the organization, but someone whose career started with a stutter-step. He came within one out of a no-hitter against the Detroit Tigers in his second career start, but after the 2000 season he was sent down to the minor leagues to be rebuilt by Mel Queen, the Blue Jays' pitching Mr. Fix-It. Queen fiddled with Halladay's arm angle, gave him two different fastball grips (a sinker and cutter) and told him to keep it simple. Halladay augmented the physical overhaul by developing an insular, almost quirky intellectual approach to his between-games routine that included Sudoku. He was unstoppable and became part of the organization's foundation, twice agreeing to contract extensions, including one in 2006 that covered the 2008 to 2010 seasons and delayed his free agency.

Corey Koskie, Troy Glaus, B. J. Ryan, A. J. Burnett, Frank Thomas: they'd all come and go as free-agent and trade acquisitions without getting the Blue Jays any closer to the top of the AL East. Halladay remained through all of it, almost sacrificial in that sense—the honest workman, punching the clock, tossing 200 innings when healthy and never once complaining about the fact that the team was spinning its wheels. Until, that is, the 2009 All-Star Game in St. Louis, when he told a media-day gathering that his Blue Jays career had become a little like *Groundhog Day* and that he was ready to "take a chance at trying to win," signalling he was waiving his no-trade clause.

J. P. Ricciardi had tried to accommodate Halladay, knowing full well that the pitcher was not likely to re-sign with the team after his contract expired. The trade talks were subject to all manner of leaks—Ricciardi didn't mince words on the record, either—and ultimately the deadline passed without a deal being struck, although Ricciardi would later claim that the trade that was eventually made essentially mirrored the deal he'd been talking to the Phillies about all along. At any rate, it was up to Anthopoulos to expedite things. A dinner Beeston had with the Halladays in Florida convinced the Blue Jays that Halladay still wanted out (his agent, Greg Landry, tightened the screws on the rookie GM by saying that if his client was not traded before February 1, 2010, there would be no talk of renegotiation nor would he approve any deal for the rest of the season). Afterwards Anthopoulos helped cobble together a four-team deal that saw Halladay end up with the Philadelphia Phillies. In return the Blue Jays got a catching prospect (Travis d'Arnaud) and a pitching prospect (Kyle Drabek), as well as an outfielder named Michael Taylor. Taylor was flipped to the Oakland Athletics for first baseman Brett Wallace, who in turn was flipped to the Houston Astros for a former Phillies farmhand that the Blue Jays had tried to acquire on two previous occasions, Anthony Gose.

Anthopoulos did well under trying circumstances. Drabek started the 2012 season with the Blue Jays before undergoing Tommy John surgery for a second time, Gose ended 2012 knocking at the major league door and d'Arnaud was ultimately the player the Mets absolutely needed to make the R. A. Dickey deal. "What the Halladay deal did for us was help jump-start our minor league system," said assistant GM Tony LaCava.

Even with these moves, the 2010 season would still be one of transition, which was presided over by Cito Gaston during his final full season as manager, and during which he managed the Blue Jays to a surprisingly successful season after replacing Gibbons halfway through the 2009 campaign. It was known going into 2010 that the season would be Gaston's last, and it was in some ways a revelatory campaign as well as a crossroads for the organization. Led by Jose Bautista's 54 home runs, the club improved to 85 wins—10 more than 2009—and had seven players with at least 20 homers en route to leading the majors with a club-record 257, which tied for the third-most in major league history. The Blue Jays also became the only team in major league history to have 20-plus homer production from all positions on the field, and only the 1927 New York Yankees had a bigger differential in homers hit and homers allowed.

Bautista, who had bounced around between organizations until the Blue Jays acquired him on August 21, 2008, for catching prospect Robinzon Diaz, found success working both with Gaston and hitting coach Dwayne Murphy. Whatever hard feelings lingered after the so-called mutiny that ended the 2009 season and likely contributed to the firing of Ricciardi, Gaston said later that the 2010 team had a special place in his heart and that it might have been one of the most talented offensive teams he'd had in his time in Toronto. They were mashers, scoring 53 percent of their runs by homers, and they had the third-best winning percentage in the American League in the second half, going 41–32 (.562).

After the Roy Halladay trade primed the pump of the club's minor league system, Brandon League was traded to the Seattle Mariners for former first-round draft pick Brandon Morrow, who had been miscast as a reliever by the Mariners. Anthopoulos continued to turn over his roster, sending Alex Gonzalez to the Atlanta Braves at the trade deadline for Yunel Escobar while setting about the process of collecting draft picks to replenish the farm.

But it was Anthopoulos's move after the 2010 season that was the biggest eye-opener: somehow, he traded Vernon Wells *and* the four years and $96 million he had left on a seven-year extension. The Blue Jays kicked in $5 million to get the Los Angeles Angels of Anaheim to send them slugging first baseman/catcher Mike Napoli and outfielder Juan Rivera, then shipped Napoli to the Texas Rangers for reliever Frank Francisco. The fact that Francisco flamed out in Toronto and Napoli went on to be an important contributor to the Rangers' first World Series appearance quickly drifted into irrelevance in Toronto: a contract that makes everybody's list of the 10 worst deals in baseball history was now somebody else's issue. But Anthopoulos would soon have his own issues, and one of them would be his new manager.

THE ARRIVAL OF JOHN FARRELL

The tipoff should have come in the manner John Farrell's hiring became public: in an email from Boston Red Sox owner John Henry to the *Boston Globe* in October 2010 before the Blue Jays could make the announcement.

"The Jays are getting a great baseball man and a great person," Henry wrote to the *Globe*, the de facto voice of Red Sox ownership. "We were able to keep John as part of our organization longer than a couple of other teams would have wanted, but it really is time for John to step up to the next level. I expected him to manage in MLB for as long as he wants to. He's going to an excellent young team, with a strong and smart hierarchy . . . I am grateful for the years John Farrell gave the Red Sox. He will be missed."

Farrell turned down other opportunities to interview for managerial jobs, but Anthopoulos felt "an immediate connection" with his would-be manager after three hours.

For two years, at least. While he would eventually end up learning a costly lesson from selecting Farrell out of a list of what Anthopoulos claims were 40 potential replacements for Cito Gaston, there was only a sense of optimism on October 25, 2010, when Farrell was introduced at a news conference at Rogers Centre.

It would emerge later that Farrell was very much a consensus pick, the product of much discussion between Anthopoulos and his lieutenants, who had identified three other finalists: Sandy Alomar Jr., the long-time catcher and brother of Roberto Alomar who was a coach with the Cleveland Indians; DeMarlo Hale, another Red Sox coach; and Brian Butterfield, the Blue Jays' ebullient, workaholic third-base coach. Farrell's case would have been easy to push: he had a player development background with the Cleveland Indians organization that, during his tenure, was considered one of the most proficient in baseball, and he was enough of a "big picture" guy that the Red Sox briefly considered him for their GM job when Theo Epstein left Boston. As the Red Sox's pitching coach, he had dealt with a disparate group and understood what it was like to compete in the American League East. Plus he looked the part. Square-jawed, physically imposing, it was easy to see Farrell commanding a clubhouse. In short? He gave good face.

Farrell was considered one of the game's bright young things when Anthopoulos hired him to manage the Blue Jays, and for an organization that was suddenly flush with young arms at the minor league level, Farrell's background as a pitcher, college pitching coach, personnel administrator and major league pitching coach was seen as a boon.

Farrell's lack of managerial experience was a concern for Anthopoulos, but the most important thing the second-year GM saw was an individual capable of exercising leadership in the clubhouse. Farrell was well-liked by both the Red Sox's pitchers and position players, fitting in nicely on a team that functioned smoothly because of manager Terry Francona's ability to make most of the daily drama stop at his office door. The Red Sox's clubhouse is a cramped, out-of-date room in ancient Fenway Park which, when coupled with the large daily media contingent, can be a wellspring of rumour and innuendo. One wrong glance can become tomorrow's lead story, yet Farrell said that Francona somehow managed to maintain the clubhouse as a sanctuary and a refuge, something he hoped to accomplish with the Blue Jays.

His inaugural campaign, however, became a season of transition. Only six weeks after Farrell agreed to the Blue Jays job, Anthopoulos sent Marcum to the Brewers in the trade for Lawrie. There would be further changes during an 81–81 season in which the Blue Jays were never more than five games below .500 or more than four games above. Centre-fielder Colby Rasmus was acquired from the St. Louis Cardinals in return for two relief pitchers who would play significant roles in the Cardinals' World Series win, Marc Rzepczynski and Octavio Dotel, with starting pitcher Edwin Jackson who had been picked up from the Chicago White Sox. Additionally, stalwarts John McDonald and Aaron Hill were traded to the Arizona Diamondbacks at the deadline in return for Kelly Johnson. Hill was one of the best first-round choices of the J. P. Ricciardi era, but he chafed under Cito Gaston's managerial style and when the Blue Jays elected not to exercise a series of options prior to the start of the 2011 season he was well aware that his time with the team was done. He had in fact suggested as much to Anthopoulos during a conversation; he and the organization had grown apart.

The season was one in which Bautista cemented his place as the team's player of note. He signed a five-year, $64 million contract in spring training and then hit 43 homers and drove in 103 runs while posting a remarkable OPS of 1.056. He was voted to the American League All-Star Team with 7,454,753 votes, shattering the record of 6,069,688 set by Ken Griffey Jr. in 1994. Bautista was made the Blue Jays' full-time right-fielder in spring training 2010, and there was no turning back.

Farrell showed a remarkable sense of self-criticism following the season, admitting publicly that game and bullpen management were two areas in which he believed he needed improvement. In fairness to Farrell, the Blue Jays went through 12 different starting pitchers, with only ace left-hander Ricky Romero showing anything resembling consistency, which put an added strain on the bullpen and often forced Farrell's hand early in games. That was a departure for Farrell, who was used to the veteran, proven starting pitchers he'd had with the Red Sox. But Farrell had some successes too: Romero earned a reserve spot on the AL All-Star Team and won AL pitcher of the month honours in August; catcher J. P. Arencibia, who set a club record for the position with 23 homers, continued to hone his defensive skills; and Lawrie was a high-energy player who seemed to have a sense of the moment with game-changing defensive skills at third base. The fact that these two players were able to keep body and soul together was no small feat. As Farrell remarked one day during spring training: "You can get pitchers the matchup you want, but you can't hide position players."

Yet whatever sense of forward movement came from that 2011 season quickly dissipated during the off-season.

MANAGERIAL DRAMA

Red Sox's president and chief executive officer Larry Lucchino frequently used the phrase "the Evil Empire" to describe the New York Yankees, but for Blue Jays fans there is little doubt that the Red Sox themselves best embody the title. The Yankees? They just spend money and win. The Red Sox . . . well, they snoop around and make life miserable for the Blue Jays. J. P. Ricciardi was given an extension a year earlier than he otherwise might have been just because of published reports in Boston that he was a candidate for the Red Sox's GM position before it went to Epstein. And with Farrell? It was felt in Toronto that the Boston media, the conduit for much of what goes on in the city, did much of his bidding.

Anthopoulos prefers to see what happened as merely a confluence of events. When the Blue Jays hired Farrell to a three-year contract, Francona was still managing the Red Sox. But by the end of that season, the Red Sox were a team in disarray, finishing 90–72 but missing the playoffs amidst reports about a lack of professionalism within the clubhouse—the now-infamous stories of pitchers such as John Lackey, Jon Lester and Josh Beckett chowing down on chicken wings and beer while in uniform during games in which they were not pitching. The team fell apart in September, going 7–20, and, making matters worse, club sources told the *Boston Globe* that Francona had been distracted by marital issues and was misusing prescription drugs. Francona quit, and the simple fact of the matter is that Farrell was the first and only choice to replace his former mentor. Farrell was out of contact most of the off-season while his son Luke underwent treatment for a brain tumour in Boston—it would later emerge that the Red Sox had a role in setting up the sessions—as stories swirled that the Blue Jays and Red Sox were working on a deal to get Farrell to Boston.

It was something of a shock to the Blue Jays, and in particular to Paul Beeston. Since the Blue Jays had been in existence, many of their executive level contracts were essentially handshake arrangements, and the unwritten rule in Major League Baseball is that while a person would be automatically granted permission to talk to another team about a job that was a promotion (a courtesy call would still be made), lateral moves could be made only after negotiations between clubs, usually involving compensation.

But Beeston had no such policy. Back in the day, it was never an issue; most people didn't *want* to leave the Blue Jays. For the first time, then, he was forced to confront a situation where the field manager wanted to leave for another team. And not only were they faced with the possibility of losing their manager after just one year, it was to a bitter, bitter division rival.

So Beeston put out a new policy: no lateral movements. Meanwhile, he ordered Anthopoulos to suss out the Red Sox's interest and made clear what the price would be—Clay Buchholz, a right-handed pitcher who was considered at worst the second-best starting pitcher on the Red Sox staff.

On December 2, 2011, the Red Sox named former Texas Rangers and New York Mets manager Bobby Valentine—who'd spent two years with ESPN after a highly successful six-year career managing the Chiba Lotte Marines of the Japanese Pacific League—as their new manager, giving him a two-year contract. Farrell would not talk about what happened during that off-season until a year later; Anthopoulos to this day will not confirm the Buchholz story. But everybody else will—including Farrell, who let the details out after he left the organization.

And so, for the time being, Farrell was managing the Blue Jays, and beyond some fanciful rumours of stealth-like attempts to sign

Prince Fielder, Toronto seemed intent on playing to Farrell's strength: pitching. The prize of the free-agent market was Japanese pitcher Yu Darvish, and the Blue Jays surprised many with what initially seemed to be a serious pursuit of the right-hander. Japanese players are subject to a posting process, in which sealed bids are submitted to the office of baseball commissioner Bud Selig, and the winning bid is paid to the Japanese professional team as a de facto transfer payment. The club then has a window of 30 days to negotiate a contract with the player; if negotiations fall apart, the Japanese club does not receive the transfer fee. Japanese players are not eligible for MLB's June draft because they are developed as professionals in what is regarded to be the second-most competitive professional league in baseball. The posting process—which has come under growing scrutiny from some baseball executives—protects the player pool within Japan while also serving as a nod toward the fact that the Japanese pro teams in fact bear the cost of developing players to the point where they are capable of playing in the major leagues. In the case of Darvish, who was 25 years old and had won 76 of his 104 decisions in Nippon Professional Baseball, negotiations dragged on before he agreed to a six-year, $56 million contract with the Rangers, at which point his Japanese team, the Nippon-Ham Fighters, received the $51.7 million high-bid that had been submitted by the Rangers.

Darvish went on to win 16 games and lose nine, striking out 221 (10.9 batters per nine innings) while finishing with a 3.90 earned run average. In the process he showed the kind of stuff and moxie that hinted at a long major league career, while also earning the appreciation of Rangers president Nolan Ryan—no small feat in itself given Ryan's status as the patron saint of the prototypical tough-as-nails Texas pitching gunslinger. Darvish certainly would have been welcomed on a Blue Jays staff ripped apart by injury, especially since landing him would have required no sacrifice of talent within the organization. Just money.

Although it is known that the organization had scouts in Japan at least twice—Anthopoulos and LaCava made those visits—the Blue Jays never revealed the amount of their bid, or indeed whether or not they had actually taken part in the process. Instead, off-the-record confirmations and guesses abounded as to the value of their bid, which according to most sources was something in the range of $25 million. Considering the manner in which the posting process's final hours played out on social media (a reporter who covered the Blue Jays' Double-A affiliate in Manchester, New Hampshire, reported at one point that the Blue Jays had won the rights to Darvish) and considering that both Anthopoulos and Beeston had always expressed confidence that ownership would provide money when the time was right to make a bold move, it was understandable that some in the Blue Jays fan base and local and national media saw in the very least a mixed message in their reluctance to bid high. In the end, the posting process comes down to a willingness to spend money, and the Rangers made it clear that a large part of their aggressiveness was the result of continued riches from a $3 billion, 20-year regional sports television deal. It was easy to see how the fact that the Blue Jays, a club owned by a company with multiple nation-wide sports channels, would not pony up could be taken as just another sign of reluctance on the part of ownership to fully engage in the process of putting together a winning team.

Beeston would later admit that the Blue Jays did not do a good job of managing expectations when it came to Darvish—particularly in light of the momentum the organization had achieved in 2011 with Jose Bautista's continued development into one of the game's premier power hitters, and Lawrie's emergence as the kind of impactful, Canadian-born offensive player that the team had never had. That momentum started a seismic shift in the public's perception of the organization, a shift reflected both in television ratings and—if such a thing even exists and can be measured—Canadian sports Q ratings.

13

THE NIGHTMARE
DREAM

DESPITE LOSING OUT ON DARVISH, THE 2012 SEASON began with a bang. The Blue Jays had the best spring training record of any team in baseball since 1997 (23–5) and were considered at least a contender for the one-game wild card playoff that had been added for the 2012 season. However, the team *did* end up needing more pitching—at least more healthy pitching. The first of the many injuries that would plague the team that season was to closer Sergio Santos, acquired in a trade with the Chicago White Sox during spring training. Santos was a virtual ghost at the major league facility during the early days of the Grapefruit League season—the Blue Jays said he was "refining his change-up" at the Bobby Mattick Training Center—but it was clear in April that there were shoulder issues, and Santos was shut down before eventually needing surgery to clean out the joint. It was a harbinger. Within the space of five days in June, three-fifths of the Blue Jays' starting rotation went down with injuries. The carnage started on June 11, when Brandon Morrow sustained a strained oblique muscle after throwing six pitches in a start against the Washington Nationals, and continued on June 13 when Kyle Drabek said he felt something pop in the back of his elbow on the 83rd pitch of a game in the same series. Two days later, 21-year-old rookie Drew Hutchison called out the team's training staff 12 pitches into a start against the Philadelphia Phillies.

Drabek, who suffered a right ulnar collateral ligament strain, and Hutchison, who suffered a sprained elbow, would both require Tommy John surgery. They would be joined by left-handed reliever Luis Perez, who had become a valuable man in the bullpen until he tore his left ulnar collateral ligament. Morrow, who was one of the best pitchers in the majors at the time of his injury, with a 7–4 record and a 3.01 ERA with three shutouts, didn't return until August 25—by which point the Blue Jays were done and dusted.

Meanwhile, Romero started the season well, going 8–1, but by the end of the campaign he was 9–14 with the majors' worst WHIP (1.67) and walks per nine innings (5.22), suffering a 13-game losing streak along the way. Morrow was the pitcher to whom Romero was the closest; possessed of a dry humour, Morrow knew exactly how to get his throwing partner to loosen up. Without Morrow, Romero seemed burdened, and it was telling that in an interview in the following off-season, Blue Jays first baseman Adam Lind suggested that leadership wasn't in Romero's DNA. It was not meant as a harsh criticism, just an honest statement of opinion.

Morrow is back for 2013, but the other pitchers won't be counted on, and the carnage of 2012 resulted in an internal, in-season examination by the organization about how it handled and developed pitching. Nobody has ever suggested the injuries had anything to do with Farrell's treatment of his pitchers or some sort of short-sightedness on the part of pitching coach Bruce Walton (who nonetheless did not return in 2013). Nor were the Blue Jays careless with their pitching prospects: in fact, they created a bit of a ripple throughout baseball when they decided to "piggyback" their three minor league gems—Noah Syndergaard, Aaron Sanchez and Justin Nicolino—with other starting pitchers at Single-A Lansing as a way of keeping them on a regular fifth-day cycle while restricting the number of pitches they were throwing. This wasn't exactly reinventing the wheel, however; bullpen coach Pat Hentgen said the Blue Jays did the same thing with him when he was coming up through the system.

Indeed, the Blue Jays are no different than most organizations, preferring to see young pitchers increase their workload by no more than 20 percent each season. But Farrell, who'd seen his own career derailed by injuries and who had been a college pitching coach before moving into player development, acknowledged that the cases of Drabek and Hutchison were food for thought. Drabek, 23, had thrown 100 or more pitches in 10 of his first 13 starts, and because of command issues was often pitching in high-pressure situations. Hutchison's battles were not quite as pronounced, but he had thrown 114, 109 and 103 pitches in his previous three starts, with spikes in his velocity. Hutchison had been expected to start the season at Triple-A Las Vegas, but the ineffectiveness of Brett Cecil opened the door for him to make his major league debut. Farrell would later say that his personal philosophy is that a pitcher should have something in the neighbourhood of 450 minor league innings under his belt before he gets promoted to the majors, but he also acknowledged that it is difficult to replicate the high-stress situations of a major league game in a major league ballpark, referring to the change of scenery and tone created by "having that upper deck."

"You do like to keep that year-over-year innings increase to roughly 20 to 30 percent," Farrell said at the end of the season, during one of his frequent dissertations on pitching. "Put a young guy in this environment, and the stress increases tenfold."

THE DEATH KNELL

Pitching injuries were only the half of it, however. On July 16, Jose Bautista suffered an injury to a tendon in his left wrist that would keep him out of action for five weeks. Bautista drilled a long foul ball down the left-field line in the eighth inning of a game in the Bronx. He turned toward the dugout and started to walk away from home plate before he dropped the bat and crouched down on his knees. Three innings into his second game back, against the Baltimore Orioles, Bautista took himself out again with more wrist pain, saying he had aggravated the injury on a first-inning swing.

Bautista would need season-ending surgery to stabilize the tendon sheath, but denied that he was either rushed back or had come back too soon, saying level of pain was the determining factor throughout his recovery, and that he'd believed he was ready to play at the time.

Bautista's original injury was effectively the death knell for the 2012 season, but it wasn't the only injury of note to a position player. J. P. Arencibia missed six weeks after suffering a non-displaced fracture in his right hand on a foul tip off the bat of the Oakland Athletics' Brandon Inge on July 25. There were near-misses too: starting pitcher Henderson Alvarez twice experienced discomfort on the mound in dramatic fashion that had the training staff, manager and his teammates rushing to his aid. And just two days after Bautista's injury at Yankee Stadium, Brett Lawrie fell six feet onto the concrete floor of a camera well near the visitors' dugout, hitting his right leg against a metal pole. X-rays were negative; the injury was ruled a calf contusion and he missed just two games . . . but he was later out from August 4 until September 7 after suffering a strained oblique muscle.

Even when the Blue Jays dodged an injury it was only for a short period of time. Romero, who fought his way through a brutal 2012 season, left his final start of the season in the third inning with what was diagnosed as inflammation in the quadriceps muscle just above the kneecap on his push leg. Romero joked the next day about how he was the last man standing. One month later the Blue Jays announced he would undergo arthroscopic surgery on his left elbow, which pretty much validated some of the whispers from scouts that Romero had been throwing like a guy who was hurt.

As mentioned, nobody laid the blame for the pitching injuries at the feet of Farrell, but the manner in which the season spun out of control certainly raised eyebrows. The Blue Jays had from the start shown signs of a lack of discipline. They became notorious among major league umpires for whining about balls and strikes, and on May 15 Lawrie found himself embroiled in an incident with umpire Bill Miller in the ninth inning of a 4–3 loss to the Tampa Bay Rays. Lawrie had taken off for first on a borderline pitch–believing it to be a ball–but was called back. Predictably, the next pitch was another called strike: after showing up an umpire in that manner the next pitch only has to be in the general area of the plate to be called in the pitcher's favour. Lawrie reacted by spiking his helmet, which bounced up and hit Miller. Lawrie had been volatile since his major league debut and it was never a surprise to see Farrell put his arm around Lawrie and have a dugout conversation.

But it was on the basepaths where most people believed the Blue Jays' randomness was most pronounced, although the statistics suggested they were no better or worse than most teams in the league. Their stolen-base percentage was 75 percent, a shade above the major league average (74). They scored from second base on a single 96 times, below the major league average of 102, and their extra-base-taken percentage (a measure of the percentage of times a baserunner advanced more than one base on a single or more than two bases on a double) was 46 percent, second-best in the majors behind only the Los Angeles Angels of Anaheim (at 49 percent). But the Blue Jays were caught stealing third base eight times, tying the Baltimore Orioles for the most in the majors. And they made 65 outs on the bases, 10 above the major league average and second to the Angels' 75.

It was a mixed bag, yet everybody associated with the team said after the season that the Blue Jays needed to be a more proficient team on the bases if they wanted to maximize their offensive potential. "When you have a pitcher telling people to run . . . sometimes it seemed as if we were running with our heads cut off, and not in the right situation," Lind said, referring to Farrell's background.

Yet that was probably Farrell's most intriguing commodity when he took over the job; the fact that he was an outsider, somebody who could be expected to bring in new ideas and a new approach, even though former pitchers and former pitching coaches have traditionally had a difficult time transitioning to manager. But as the dalliance with the Red Sox kept rearing its head, all those issues that had surrounded Ricciardi's tenure as GM resurfaced, including the sense of entitlement that many in the Toronto media and Blue Jays fan base perceived from their counterparts from Boston.

FARRELL RUMOURS . . . AGAIN

By mid-season, it was open knowledge that Bobby Valentine was going to be fired at the end of the season (if not sooner) as Red Sox manager, and Farrell never really pledged allegiance to the Blue Jays as the rumours percolated—other than pointing out that he was under contract. On September 7, the Blue Jays went into Fenway Park for a three-game series with the Red Sox and Farrell was asked about his interest in the Red Sox's job. It was a vintage performance, with Farrell saying he was "somewhat aware" of the speculation, while adding, "There's a lot of speculation, but as I said last week in Toronto, I'm the manager of the Blue Jays. This is where my focus is. I'm under contract; that's obvious, because if I wasn't I wouldn't be sitting here today. I can understand the natural connection because I've worked here in the past, but my focus is clearly with the Blue Jays."

Though Farrell maintained that his sole focus remained on the Blue Jays, it later became public that he had asked the Blue Jays for permission to speak to the Red Sox about the job the previous season. Here's where it gets murky: while Farrell is clear that he told the Blue Jays it would be his "dream job," and published reports suggested the Blue Jays took it seriously enough that they had asked the Red Sox for Buchholz in return, the Blue Jays maintain that it wasn't until after the 2012 season that Farrell made his interest known. As recently as the winter meetings in Nashville, Tennessee, the two sides stuck to their stories, with Farrell saying clearly that he had asked the Blue Jays twice to pursue the job. One thing was certain: at no point when Farrell was asked about the Red Sox's job by reporters did he ever close the door entirely, not even after the *Boston Globe* published an article in early September quoting major league sources as saying the teams had spoken informally the winter before, and making clear not only that Farrell would welcome a move to Boston, but also laying out ways in which it would happen.

While Blue Jays executives say both on and off the record that they did not detect a deterioration in Farrell's work as the season wound down, the Blue Jays were nonetheless a mess in the month of September–they were 10–18, after a 9–19 August–and when the season was finally over, first baseman Lind said the club was aware of the rumours involving Farrell.

"I mean, that's his only coaching experience at a major league level, in Boston," Lind said in an interview on Toronto sports radio station Sportsnet 590 The Fan. "You always kind of love your first love, and it was clear he enjoyed his time in Boston.

"You could tell, because when we were in Boston playing he had a little pep in his step. That was a little disappointing to guys like myself and Casey Janssen. It's like: 'Man, would you *be* a Blue Jay instead of a guy *working* for the Blue Jays?'"

So it is natural that people will wonder about the issues that surfaced later in the year–particularly the storm created when shortstop Yunel Escobar took the field for a September 15 game at Rogers Centre against (who else?) the Red Sox with a homophobic slur written on his eye-black. It was only when a fan posted a picture on a social media site that the Blue Jays suspended Escobar for three days without pay. The announcement was made three days later at a news conference at Yankee Stadium before a game against New York and it was a ham-handed affair, with Farrell uttering a particularly lame answer to a question about whether he thought there was homophobia in sports. Farrell said that nobody took notice of the message because Escobar was always writing messages of an "uplifting" nature on his eye-black, while Escobar himself claimed it was a matter of misinterpretation, that cultural differences meant the words were less pejorative in his culture than in others. Among the players who rose to Escobar's defence was Omar Vizquel, the Hall of Fame–bound shortstop who played out the string in 2012 with the Blue Jays.

But Vizquel wasn't done. When the Blue Jays returned to Toronto for the final series of the season, he blistered Farrell and the clubhouse culture, saying that far too many mistakes were simply let go.

"It's part of the inexperience," he told reporters gathered in front of his locker. "If you make mistakes and nobody says anything about it—they just let it go—we're going to keep making the same mistake over and over again. We have to stand up and say something right after that mistake happened. We have to talk about it at meetings. We have to address it in a big way in the clubhouse. Sometimes you have to punish players because they're making the same mistake over and over again.

"Obviously," he continued, "they need some veteran leadership in here. I tried to do my best, a little helping here and there. But I think the coaching staff have a big responsibility to kind of get in there and tie things up a little, have a little bit more communication with their players."

Needless to say, the comments rankled Farrell, who called a closed-door meeting the next day, after Vizquel visited the manager's office personally to apologize. Yet Vizquel, whose comments were more or less supported by veterans such as Janssen and Jason Frasor, did not pull back after the meeting, telling reporters he'd apologized to Farrell and the coaching staff without suggesting he'd changed his mind about the correctness of the sentiment.

THE END OF THE LONG GOODBYE

It was against that background that the Blue Jays went into an off-season with a fan base on the cusp. Much of what the organization had done had proven to be a critical success: the return to a more traditional Blue Jays uniform, including the re-institution of the Maple Leaf on the cap and jersey, as well as a series of catchy, well-produced television advertisements and the lure of its first-ever Canadian-born marquee player. Anthopoulos had a huge amount of currency with the fans, in part because he himself was Canadian, but also because he seemed to represent a balance between old school scouting and new-fangled analysis. Interestingly, some of that currency had been chipped away during the mishandling of the Darvish situation, and when Anthopoulos sent out a strange message at the winter meetings in Dallas that appeared to suggest fans had to start coming out to games before the team's payroll would be raised. It is fundamental economics, of course, but the timing and tone of the statement was surprising. Anthopoulos later de-linked payroll from attendance and said it was related to overall revenue, but some of the damage had already been done.

But the song and dance with Farrell was becoming perhaps the biggest black eye of Anthopoulos's tenure, and he finally ended it by trading Farrell to the Red Sox. Technically, the Blue Jays released him from the final year of his contract in exchange for journeyman infielder Mike Aviles—who they in turn traded to the Cleveland Indians for right-handed pitcher Esmil Rogers. Not much for a manager, eh?

In retrospect, there had been something unsettling at Farrell's introductory news conference, something that created future issues for the Blue Jays: the terms of his contract, specifically the length of the contract, were not released.

Player contracts, including term and financial details, have been made public for years, ever since the MLB Players Association realized the public disclosure of contract details actually benefitted the players by providing leverage when negotiating. The length of managers' contracts are almost always released, as at times are the length of GMs' contracts. But Anthopoulos, probably influenced by Beeston's laissez-faire approach to executive contracts, does not believe a manager's contract or those of his coaches need to be made public. Conventional wisdom was that Farrell had been given a three-year contract, but that was never formally acknowledged by either side until the middle of the 2012 season when an exasperated Farrell answered "yes" to a straightforward question about whether he had a year left on his deal.

Anthopoulos was not chastened by his experience with Farrell, but he did learn something about himself. In many ways, this was another one of those Jeremy Giambi moments. Much as the sight of Giambi taking batting practice at Olympic Stadium all those years ago had shown the then Montreal Expos intern the fallacy of a doctrinaire approach based on statistics, so too did the experience of hiring and then trading Farrell reveal to Anthopoulos that he needed to do a better job, simply put, of being his own man. Anthopoulos had inherited Cito Gaston with his job when he replaced J. P. Ricciardi, and had surrounded himself with advisors by the time it came to hiring a new manager. Anthopoulos never came out and said he regretted hiring Farrell—he's not wired like that—but those close to him believe that if he had made the hiring decision on his own, Farrell wouldn't have received the job. Perhaps, those friends say, there is a reason Anthopoulos never once broached the subject of a contract extension as a means of figuring out Farrell's true intentions, a reason beyond his stated explanation, which essentially boils down to him having other things on his list besides dealing with a manager already under contract.

"Looking back on the whole thing, I realize now that what I didn't do was go with my gut," Anthopoulos said in a candid interview just days after Farrell was traded. He professed that it would be different the next time, that he wouldn't worry about how the hiring looked or how good the manager looked on television.

Anthopoulos holds his fire whenever the topic of Farrell's exit comes up, simply painting it as one of those "it's just business" things. But some of his friends in the industry say he was enraged at the position Farrell put him in—with Farrell openly talking about the team knowing about his interest in the Red Sox before the 2012 season and his replaying of a line from Anthopoulos during their final conversation, in which the Blue Jays GM seemed to equate the lure of the Red Sox's managing gig for Farrell to the lure he would feel if the Montreal Expos were still in existence and looking for a GM.

Regardless of who said what or how anyone felt, Montreal might as well have been a distant memory for Anthopolous in the winter of 2012 and 2013. It was in Toronto where he was about to make his mark.

MAKING HIS MARK

No one saw it coming. This is how Anthopoulos does business. In an industry where trade rumours are often the currency of the media realm, he fancies himself as leak-proof, to the point that very early in his tenure he boldly told reporters that if they heard a rumour about a big move, it meant it wasn't happening.

That notion was born, Anthopoulos would tell you, from his experience as assistant general manager to J. P. Ricciardi, watching the implosion of a potential trade at the 2007 winter meetings in Nashville that would have seen future National League Cy Young Award–winner Tim Lincecum join the Blue Jays from the San Francisco Giants in return for All-Star outfielder Alex Rios. Lincecum would go on to become one of the most dominant NL pitchers of the era; Rios ended up signing an inflated contract and was dumped on the Chicago White Sox.

Both Ricciardi and Giants GM Brian Sabean were unusually glib and forthcoming about the potential deal, before Sabean experienced an acute outbreak of common sense that was rumoured to have seized him only after ownership became involved, and after he was repeatedly asked by his peers in one of the many lobbies and hallways of the Gaylord Opryland Hotel whether it was indeed true that he had lost his mind.

Anthopoulos's ability to keep a secret is all the more remarkable given the expansion of the team's scouting and evaluation department during his reign. It is true that more scouts and advisors mean more eyes and more sounding boards; it also means more mouths and, possibly, more agendas. Nobody in the baseball media in Canada or the US knew that Anthopoulos's 12-player deal with the Marlins had taken shape at the general managers' meetings in Indian Wells, California, soon after the World Series. But the signing of R. A. Dickey didn't hold to form:

the Blue Jays' status as a serious contender was established at the winter meetings by many of the national opinion-makers in the US, and stayed in place even with signals from Anthopoulos to the contrary. Anthopoulos didn't get the agreement of Dickey and agent Bo McGinnis on a contract extension until three days after the Mets and Blue Jays had agreed on the players, and by then the identities of the prospects going to the Mets for the 38-year-old knuckleballer (Travis d'Arnaud and Noah Syndergaard) were known. It was an untenable position for Anthopoulos; the baseball world knew he'd made the deal—the prospects he was sending to the Mets knew all about it—and now he had to finalize the contract or risk having it fall apart.

After signing his contract—$12 million per year for 2014 and 2015, with a $1 million signing bonus tacked on to the pre-existing $5 million he was going to earn in 2013, and a club option for 2016—Dickey remarked how impressed he was that Anthopoulos had flown down to his off-season home in Nashville, Tennessee, to press the Blue Jays' case. Indeed, Anthopoulos, manager John Gibbons and director of scouting Perry Minasian (who was employed by the Texas Rangers when Dickey was with the organization) met with Dickey for a cup of coffee that turned into a four-hour discussion before Anthopoulos and McGinnis went into the wee hours of the morning talking about the extension, then revisiting it later in the day.

Dickey's knuckleball is harder and has more variety than those thrown by some previous practitioners of the pitch, and that's fitting because he himself is a different cat. You no longer just need to read books to be considered an intellectual in a baseball clubhouse, but Dickey's backstory—he is a published author who has detailed a background that includes sexual abuse and coming from a broken home, and has travelled extensively—certainly appears to make him subject to different sensibilities than the run-of-the-mill professional athlete.

The meeting, Dickey said, "allowed me to look him in the eye and hear from his heart where he thought I fit into the scheme of things with the organization, where he envisioned us going in the near future and how important he felt like I was to that vision."

There are echoes in that statement that must surely take Blue Jays fans of a certain age back to the early 90s, when the organization was a destination not because it was willing to overpay—as was the evaluation made by Ricciardi—but because it was viewed as a destination that offered a decent chance of winning. It's also why Anthopoulos was fully comfortable with the fact that Josh Johnson, one of the centrepieces of the deal with the Marlins—no, the centrepiece—is eligible for free agency after the 2013 season. If the Blue Jays win, Anthopoulos reasoned, it will open up the possibility of getting Johnson signed to an extension.

The trip to Nashville was not Anthopoulos's first selling trip of the off-season. He had in fact flown to south Florida to meet with another free-agent pitcher, Anibal Sanchez, before the Marlins trade was finalized. While no offer was forthcoming, Anthopoulos did glean some information about Sanchez's former Miami Marlins teammate Emilio Bonifacio, who would become part of the 12-player deal. This was a trademark of Anthopoulos's climb to the top: a willingness to absorb information and listen. It was one reason that Anthopoulos quietly scheduled a meeting with the agents for Jose Reyes, Peter Greenberg and Chris Leible in the winter of 2011 even though Anthopoulos knew the Blue Jays would not be in the bidding at the time for Reyes, who was a free agent that winter and eventually signed with the Marlins. He wanted to meet with Greenberg . . . well, he wanted to meet with him just because. It's a leap to say Anthopoulos knew back then that the Marlins would embark on a fire sale the very next season, but given the fact that he spent much of that winter telling everybody that the notion that he had an open chequebook was nonsense, it was in the very least slightly prescient.

When the Marlins deal was finalized, Anthopoulos had acquired the lead-off hitter the organization has craved for years in Reyes, a shortstop who was a year removed from winning the National League batting title; a veteran left-handed pitcher, in Mark Buehrle, with a long track record of success in the American League and who can tutor another lefty starter coming off a difficult year (Ricky Romero); and a high-energy utility player in Bonifacio, whom some see as an everyday second baseman. He also acquired catcher John Buck, who was then dispatched to the Mets in the Dickey trade. By the time Christmas Day rolled around, the Blue Jays payroll sat at $108 million without non-arbitration raises factored in. It is only the second time in club history that payroll has exceeded $100 million, and comes after being well under the major league average in payroll the previous two seasons, including $17 million under in 2012. By New Year's Day the club had $30 million more in commitments for 2013 than the major league average. That will be the case for the next two seasons, as well. All told, Anthopoulos's signings and trades saw the Blue Jays take on $220.85 million in guaranteed money, including buyouts, with Reyes's remaining five years and $114 million (there is a club option at $22 million for 2018 that carries a $4 million buyout) topping the chart.

It was the Vernon Wells trade that earned Anthopoulos the good housekeeping seal of approval from management, though that deal seems so long ago given what happened in the 2012 off-season. When his work was done, Anthopoulos sat back one day and said he was a little concerned about his overhaul—a potential seven new additions to the 25-man roster resulting from two trades and the free-agent signings of Melky Cabrera and Maicer Izturis—because it meant the team could no longer fly under the radar.

"Everybody thought Omar [Minaya] made a great deal when he got Bartolo Colon from the Cleveland Indians," Anthopoulos said, referring to a trade Minaya made in the Montreal Expos' final year in Montreal that saw future All-Stars Cliff Lee, Grady Sizemore and Brandon Phillips join the Indians.

Truth is, Anthopoulos had had an inkling that he would be able to add to payroll based on his discussions with Paul Beeston and ownership in the previous winter. The Blue Jays made a run at Carlos Beltran, a free-agent outfielder who ended up signing with the St. Louis Cardinals for two years and $26 million (in part because he didn't want to play on the artificial turf at Rogers Centre). Anthopoulos, a friend said, believed he had already jumped through the necessary hoops in setting the stage for adding payroll—especially since the Blue Jays experienced a 15 percent growth in attendance from 2011 that was the largest one-year jump in club history—and improved revenue from television ratings and the new national network TV contract had answered some of the preconditions Anthopoulos tried to lay down the winter before with his buzz-killing linkage of payroll to attendance. Until that winter, he had been the "ninja GM," the guy who had acquired Brandon Morrow for Brandon League, Lawrie for Marcum, stuck the Angels' Tony Reagins with the type of contract that gets a guy fired—which the Vernon Wells deal did—and who gambled and won when he signed Jose Bautista to a five-year, $65 million contract on the basis of one good year. "I had players ask me if I was nuts," he said, shrugging.

Anthopoulos was right: Beeston was able to get Blue Jays ownership to sign off on a deal for Chicago White Sox pitcher Jake Peavy that fell through, but he put the money to good use by pursuing the Marlins. Anthopoulos said his concern in making the Marlins deal wasn't the impact on the 2013 payroll as much as it was the long-term commitments the team was assuming. Just as Pat Gillick's signature acquisition of Alomar and Carter from the San Diego Padres in 1990 started out as talks focusing on Carter, so too did the Marlins trade stem from Anthopoulos's interest in one particular player: in this case, right-hander Josh Johnson, whom the Marlins had put on the trade block at the July 31 trade deadline. The Blue Jays asked about him then and were told that it would take d'Arnaud to get the deal done. When Anthopoulos heard that the price would also include one of his three top pitching prospects (Justin Nicolino, Aaron Sanchez or Noah Syndergaard) as well as Hechavarria, widely touted as the best defensive shortstop not playing in the majors, he decided to expand the deal. The Marlins wanted Syndergaard, a big, hard-throwing Texan who had been compared to Chris Carpenter and Halladay by Blue Jays advisor and former Cy Young winner Pat Hentgen. But Anthopoulos knew that they also had a soft spot for Nicolino, and liked outfield prospect Jake Marisnick. Would the Marlins, he wondered, be interested in parting with Jose Reyes?

There was a great deal of discussion among the Blue Jays people as they left the Marlins villa at the Hyatt Grand Champions Resort. Some voices were raised in dissension at the thought of giving up so much of the farm system. Better, he was told, to try and address the team's issues through the free-agent market. But the experience with Beltran was still in Anthopoulos's mind; so, too, an experience with a free-agent reliever (Joe Nathan) in which myriad conversations with the agent couldn't overcome issues of geography and family. Plus, Anthopoulos realized he was addressing core issues surrounding his team well *before* the free-agent feeding frenzy would start toppling dominoes that might impact the market for the Marlins players. It was a thin free-agent market at the top end to begin with, which meant expectations were inflated and returns overstated. Less of a factor, he maintained, was the kind of torpor that had set in over the traditional free-agent market drivers in the AL East, the New York Yankees and Boston Red Sox. "There is a value to getting the bird in the hand," he said later. "You don't want to leave things hanging around, where it starts to get involved with other things."

Still . . . Jose Reyes? Five years and $96 million guaranteed remaining on a contract for a player with a history of leg issues that would seem to leave him exposed playing on artificial turf? "You just had to throw Reyes's name in there, didn't you?" Anthopoulos remembers assistant general manager Jay Sartori saying as the Blue Jays brain trust left their discussions with the Marlins.

Why not? "Jose Reyes is one of my favourite players," Anthopoulos said, his hands open in admission. "He always has been. I can tell you there were people in our group who didn't like this deal, and there was a lot of debate about Jose—how he would age, how we thought he might be at the end of the deal. But . . . I don't know. I just always liked him. He's an electric player. You talk about guys like that in the draft—electric—and it's a synonym for exciting, quick-twitch muscle, high-energy guys. He's a shortstop—which has kind of been a black hole for us—and a lead-off hitter. The captain and catalyst of the infield."

Anthopoulos admits that the longer he stays in the game, the more he becomes a fan of athletes. "Guys who bring energy to the ballpark every day of a long season." It was that energy that drew him to Bonifacio as well. In making the Marlins deal, Anthopoulos remembered a discussion he'd had with Pat Gillick (still the standard against which all Blue Jays GMs are measured) focusing on the importance of outfielder Hunter Pence to the Philadelphia Phillies 2011 season. Pence had a funky swing and was something of a wing nut, but Gillick's message to Anthopoulos was clear: you can't have too many high-energy players. Pence brought that commodity and then some.

As is often the case in complicated deals, it is the details that can sometimes scupper the transaction. Anthopoulos was prepared to walk away if the Marlins didn't include Bonifacio, a 27-year-old switch-hitter. Some of his own people were telling him he'd be fired if Paul Beeston—who'd made the successful move to get ownership's approval—found out he let the deal die because of Bonifacio. But Anthopoulos's response, as relayed by somebody familiar with the debate, was, "I'm already uncomfortable giving up the guys we're giving up, and nobody else is going to give these guys (the Marlins) the type of players we're giving them."

Is there an art to making a deal like this? Anthopoulos shrugged. Truth is, the dealings with the Marlins tested some of his basic tenets. "Anybody can make a trade," he said. "I don't think it's a skill. I never try to sell a trade, because I think it's a slap in the face. I can't imagine the guy on the other side of the table saying to his owner, 'Look, Alex told me to go get this guy.' It's something I learned from [Chicago White Sox] GM Kenny Williams my first year on the job. We were looking at a deal and he was reluctant to put a third or fourth player in and I said, 'Kenny, this guy is this, this and this.' He said, 'Well, if he's that, then leave him alone. Leave him alone.' It was a utility guy and he was reluctant to include him. The guy's a GM; he knows what he's willing to do and there's really nothing you can do to get him to change his mind."

This deal was a test. Just as the Marlins were reluctant to part with Bonifacio, so too was Anthopoulos reluctant to move catcher Jeff Mathis, whom the Marlins wanted in return.

Yes, Jeff Mathis: he of the .198 career average, $1.5 million annual salary and the type of bedside manner that makes pitchers weep with joy. Mathis for John Buck: the catcher who was scheduled to earn $6 million this season had to be part of the deal. "We'd just signed Jeff, and that was my issue," Anthopoulos said. "I mean, I felt like a shithead doing it. Mathis was the last piece introduced . . . and it was the principle that we'd just signed him. He was a good guy who knew his role and accepted his role and besides that, part of me felt, 'Are these guys really not going to do this deal because of John Buck and Jeff Mathis?' I didn't feel right doing it, and I talked to Paul Beeston about it and he said, 'You have to do it. This is the biggest trade this organization's made.'

"So I rationalized it. I told Jeff, 'Go ask the Marlins if we shopped you.' I just realized: if I'd lost this deal, Paul would have fucking choked me. He really would have."

It remains to be seen whether or not the Blue Jays won the World Series during those hectic two months when they acted like the big-market franchise Paul Beeston wants them to be. But they won the off-season. If you'd told Blue Jays fans, at the end of the 2012 season, that this would be the case, they might not have choked you, but they sure would have had a laugh at your expense.

THE RETURN OF JOHN GIBBONS

But now that the Blue Jays had had their biggest off-season haul in franchise history, who would manage them? Although the hiring of the new Blue Jays skipper wasn't the biggest story of the 2012 off-season, it was certainly the most stunning. While the fans and the media looked to the future, Anthopoulos looked into the not-so-distant past—and John Gibbons was on no one's shortlist but his. In true Anthopoulos form, his decision to hire Gibbons would likely have been kept under wraps right up to the news conference had the two men not been spotted dining in Toronto a couple of evenings earlier—not early enough to make anybody's newspaper, but not too late that the *Toronto Sun* couldn't have the tidbit on its website the morning of the announcement.

Later, Anthopoulos would admit that the idea of hiring Gibbons as manager had occurred as far back as his first year, that in his spare time he would muse about how the hiring would be greeted: he thinks it would have been one hard sell to Paul Beeston. But Anthopoulos, like most of the holdovers from Gibbons' previous sojourn with the team, regards Gibbons as a masterful maker of in-game decisions regarding the bullpen. And as a former catcher, he's expected to help the Blue Jays become more proficient on the bases. Gibbons spent three years as a bench coach with the Kansas City Royals before moving on to manage the San Diego Padres Double-A affiliate in his hometown of San Antonio, Texas, and when he flew up to Toronto to have dinner with Anthopoulos one weekend in late November, he thought he was being offered a coaching job. (Anthopoulos had also, at one point, considered hiring Gibbons as an advance scout; he remembered how as a manager Gibbons would be remarkably accurate in giving off-handed analysis of a particular players strengths and weaknesses.)

Gibbons is a breath of fresh air after the stuffy Farrell; a casual Texan given to wearing cowboy boots and jeans and a fond teller of stories from his days as a New York Mets catching prospect, when his teammates at various times included Billy Beane (who once purchased a raccoon and brought it home when the two were roommates), Darryl Strawberry, Kevin Mitchell and, as mentioned, J. P. Ricciardi. Gibbons has perfected the whole "dumb as a fox" thing, and he has a competitive edge that was revealed in his previous tenure during the incidents with Lilly and Hillenbrand.

"Actually," Anthopoulos remarked at Gibbons' introductory news conference, responding to a question about Gibbons' history (and perhaps with an eye toward the waywardness of the 2012 team), "I'm not certain that's all that bad."

Gibbons goes into 2013 with his work cut out for him. This Blue Jays team is very much new, with players of impressive pedigree:

veteran pitchers with World Series rings and Cy Young awards and perfect games; a position player with a batting title; and another who might have won a batting title had he not been suspended for failing a drug test. There were other managerial candidates whose names were made public—Sandy Alomar Jr. (again); DeMarlo Hale (again, although he will be Gibbons' bench coach); Don Wakamatsu; long-time Blue Jays coach Brian Butterfield; Tim Wallach; and even Mike Hargrove. Gibbons had fun with the hunt at his news conference, gently chiding Hall of Fame member and *Toronto Sun* columnist Bob Elliott by saying he was "digging up dead people" in reporting about the identity of some of the candidates. At the winter meetings in Nashville, Gibbons walked up to an acquaintance after checking in to the Opryland Hotel and said, "Bet you never thought you'd see me at one of these again—unless it was for a minor league meeting."

Anthopoulos's friends and people who have covered the team noted that the GM looked happier and more relaxed at the news conference to announce Gibbons' hiring than he had in two years. Yes, he had gone to school on what had happened with Farrell. It was a not-so-subtle reminder that the learning curve never ends.

"Hiring John . . . it was like I was trying to get a five-tool player," Anthopoulos said over lunch a few days after Gibbons' hiring. "You know, you try to check off the boxes: good with the media, smart, somebody who can connect with players. John [Farrell] did all that. But what I learned from the whole thing was that you aren't hiring a player or acquiring a player; you have to look for a fit for your organization."

Anthopoulos paused. "It's not just about working from 7 to 10, during the in-game. There's all sorts of other components. The last time, I sat there and looked at the big-time managers in our division. New York had Joe Girardi, Baltimore had Buck Showalter . . . there's Joe Maddon in Tampa and Terry Francona was still in Boston. It really was like I thought I was adding a player, somebody to our lineup. But the thing is, a player can go to any team, because of his skills. It doesn't matter what a player's philosophy is, right? It's what you do when you get in the box and on the mound. A manager can't be like that, though. What works for one city or one team doesn't always work someplace else. Ultimately, you have to be able to manage the game. That goes without saying. But you also have to fit the team, and maybe that's what I didn't ask the first time: 'Do you fit here?'"

Really, we've all just about had enough of Boston, don't you think?

14

OVER-HYPED . . .
BUT BETTER
THAN THIS

THIS WAS WHEN IT STILL ALL SEEMED SO BELIEVABLE.
When the odds-makers and chattering classes had no reason to
doubt that the Toronto Blue Jays had to be—must be—one of the
favourites to win the 2013 World Series. In the spring, Jim Leyland,
a manager who has both won and lost World Series, was behind
the batting cage before a Grapefruit League game between his
defending American League champion Detroit Tigers and the Blue
Jays. He'd already greeted John Gibbons warmly in that trademark
voice that revealed years of well-intentioned yet failed attempts to
quit smoking—"You got your fucking Series ring sized up already,
Gibby?" he'd asked. "Bet there's a big, fucking red Maple Leaf in
the middle, huh?"—and now he saw Alex Anthopoulos. "I just want
to congratulate you for having the biggest set of balls of anybody
in the game," Leyland said, extending his hand to the Blue Jays'
general manager. "You'd have to, to hire this guy back."

Two things were noticeable during the spring of what was supposed to be the Blue Jays rebirth: baseball people to a man were
happy to have Gibbons back in the fold. And they were keenly interested in how—and, yes, if—Anthopoulos's Fantasy League off-season
would bear fruit.

Fast-forward to the final two weeks of the regular season, with the
Blue Jays about to finish dead last in the American League East for
the fourth time since their 1993 World Series title, and with only a
single win (74) more than the mess that was 2012. Gibbons is seated
in Toronto's Real Sports Bar & Grill, picking away at a salad. His team
will leave in a few days for their final road trip, where they will see
John Farrell and the Boston Red Sox clinch the American League East
title at Fenway Park. Sometimes when that happens, the television
cameras will find a player sitting in the losing dugout looking out at
the celebration scene on the field. Veteran infielder Mark DeRosa had
suggested to his teammates that some of them might want to do so to

let it sink in. But none of the Blue Jays watched the Red Sox. None wanted to see Farrell and former Blue Jays coaches Brian Butterfield and Torey Lovullo celebrate on the field.

Days before that, Gibbons was asked about his biggest disappointment of 2013. He shrugged. "I'm just disappointed we weren't as good as we were expected to be," he said. "Look, we were overhyped. But we should have been better than this."

There is no great mystery to why the 2013 Blue Jays were so bad, although finding the reason *behind* the reason gave Gibbons, Anthopoulos and—make no mistake about it—ownership cause for concern as the season wound down. Offensively, the Blue Jays were 10th in average (.252) and ninth in OPS, eighth in runs and fourth in home runs, despite the fact that J. P. Arencibia and Adam Lind were the only position players to not miss significant playing time due to injuries. That doesn't explain a 74-win season. No, momentum in baseball is a sports-writing cliché and doesn't exist beyond the identity of the next day's starting pitcher. A winning or losing streak starts, continues or ends depending on the man on the mound, and the Blue Jays had the second-worst starter's earned run average (4.81) and the team's starters pitched the third-fewest innings in the major leagues. There's the rub.

Spring training was a decidedly laid-back affair, with the exception of a million-dollar television advertising campaign that required each player to head over to a tent behind the visitors bullpen at Florida Auto Exchange Stadium to be filmed on a huge soundstage surrounded by lights and microphones and extras hired to wave flags and cheer as the players went through impromptu and prompted motions. "I'm going to have nightmares after that," Mark Buehrle said following his session. "I had to act. I had to narrate stuff. Those are two things I'm not good at." Veterans weren't required to make the long bus rides to Fort Myers: get in early, get your work done quickly and go home, was the mantra. Gibbons was asked one day earlier in the Grapefruit League campaign whether or not he was worried that the attitude might be too relaxed. His response was that this wasn't a young team; that the Blue Jays were largely a veteran group comprised of players who should know what they need to do to get ready. One of Gibbons' coaches said that part of the manager's thinking was that with so many new bodies in camp, it was important to let clubhouse cliques get established and broken down, and for that reason the manager was taking a largely hands-off approach.

A MESS OUT OF THE GATE

While it seemed to be pretty much just like any other spring in terms of drills, there was a sense of interruption created by the World Baseball Classic. It was a hint of things to come. The Blue Jays sent five regulars to the WBC—Brett Lawrie, R. A. Dickey, J. P. Arencibia, Reyes and Encarnacion. Lawrie injured his rib cage diving for grounders in practice for Team Canada and was on the 15-day disabled list when the season started; Encarnacion hurt his finger playing for the Dominican Republic and started out with two hits in his first seven games. Coupled with Reyes missing 66 games with a sprained ankle suffered on an awkward slide into second base in an April 12 game against the Kansas City Royals (which Gibbons later called "the death blow"), it meant that the first time Lawrie and Reyes—the intended starting left side of the Blue Jays infield—actually played together in a game was July 13. Only Lawrie, who had a second stint on the 15-day disabled list with a left ankle sprain, was at second base—not third—because the tandem of Emilio Bonifacio and Maicer Izturis had been such an offensive and defensive liability that the Blue Jays moved their prized young player back to the position he'd manned with the Milwaukee Brewers. Lawrie's rehabilitation option in the minor leagues and a suggestion on the part of Jose Bautista that he (Bautista) move in from right field to third to shore up the left side of the infield in Reyes's absence provided the pretext. But Bautista hurt his back in the first game he played at third, and the experiment lasted all of a week before Lawrie was back at the hot corner, with second base a hodge-podge that included journeyman Japanese infielder Munenori Kawasaki before minor leaguer Ryan Goins came up and supplied the type of offensive and defensive balance for which the Blue Jays had been searching. (Nicknamed "The Mascot" when he was with the Seattle Mariners, the quirky, twitchy Kawasaki became a fan favourite, much like John McDonald used to be.)

It was all unhinged. Nothing was as it was supposed to be, almost from the start. The addition of Reyes and Bonifacio and Izturis was supposed to make the Blue Jays better defensively—yet they were a mess out of the gate, and advanced defensive metrics showed them to be among the worst defensive teams in the game. Josh Johnson—whose availability from the Miami Marlins served as the impetus for the multi-player deal Anthopoulos made in the winter—had a 6.86 earned run average in his first four starts, went on the 15-day DL with a triceps inflammation, and finished 2–7 in 16 starts, after which he was shut down with a forearm strain. Brandon Morrow made 10 starts and suffered a frightening decrease in velocity before his season ended with what turned out to be a nerve injury; Ricky Romero, just two years removed from the All-Star Game, couldn't throw strikes at either the major league or Triple-A level; and Buehrle and Dickey stutter-stepped out of the gate. The Blue Jays were 10–17 in April, when their starting pitchers had a 5.37 earned run average.

The Blue Jays spent all but 15 days in last place in the American League East, with the high-water mark coming on June 23 when, after a 13–5 home win over the Baltimore Orioles that was their 11th consecutive victory, they found themselves a season-high two games over .500 at 38–36. It was their 15th win in 18 games, a stretch during which their offence seemed to find its stride. Gibbons had moved slugger

Bautista up to second in the batting order and inserted Encarnacion into the cleanup spot. "I have been waiting for this," Encarnacion told reporters after the game, as the Blue Jays packed up for a seven-game road trip to Tampa Bay and Boston. "I know what this team can do." The key during that stretch was the same thing that dragged the Blue Jays down for 90 percent of the season: starting pitching. During that winning streak, the Blue Jays starters allowed 20 earned runs over $73^{1/3}$ innings (2.45) and had seven outings of at least seven innings in length. "It all came together for a two-week period," Gibbons said. "But then, even bad teams run off a streak every now and then. It just didn't happen enough."

The streak should have been a starting point. It matched the longest-ever in club history and it occurred just a week before short-stop Reyes was expected to return. Excitement was palpable going into Tampa, where the Blue Jays promptly lost two of three and then lost three of four at Fenway Park to the Red Sox. Up next? The first of two seven-game losing streaks that would have Buehrle looking around the clubhouse and suggesting that maybe the team wasn't as good as it thought. Yeah, well . . . you think? By the end of the season, there were the same whispers as those that emanated from the 2012 clubhouse—only this time, instead of Omar Vizquel, it was play-ers such as Mark DeRosa suggesting (albeit in much gentler tones) that there needed to be a greater emphasis placed on responsibility.

"To be honest with you, I've never been in this situation," DeRosa said after calling a players-only meeting on April 29, back before the winning streak and losing streaks that followed. "I'm not used to putting on my uniform and expecting things to go wrong. I expect them to go right, and there's no reason that should not happen."

It all seemed a little rinse and repeat. Lawrie struggled at the plate and in the field, and was taken to task publicly by Gibbons after star-ing down third-base coach Luis Rivera and Adam Lind when Lind didn't tag up on a Lawrie fly ball. Jose Bautista, who was put on notice in spring training by Gibbons that his overreaction to umpires' calls needed to be tempered, raised eyebrows early in the season when he said: "Sometimes I have trouble more than other players dealing with my production being affected by somebody else's mediocrity." But he finished the season once again on the disabled list. And while he was the highest-rated Blue Jays player in WAR (wins above replacement), he was only 32nd in the majors in that category. Colby Rasmus and J. P. Arencibia seemed to be in a race to lead the American League in strikeouts before Rasmus settled into a quietly effective season. Arencibia, however, regressed defensively and offensively and had one of the worst offensive seasons in history: a .194 batting average in 474 at-bats with 148 strikeouts, 18 walks and an OPS of .592. Arencibia also became embroiled in a controversy with television and radio analysts Gregg Zaun and Dirk Hayhurst, which became bitterly personal.

POST-SEASON SCRUTINY

The similarities between 2012 and 2013 suggest that a search for common denominators might be in order, but it's not entirely surprising that the newcomers would bear the brunt of the post-season scrutiny. Buehrle gave the Jays 203²/³ innings and pretty much turned in a representative season, although his WHIP (1.345) was his second-highest in seven years. Reyes finished without a triple for the first time in his major league career, but hit above his career average over 93 games and moved around much better late in the season once his ankle was fully healed. (True to his character, and despite all the unrealized expectations and a season on unforgiving artificial turf, Reyes pronounced, "I can't wait for 2014" on the final day of the season.) Meanwhile, Bonifacio and Izturis turned second base into a black hole: Bonifacio was traded to the Kansas City Royals for cash or a player to be named later, and minor leaguer Ryan Goins opened eyes as the team's everyday second baseman down the stretch. Josh Johnson was a disaster and needed surgery to remove loose bodies from his elbow after the season. Melky Cabrera? Anthopoulos's two-year, $16 million gamble on a player coming off a 50-game suspension for the use of performance-enhancing drugs turned up snake eyes: Cabrera was an offensive passenger who moved stiffly around the outfield until he was diagnosed with a tumour in his lower back.

Then there was R. A. Dickey, the 2012 National League Cy Young Award winner for the New York Mets who was acquired for the Blue Jays' two top prospects (pitcher Noah Syndergaard and catcher Travis d'Arnaud) and who agreed to a two-year contract extension with a club option for a third year. Dickey's discordant outing in the home opener set the stage for the 2013 season, but afterwards he spoke optimistically: "We're family in here. We're going to stay positive." Dickey adopted a "season isn't over one game in" tone in his post-game media session—which was odd since, well, nobody had suggested it was. It wouldn't be the first time that there was a tinge of melodrama to a post-game session with the knuckleballer, who lasted all of $4^{2/3}$ innings in his second start, a 13–0 loss to the Boston Red Sox at the Rogers Centre that seemed unsettlingly definitive.

Dickey's early performances raised unsettling questions. This was not the National League East anymore, and the Rogers Centre is not the pitcher-friendly park that Citi Field was when Dickey won his Cy Young Award. As the Blue Jays' season deteriorated and it became time to take a more detailed look at what had gone wrong, the spotlight settled eventually on Dickey's effectiveness at home with the Rogers Centre roof open or closed. Dickey's performance over the second half was much-improved. In his last 20 starts, he had a 3.62 earned run average and walked 36 batters, after walking 35 in his first 14 starts in a season in which he posted his highest walk rate since mastering the knuckleball (or, in his words, "having a relationship with it, because you never master the knuckleball"). At home with the roof open, he had a 5.73 earned run average; closed, his ERA was 3.51. Dickey spoke a great deal toward the end of the season about wanting to sit down and digest the numbers at the end of the season, saying the fact that he was hampered by an upper-back strain early in the season—not to mention tipping his fastball—might have skewed the numbers. The Rogers Centre roof is open or closed at the call of president and chief executive officer Paul Beeston and the building's operations staff (once the game starts, the decision is in the hands of the umpiring crew chief, and during the post-season the commissioner's office makes the call). Nobody seemed much interested in discussing what would happen if, in a big game on a gorgeous, unseasonably hot September day, Dickey decided he wanted the roof closed.

Not that it mattered in September of 2013. "I had some foresight about this," Dickey said at the end of the season. "I knew what expectations would be for this time in general. But next year, we won't have the WBC. I will take my normal amount of time to get ready. We played together for a year now, and that's a big deal. We know how to challenge each other and hold each other accountable."

Dickey dismissed suggestions that moving into the AL East was ill-advised. "I knew this was going to be a ginormous challenge and that's one of the reasons I signed here," he said. "I saw what my knuckleball could do in the NL East and felt like I had it at a point where it would be exciting to challenge the best hitters day in and out. I never thought, 'What have I done?'"

For his part, neither did Anthopoulos second-guess his decision to go all-in. While some saw a cautionary parallel to the profligate spending of his predecessor, J. P. Ricciardi, the Blue Jays' GM said he believed the time was right to add to a core of Jose Bautista, Encarnacion, Morrow and a bullpen that turned out to be a strength, and not the weakness everybody thought it would be.

"It's fair, when you look back at the results, to ask if we jumped too soon," Anthopoulos said. "But when you look at the guys we had under contract, their ages and the fact that we had control of so many of them for two, three and four more years, being in the middle didn't seem like an option. Either you trade and go young and stockpile prospects, or you try to move it forward and get better."

But what 2013 did prove to Anthopoulos was that the team needed to pay more attention to how it graded players defensively, given the issues that Bonifacio and Izturis had on turf. The Rogers Centre will eventually get a natural grass playing surface—the Canadian Football League's Toronto Argonauts have already been warned they will have to vacate the facility—but until then the team will need to live with an artificial surface that degrades each time it is taken up for events other than baseball. The season also caused Anthopoulos to look into ways that the team might better manage risk, although he said the organization did as much due diligence as possible on Cabrera and Johnson. "Very few players are 'clean,' in terms of their medical reports, when you look at signing or acquiring them," Anthopoulos said. "But in light of what has happened here the past two years, we might manage risk more."

What does the immediate future hold for the Blue Jays? Team owners Rogers Communications welcomed a new chief executive officer at the end of 2013, and while in some quarters that was taken as grounds for worry, the fact that the Blue Jays were specifically excluded from a company-wide round of belt-tightening by Rogers Media was seen as a positive sign. The Blue Jays finished 2013 with $110 million committed to 14 players in 2014 and a further $91 million to 11 players in 2015, and privately, Blue Jays executives were bullish on a payroll increase. In his year-end post-mortem with reporters, Anthopoulos pointed to the fact that in drawing more than 2.5 million spectators to the Rogers Centre in 2013, he believed the argument about whether Toronto was a big or small market had been settled "once and for all." Perhaps. One thing is clear: after spending lavishly to prop open what the Blue Jays have sold to their fans as a three-year window, the context of the discussion—and fan expectations—have changed unalterably.

THE GAME
GROWS UP

FOR THE MAN WHO OVERSEES MAJOR LEAGUE Baseball's Canadian scouting bureau, it hasn't always been as clear-cut as Brett Lawrie. Walt Burrows doesn't always get the best athlete.

There was, for example, this 14-year-old hockey player from Nova Scotia. Nothing against his guy in the Maritimes, Ken Lenihan, or the kid from Cole Harbour–a shortstop/catcher/centre-fielder who batted left and, in Lenihan's words, "can really hit." It was the rest of the description. "The kid," Lenihan told him, "is a pretty good hockey player."

Burrows chuckles. He wishes he had seen Sidney Crosby play baseball, just to say he had, just to put together a scouting report. After all, he had a pretty good record with guys from other sports. He'd once tried to convince a young Steve Nash that he had a future in baseball, before he went on to become a sure-fire NBA Hall of Famer. As a basketball referee in British Columbia, Burrows had plenty of time to keep tapping the kid on the shoulder, preaching the virtues of baseball. "A Canadian shortstop," Burrows sighed. "I remember talking to somebody about him, and the guy says, 'They just don't exist.'"

Still, Burrows has won his share of multi-sport battles, a feat that became easier to accomplish once Baseball Canada and its visionary general manager of national teams, Greg Hamilton, established a full-time junior development program offering high-quality opposition and exposure. But hockey was different. Burrows had scouted baseball in Canada long enough to know that when Lenihan told him the kid from Nova Scotia was a "pretty good hockey player," it was time to ask the follow-up.

"I asked him 'How good do they say he is?'" Burrows said. "Ken pauses, and says, 'Well, they say he might be the next Wayne Gretzky.'"

Gretzky, of course, played baseball in the summers in Ontario's Intercounty Baseball League. And like Gretzky, Crosby was on to bigger things.

Luckily, there was no such issue with a certain sports prodigy from Langley, British Columbia—Brett Lawrie. Canadians like to make a big deal out of the "hockey attitude" their major leaguers bring to the game, but what drives the Toronto Blue Jays' third baseman isn't some carry-over from the ice. He never *played* hockey, as his father Russ says. Basketball? Yes. Soccer? Good enough that Russ remembers a guy from the Canadian junior team asking him one time if his 14-year-old son wanted to train with the club. But Russ, a burly rugby player, had an inkling about what was in store for his son. "It was always about throwing stuff or hitting stuff with that kid," Russ said.

There are a few things Russ Lawrie would like you to know about his son, who has as much as anybody played a role in helping the Blue Jays re-establish their brand across the country. Despite the impression left by the way he flies around the bases or the fearlessness he shows venturing into foul territory, he does have a sense of self-preservation. "He knows you don't win the series in the first game," Lawrie said. "Frankly, the baseball field's the one place I don't worry about him."

MOSTLY MISSING OUT ON HOMEGROWN TALENT

Brett doesn't make a big deal about it, but he is acutely aware that according to Major League Baseball and the Major League Baseball Players Association, he was 20th in jersey sales after the 2012 All-Star Break (teammate Jose Bautista was number 16). He also understands that he is uniquely positioned; that he can be, in Russ Lawrie's words, "a kind of conduit from coast to coast." An explosive, barrel-chested bundle of quick-twitch muscle, he has shown flashes in his first two major league seasons of being the Canadian-born star that the Blue Jays have never had, not even in their back-to-back World Series seasons.

This up-until-now lack of a Canadian face for the franchise is remarkable, given the financial, technical and moral support the Blue Jays have provided to the sport throughout their existence. Pat Gillick has been rightly described by president and chief executive officer Paul Beeston as being "a disciple," helping to spread baseball across the country by attending banquets and fundraisers in every corner. And the Blue Jays' success meant that the organization eventually dwarfed the Montreal Expos in the country's sports consciousness, despite the fact that it was the latter who signed and developed the greatest Canadian-born baseball player of his generation, Larry Walker.

The Blue Jays have had limited success drafting and developing Canadian-born players. In fact, it is somewhat symbolic that the highest-drafted Canadian in club history—a left-handed pitcher from Ladner, BC, by way of the University of Kentucky, named James Paxton (selected 37th overall in the 2009 draft)—didn't even sign with the team. Paxton, who was advised by super-agent Scott Boras, wanted $1 million, $125,500 more than the Blue Jays were said to be offering. He returned to Kentucky, ended up pitching in Independent baseball for the Grand Prairie (Texas) AirHogs due to an NCAA investigation surrounding Boras' involvement, and was eventually the fourth pick of the Seattle Mariners after re-entering the draft, signing for $942,500. It was in the same 2009 draft that the Blue Jays snagged another Canadian pitcher, Jake Eliopoulos from the Toronto Mets organization; he, too, failed to sign. In fact, Eliopoulos would be drafted again by the Jays in 2011 after the Los Angeles Dodgers drafted him in 2010, by which time he was playing at Chippola Junior College in Marianna, Florida. The

Blue Jays failed to sign another local pitcher in 2012, when Ryan Kellogg of Whitby, Ontario, elected to go to college baseball power Arizona State University rather than sign with his hometown team, which had chosen him in the 12th round. Kellogg was highly touted heading into the draft, but teams shied away, believing they'd have to overpay to get him to forego college.

Besides Lawrie, 16 Canadian-born players have made an appearance in the majors in the Blue Jays uniform, with reliever Paul Quantrill the most successful. The Port Hope, Ontario, native was drafted in the 26th round by the Los Angeles Dodgers in 1986 while at the University of Wisconsin, but stayed at school and was later taken in the sixth round by the Boston Red Sox in 1989. A sturdy middle reliever, Quantrill's sinking fastball earned him a trip to the 2001 All-Star Game in his final season with the Blue Jays, who had acquired him in 1996 from the Philadelphia Phillies in return for Howard Battle and Ricardo Jordan. Quantrill made 386 of his 841 major league appearances in a Blue Jays uniform before being traded to the Dodgers along with shortstop Cesar Izturis in one of the first deals struck by J. P. Ricciardi, who in return acquired pitchers Chad Ricketts and Luke Prokopec.

Outfielder Rob Ducey, from Toronto, signed in 1984 as a free agent and played 188 of his 703 major league games with the Blue Jays over two stints. But he was traded in July 1992 to the then California Angels along with Greg Myers in return for reliever Mark Eichhorn, missing out on the two World Series wins. Toronto's Butler brothers, Rob and Rich, had limited success in the majors, though Rob did win a World Series ring and get a hit in the 1993 Series. Corey Koskie from Anola, Manitoba, as we know, signed as a free-agent third baseman and offered modest returns.

The Blue Jays had a Canadian-born player, Vancouver's Dave McKay, on their first-ever Opening Day roster after he was claimed in the expansion draft from the Minnesota Twins, but if anybody thought it was a sign of things to come, they were wrong. The Blue Jays missed out on Larry Walker; Jason Bay of Trail, BC; Russell Martin of East York, Ontario; Eric Gagne of Mascouche, Quebec; Justin Morneau of New Westminster, BC; and Joey Votto of Etobicoke, Ontario—all of whom went on to win individual awards or be on All-Star teams in other major league uniforms. The Blue Jays didn't get a shot at two other highly drafted Canadians: left-hander Jeff Francis from the University of British Columbia was chosen ninth in 2002 by the Colorado Rockies (five spots ahead of the Blue Jays' selection, shortstop Russ Adams); and Adam Loewen, who went fourth overall in that draft and wasn't expected to fall to the Blue Jays. They also missed on Lawrie, who was taken 16th in 2008 right in front of their selection. They settled for first baseman David Cooper from the University of California, Berkeley, but eventually traded for Lawrie, who is now their everyday third baseman.

Each year before the draft, Beeston reminds his front office that while he doesn't expect them to give preference to Canadian-born players, neither does he want their birth certificate held against them. "We never really had arguments about Canadian baseball players the way you'd have, say, arguments about kids from California," said Beeston, whose admonition to his scouts was always the same: "Don't pick a kid just because he's from Canada, but don't hold it against him, either."

It was the same message he'd impart to Gillick. Gillick actually *did* draft a Canadian player 36th overall one year—but that was in 1997, when he was GM of the Baltimore Orioles and reached for a Montreal power prodigy named Ntema Ndungidi, who would flame out in the minor leagues.

J. P. Ricciardi believes criticism of his predecessors for failure to draft a Canadian star overlooked the fact that so many of the Blue Jays' initiatives involved growing and marketing the game across the country. "It's tough to be all things at once," he remarked.

Toronto-born Gord Ash, whom Ricciardi replaced as GM, said that while his predecessor, Gillick, paid special attention to Canadian players and was tuned in to the nationalist sensibilities of owners Labatt Breweries, he was also strongly against what Ash described as "novelty acts."

"So somebody like Brett Lawrie would likely have been a Blue Jay," said Ash. "But part of it is just evaluating too. We did not have Larry Walker highly ranked. I believe the story is that when Bob Prentice saw him, he was not 100 percent, physically. We didn't see him enough, and that happens. Others? Like Morneau? We were just beaten on him. That's all. And that happens too."

A NARRATIVE WAITING TO EXPLODE

It is understandable, then, that Lawrie is a big deal. Acquired at the 2010 winter meetings for Shaun Marcum, Lawrie made an immediate impact in the spring of 2011, so much so that manager John Farrell mused openly about him making the team out of spring training. But that was a battle he lost with Anthopoulos. Lawrie started out in Triple-A, hitting .353 with 40 extra base hits in 69 games at Las Vegas, but suffered a non-displaced fracture in his left hand when he was hit by a pitch twice in the same game. He was called up to the big leagues on August 4, 2011, but his stay ended prematurely, on September 21, when he fractured his right middle finger taking infield practice. In his time with the club he hit .293 with nine home runs and 16 RBIs and had a .953 OPS in 43 games. Included in those stats was a memorable grand slam against the Oakland Athletics in an 8–4 win on August 10, and a walk-off homer against the Boston Red Sox on September 5. Lawrie's celebration after his grand slam was something else: he charged down the dugout fairly punching high-fives along the way, and slammed his batting helmet down, sending his teammates howling as they ran for cover. "A knack for the flair," was how manager John Farrell described Lawrie's sense of the moment.

Russ Lawrie had seen it before. When his son was 11 years old, he made a play that was so audacious that the teams just walked off the field even though there were only two out in the inning. Well, why not? Lawrie joined the Blue Jays as a narrative just waiting to explode: a catcher who was converted to second base by the Brewers before being moved to third by the Blue Jays; the guy who'd hung up on the Brewers GM Doug Melvin after a phone call to his minor league clubhouse; internet pictures that made him look like a bit of a yob–backward hat, shirt off and what appeared to be a beer bottle taped to his hand; brother of Danielle Lawrie, a member of Canada's women's fastball team; tattoos everywhere, including one in memory of a sister whose passing predated his birth. Then, there's the Glosette's box.

Lawrie and his sister took part in the Honda Hit, Run and Throw Program and, as regional winners, made the trek to the Rogers Centre. "He was being a little dick, actually," Russ Lawrie said, laughing. "He was running around. He got on the bullpen telephone and got shit for that. He found one of those Glosette's boxes, ran on the mound and poured a bunch of the dirt in the Glosette's box and got shit for that too. He gave it to his mom. Mom kept it. She told me one day, 'We still have that thing and should put it back.' Brett told me that night while we were in the hotel that he'd play on that field someday. I just said: 'I bet you will, son.'" Maybe life really is a box of chocolates.

But Lawrie is no cartoon character. "I've known the Lawrie family since Brett was 14, and they are solid, solid people who wear it on their sleeve," said Greg Hamilton, Baseball Canada's general manager of national teams. "He is a guy who does things that are easy to misconstrue. He is easily misunderstood if you don't take the time to dig deeper. If he can become a bona fide star playing in this country, well, he could have a tremendous impact on baseball in Canada."

Lawrie has learned that precociousness can sometimes carry a price—at least in terms of broader perception. He took himself out of a game in spring training in mid-March of 2012 with a groin strain and was taken aback when he was asked whether he would have done so in his rookie season. Of course he would have, he said. Indeed, while everybody else stands around waiting for the next calamitous base-running decision or explosive moment, his teammates, manager and coaches talk about his instincts and decision-making as a fielder. The first pitcher Lawrie saw in live batting practice this past spring was newly arrived knuckleballer R. A. Dickey. Lawrie shifted slightly as he stepped into the batting cage in Dunedin, creeping up in the batter's box a step or two before Dickey delivered his pitch. Lawrie was one of the few Blue Jays hitters to make hard contact off Dickey, and Dickey later commended Lawrie for his approach. "I tried it a couple of times against Tim Wakefield, and it seemed to work," Lawrie said later, referring to the former Red Sox knuckleballer. "R. A.'s knuckler is harder . . . it was just something I thought about."

John Farrell was a big believer in utilizing defensive shifts, and would often move Lawrie from third base into a position in shallow right field, between the first baseman and second baseman, against a pull-prone left-handed hitter.

"You take the guy and put him in the most prominent lane that the over-shifted batter will hit into," said Brian Butterfield, the former Blue Jays third base coach. "Brett's such an explosive, quick-twitch athlete that he's perfect for the role.

"He thinks the game far ahead," said Butterfield, who worked with the young Derek Jeter while a coach in the New York Yankees organization. "We give these guys a defensive sheet before the game, but you know sometimes you have to crumple that paper up and throw it out. You have to see the game. If the guy on the mound can't locate his two best pitches in that game, you throw the paper out. Brett can do that. And offensively, a lot of young kids, if they need to get a read on a play at second base, they'll wait for the ball to fall before deciding what they're going to do. You end up having to hold them up at third. Brett . . . I could trust him to make the right read right away."

Butterfield had as much individual time with Lawrie as anybody in uniform through Lawrie's first two years as a big leaguer, and he admits that Lawrie can be hard to read. "There are times when you're doing a lot of work with him and you'll be talking to him and it's like he's looking off someplace else. Right away you're saying to yourself: 'Aw, geez, I've lost him.' You think, 'What is it with this guy? He have ADD [attention deficit disorder] or something?' But just when you think you need to back off a bit, he goes out and applies it that night. It's like he's listening when you think he's not."

What it comes down to are Lawrie's instincts, and much as Larry Walker was never given full credit for his baseball instincts—although managers such as Tony La Russa, Don Baylor and Jim Leyland stand ready to provide testimony—so, too, is there a sense that Lawrie won't get credit for similar strengths. But as long as Lawrie's career isn't beset by the type of injuries that robbed Walker of several hundred at-bats, it might be a trade-off worth making.

"I've always had a pretty good feel for the game," Lawrie said in the fall of 2012. "I have a good internal time clock; I know who's running, and when to get rid of the ball or eat it. It's like I can picture stuff in my mind before it happens, then once I've done it once it's stuck in there. It's all muscle memory, after that. People always talk about how everything is a learning experience, but the thing with baseball is that you learn different things at different times of the game. I mean, I know I've learned a lot. I just have a difficult time explaining all the things I've learned."

Lawrie's 2012 season was Roller Derby, and 2013 was not much better. The 2012 season was as much about run-ins with umpires as it was about injuries. He had the celebrated run-in with umpire Bill Miller on May 15 that saw him suspended four games for his thrown helmet; he suffered a leg contusion on a scary-looking fall into the third-base camera bay at Yankee Stadium (missing just two games); and he missed more than a month when he suffered a right oblique strain in a game on August 3 at the Oakland–Alameda County Coliseum. In 2013, though, it was all about staying healthy.

Lawrie received an early indication of how his season would transpire when he strained his rib cage playing in an exhibition game in the World Baseball Classic. That put him on the 15-day disabled list to start the season, and when he was rushed back because of the team's defensive issues, his bat was not nearly ready—as the Blue Jays front office would later admit. But Lawrie's travails weren't over: in addition to seeming uncomfortable at the plate, Lawrie had the "stare down" incident with Adam Lind and third-base coach Luis Rivera . . . and the very next day, Lawrie sprained his left ankle as he slid awkwardly into second, trying to steal in the sixth inning with a five-run lead over the Atlanta Braves. That resulted in a six-week stint on the disabled list.

This time, it was a different Lawrie who returned to the Blue Jays clubhouse. His approach at the plate was much quieter; he had, it seemed, digested the constant preaching of the coaching staff. Hitting coach Chad Mottola, who was fired by the Blue Jays at the end of the 2013 season, regularly admonished Lawrie to "let yourself breathe up there." There were fewer twitchy, moving parts. On the field, Lawrie still played with the same defensive intensity, but there was a distinctly professional air to him that was not always readily apparent in 2012. Indeed, by the end of the 2013 season Lawrie had decreased his strikeout rate noticeably, from 37 in 148 first-half at-bats to 31 in 258 at-bats in the second half. In a season of few positives, no other statistic from 2013 might carry as many good signs heading into 2014.

Many around the Blue Jays credited Mark DeRosa for the transformation. A 38-year-old former Princeton quarterback and infielder who made the Blue Jays his eighth major league stop—"my father always told me to follow the good pitching when I was picking teams," he joked in spring training—DeRosa had been brought in by the Washington Nationals to smooth over some of Bryce Harper's rough edges. In Toronto, his locker was next to Lawrie's. "Both of these guys have similar personalities," DeRosa said of Lawrie and Harper, the latter of whom is one of the game's transcendent personalities. "Bryce is a little more laid back than Brett, but their passion for the game—their passion for wanting to be the best there is, for playing the game hard and playing it the right way—is very similar.

"Tools-wise, Brett does everything you can do on the field," DeRosa said. "I guess what I'd like to do is expedite things."

There have been false springs with Lawrie before, of course. But perhaps DeRosa's constant reminder that the intensity Lawrie brings to his defence needs to be tempered when he's at the plate has started to pay off. Indeed, Farrell, who believes Lawrie will eventually bat out of the third spot in the order—the place often reserved for a team's best hitter—said that Lawrie was still trying to find the "right level of intensity." Translation: as popular as he is and as many jerseys as he's sold, he is a work in progress. His power will come, Farrell said, in part when he tempers his aggressiveness and gives his swing pattern more consistency. Farrell also said the club had asked him to make adjustments that would maximize his power, after noticing he was taking his contact point deeper in the strike zone than is ideal.

Lawrie's rapport with umpires also needs to improve, his former manager admitted, and that means an adjustment (as opposed to complete eradication) of his headstrong nature. "It's important he know who he is," said Farrell, "because he's already turned himself into one of the best defensive third basemen in baseball."

And then Farrell said something that wasn't directed solely at Lawrie, but in many ways was a reference to Omar Vizquel's sharp-edged rebuke of the manager in the final week of the 2012 season: that Farrell's clubhouse culture led to a lack of acceptance of responsibility. That criticism would seem ironic one year later, when Farrell led the Red Sox to a World Series victory, earning plaudits for stabilizing a clubhouse that lost its way under Terry Francona and Bobby Valentine. Yet in 2012, for those around the team, one of the most egregious examples of "lack of discipline" was Lawrie's attempt to talk his way out of a base-running error on September 14, when he was thrown out at third in the eighth inning of a tie game against the Boston Red Sox trying to advance from second with the ball hit in front of him. "The game has to be one of the top three priorities in a player's life," Farrell said. "It is not a vehicle to a lifestyle."

Lawrie smiled when asked to name the best thing about being a major league baseball player. "It's that every day is an event," he said quietly. "It probably makes sense, because I don't think anybody considers the minors to, you know, be their end goal. When you get to the bigs, people care because you can't go any higher. You feel like you're with a family for that reason. It's not the minors; it's not just the path you are on that counts anymore. It's about who you play with—team, all those things. It's in the majors where you're with guys you live and die for. That's how I feel, anyhow."

WIDENING THE POOL

To hear his own family speak, Lawrie was destined to be an athlete. Luckily for him, and for other Canadians who have managed to carve out a career in the sport, Baseball Canada gave him an avenue to pursue that goal. There is still an element of randomness to making it to the majors, and while Canada has been producing major league ballplayers since the 1890s, the depth of talent has never been as deep as it is currently. The highest-paid Canadian professional athlete isn't a hockey player; it's Votto, the Cincinnati Reds' first baseman, whose new 10-year, $225 million contract kicks in in 2014.

The 2013 draft saw just 20 Canadian-born players selected, the smallest total since 20 made the cut in 1992. Part of that may be the result of a new collective bargaining agreement that eliminated 10 rounds of the lengthy process; it may also be that, like anything else, the game in Canada is cyclical at the developmental level. Sometimes it is BC-born players that lead the way—the BC Premier League is a model of development—but in recent years Ontario-born players have come to the fore. There have been seven Canadian-born first round draft picks—including Lawrie—and 23 Canadian born players appeared in the majors in 2012. According to canadianbaseballnetwork.com, a further 123 played for minor league teams affiliated with major league clubs, while just under two hundred played US college baseball in Divisions I, II and III. Those numbers do not include Canadians playing in junior colleges.

A major change occurred in 1991, when Canadian players were made eligible for the June draft. The draft had been in existence since 1965, but until 1991 the only Canadian-born players subject to the draft were those who attended four-year US colleges, where they were governed by the same rules as US-born collegians (could not be drafted until after their junior or senior year, or until they turned 21). Those players who weren't in college were considered free agents, able to sign for whoever offered them the greatest amount of money. In 1989, Puerto Rican players (and those from other US territories) were added, and it made sense to put Canadian-born players into the same category. From that point on, teams had to draft any Canadian-born high school player just like any US high schooler: they had to wait until the player was in his senior year, and were unable to sign the player once he attended a US college.

"Signing bonuses were starting to escalate in the late 1980s, and there was a real move made to close loopholes and contain their growth," said Allan Simpson, the BC-born founder of *Baseball America* (which grew into the paper of record for the scouting and development fraternity) and who now works for Perfect Game USA, a scouting resource centre.

Indeed, the game had reached something of a tipping point in 1985, when Pete Incaviglia refused to sign with the Expos after they drafted him eighth overall, leading to his trade to the Texas Rangers. As a result of that brazen move, baseball put in place a one-year waiting period during which players who chose not to sign had their rights retained by the drafting team. If a deal was not reached with that club by a deadline, the player had the right to re-enter the draft the next year. The Blue Jays had given John Olerud a $250,000 bonus as part of a $1 million contract that took him directly from Washington State University to the majors after picking him in the third round of the 1989 draft, while Scott Boras was busy getting $1.2 million from the Oakland Athletics for pitcher Todd Van Poppel and $1.55 million from the New York Yankees for pitcher Brien Taylor.

Walt Burrows estimates six to seven hundred Canadian players have been drafted since they were added to the pool of draft-eligible players.

"Canadians in general were put down as having crude skills, of being a bunch of hockey players who just didn't play that much," Burrows said. "What the draft did is it brought Major League Baseball—myself and all the teams—up here. It probably didn't make a big difference to the Ryan Dempsters or the Brett Lawries, but it did make a difference to the next tier of Canadian players. This opened the floodgates to a level of players that otherwise wouldn't have the opportunity. And if you look at the success of Canadian players, a lot of them weren't picked in the early rounds. They were selected later on in the mix."

Ash, the Blue Jays' assistant general manager when Canadians were part of the widening of the draft pool, said that the Blue Jays were not in favour of the move at the time, but realized it was part of a philosophical shift within the industry aimed at, in his words, "levelling the playing field." Truth is, the Blue Jays established the National Baseball Institute (NBI) not only for what Ash described as "the common good," but also for selfish reasons: keeping quality Canadian-born players out of the US college system while letting them develop their skills maintained their free-agency status as long as possible. That the Blue Jays were unable to land an impactful Canadian despite the edge the NBI gave them is another matter. From his perch, Simpson suggests it was the Blue Jays' success in Latin-America—not Canada—that might explain why the team would have preferred that Canadian and, by extension, Puerto Rican players remain outside the draft pool.

Burrows and other people involved in the game in Canada point to Baseball Canada's establishment of a year-round junior program in 1999 as a turning point in the development of Canadian players. It was spearheaded by Greg Hamilton, a native of Peterborough, Ontario, who went to Princeton as a freshman hockey player and pitched for the school's baseball team before embarking on a quirky career that included a stint as pitching coach and general manager for a team in the French elite league. The program identifies players as young as 14 and 15 and provides what Hamilton calls "a legitimate competitive outlet" for the critical development age from 14 to 18. As part of the program, the Canadian junior team makes annual trips to Florida—one during Fall Instructional League, another during spring training–where they set up shop at Disney's sprawling World of Sport facility and play against minor league teams around the state. In 2012 they played an exhibition game against a Toronto Blue Jays squad that included Lawrie, Jose Bautista and J. P. Arencibia, and another against the Dominican Republic, where they faced the best young players from the various academies of major league teams. This, of course, is in addition to the world championships and other International Baseball Federation events, as well as whatever competition the players get from their regular travel teams in Ontario, British Columbia, Quebec and now Alberta too.

"I don't like to say we compete with hockey, because hockey is hockey in Canada and you can't spend your days worrying about it," said Hamilton. "What we did was try to learn why kids migrated to hockey; what is there in it for them?

"I thought initially we needed something to go out and compete in the athletic marketplace for good, quality athletes from 14 years old and onward, where we could provide something comparable to the environment kids get in the hockey world. What the year-round program has done is allowed us to look at a kid and take his passion for baseball and give him an outlet for growth and realize his potential and move forward, at a minimum to the college level. I mean, hockey's almost a 12-month endeavour now. So you need to give the kids something they can really sink their teeth into."

Burrows is effusive in his praise of Hamilton. So is Ash. Heck, so are Russ Lawrie and Ryan Dempster, the latter of whom was drafted in the third round (66th overall) of the 1995 draft by the Texas Rangers and has made two All-Star appearances in his 15-year career. Dempster, who was born in the tiny southwestern BC coastal town of Gibsons–the setting for the iconic CBC-TV series *The Beachcombers*–remembered that his big break was being chosen for a select team at a national tournament due to the illness of another pitcher. "I think the year-round program means there's less chances of somebody kind of slipping through the cracks," Dempster said.

"I've been around forever, and the success of Canadian baseball tracks back to him [Hamilton] and Baseball Canada," said Burrows. "That first full-year team he had in 1999 had Justin Morneau and Jeff Francis in the group, and there was a camaraderie there that you see with everybody who has come through.

"We've had more position players in recent years that have come from Canada. Who are the kids that develop into position players? Your best athletes. We weren't getting the best athletes before. What Greg and Baseball Canada have done is identify the kids early and simply show some interest in them. That's a step toward not losing the kid." Added Ash: "Greg made it a true development system. It used to be that the big scouting opportunity for Canadian kids was the Canada Cup. Now you get a lot of looks at a kid against much better competition. Plus, having that clear-cut system means you get less regionalization and more co-operation."

Ask the people who run soccer in Canada about the importance of clarity. It's no wonder that Baseball Canada—and the loyalty it engenders from its former junior national team members—is the model for development for sports in a hockey-mad country. (That's why the decision by Russell Martin to pull out of the 2013 Canadian entry in the World Baseball Classic when the team would not grant him his wish to play shortstop instead of catcher—the position he's played in the majors and the position at which he helped take the Pittsburgh Pirates into the 2013 post-season—was such an anomaly.) Beyond that, Burrows reckons that the level of preparation a Canadian baseball player has heading into the draft can separate him from some other high school players.

"The Canadian kids' pre-draft schedule is the hardest of anybody out there," Burrows said. "They're not playing high school kids; they're playing games against pro players with wood bats and all that, not facing some 82-miles-per-hour guy.

"You think about it," Burrows continued, "and to make it to the majors there's possibly six levels you might need to go through in the minors. You can't afford stage fright. You have to be able to survive right away; it doesn't matter how much bonus money you get or where you're drafted, you need to get to that high-A level as soon as you can. So a kid like Brett Lawrie, for example, had two hundred at-bats against pros by the time he was drafted. He wasn't intimidated by much."

What Hamilton and Baseball Canada have created, in Hamilton's words, are "scale economies both financially and in terms of scouting.

"We're able to take the critical mass of the most talented players in the country and bring those players into one environment and one venue so they [scouts] aren't chasing everybody around. For the visibility of Canadians, that's been critical."

After that 1991 decision to change the draft rules, the next major development came about as a result of lobbying that reached as far up as the highest political office in the land. While foreign-born players on 40-man rosters had little difficulty getting US P-1 visas to play in the majors—the visas were received for elite athletes and entertainers—minor league players born outside the US, including Canadians, needed H2B visas to play in the States. Those visas, for seasonal workers, were capped annually by the American government, and normally there were enough to go around for major league teams to stock their minor league affiliates. Baseball would ask for a thousand to twelve hundred visas and in October or November call around to major league teams for an estimate as to how many each team would need. "We'd try to petition for the same amount of visas we had the year before, and maybe a few more," said Charlie Wilson, the Blue Jays' Ottawa-born director of minor league operations. "In 2006, I think we had 38 and the Washington Nationals had 50, for example. Baseball would often request an extra hundred visas and keep them for Canadian players, as a kind of protection." Sometimes, the Blue Jays would ask for a visa for "unnamed player," and put it in the major league database to be used if they were planning to draft a Canadian in the June draft.

Ash remembers a trade he made with San Diego in which the future considerations he received in return were three visas. The Blue Jays at one point had a Rookie League team based in Medicine Hat, Alberta, to get around the issue.

"You always looked to get extra ones or borrow them from other teams," said Ash. "It was part of baseball's goal to create a level playing field, because there were some significant disparities in the amount teams had. We always tried to borrow from clubs, and that kind of thing. I don't think it ever stopped us from signing a particular player, but it created development issues in terms of where we had to send a player or making us keep a player for a year at a level below where he should have been."

Ash said it only stands to reason that for some teams there would be a reluctance to use one of those visas on a Canadian player rather than, say, a prospect from the Dominican Republic. Burrows agrees, saying the marginal Canadian player was more affected than an elite player who was highly touted and heavily scouted. But Canadians managed to stake their claim to a spot in the game regardless of the restrictions at least until 2004, when the US government, which had flaunted its self-imposed limits on temporary workers' visas at times, tightened visa requirements as a result of the new security consciousness that set in after 9/11. There was real concern in the commissioner's office that even with President George W. Bush, a former baseball owner, in the White House, further tightening would impact the ability of teams to use players from Central and South America, the Caribbean and Mexico, and Canada. "It was getting tight," said Wilson. "I remember there was a lot of correspondence with the commissioner's office."

Finally, in January of 2007 the US government granted access to P-1 visas for all professional ballplayers, removing that impediment. "It's flushed itself through by now, but it was very restrictive and people were very worried," said Hamilton. "I think it's back now to where it should be: assessing talent as opposed to counting visas. Take a look at Michael Saunders [a left-hand hitting outfielder from Victoria, BC, who went in the 12th round to the Seattle Mariners]. When you look at the talent he had as a high school player and where he ended up going in the draft, a lot of it had to do with the visa issue. There was a kind of knee-jerk reaction, where people panicked about the Canadian marketplace."

So it is not just enough, then, to chalk up the success of Canadian-born baseball players to the hardness of a hockey mentality, which has emerged as one of the narratives favoured by those on both sides of the border as they attempt to explain the fact that the game has enjoyed growth at the elite level even as it stagnates slightly at the youth level. Systemic changes both in the US and at home have helped pave the way for the Vottos and Morneaus and Lawries, and, in the case of the changes brought on by Baseball Canada, it has not been by happenstance.

PAYING IT FORWARD

There is nothing fluky about the manner in which a Canadian-born player makes it to the majors; the days of a player such as Larry Walker crapping out as a junior hockey goalie and throwing in his lot with baseball are history. Athletes such as Lawrie will have spent three-and-a-half years in the junior program before they are drafted; Adam Loewen, in fact, spent four years—as will have Gareth Morgan when he is drafted in 2014. As was the case with Lawrie, who spent time bunking with Russell Martin in Arizona one year, many of them will have gone through a mentorship program in which a draft prospect spends a week or two in the off-season with a Major Leaguer and gets to pick his brain about the game and approaches to conditioning. The loyalty is returned: one year's apprentice becomes a mentor down the road. Furthermore, barring injury or rehabilitation concerns, Canadian players queue up to play for Team Canada at the World Baseball Classic and enjoy the now-legendary games of road hockey that are a staple of the team; minor leaguers or those players competing in international leagues return to play for Canada. And every January, Baseball Canada—which lost some of its government funding when the International Olympic Committee voted to remove the sport from the summer Olympics—holds a fundraising dinner for which many of its alumni return.

Hamilton knows he can call on alumni to give of their time or even cut a cheque for the bettering of the program. "The base is still supported by the government, but the really critical components—the trips to the Dominican Republic, our spring training trips—are tied to the alumni program and private sector. People want to associate with passion, and they'll embrace a program that will bring tears to the eyes of Larry Walker and Justin Morneau."

It is a strange dichotomy, the way Canadian baseball has churned out elite players even as the Blue Jays fight mightily to escape the no-man's land of the American League East, and as the number of affiliated minor league teams has shrunk to one, a product of the vagaries of the Canadian dollar and concerns about travel expenses. It is no longer necessarily the summer sport of choice, either, the way it was when Wayne Gretzky played in the Intercounty League. But the game is proceeding apace, and Hamilton said that having a Blue Jays general manager who is a born-and-bred Canadian has been a help.

"The Blue Jays have always been here for us, which is huge," said Hamilton. "But in J. P. Ricciardi's tenure, I think there was a change in the relationship. J. P. viewed himself as GM of the Toronto Blue Jays, not somebody who was here to develop amateur baseball. Alex being Canadian has, I feel, made a difference."

A BLESSED CONVERGENCE

Who knows where the game can go if the Blue Jays get back on top with a bona fide Canadian-born star? Who knows what will happen if Brett Lawrie's whispered about, transcendent qualities manifest themselves in the context of a world title with the Blue Jays? The game in this country has deep, deep roots, but it has never had the baseball gods grant it that blessed convergence. As Dr. Colin Howell—academic director at Saint Mary's University's Centre for the Study of Sport and Health, and an authority on the history of the sport in the Maritimes—explains, baseball developed in Canada along a north-south axis, largely because of affiliation with and interest in US-based teams. That was the way until the 1950s, when a national sports culture emerged that would ultimately spawn the Canada Games and cause sports in general to move along an east-west axis. There's a great deal of history—planned and unplanned—represented by Brett Lawrie, and it's a lot to hang on the shoulders of a kid.

"Aw, he's learning," said Russ Lawrie when asked if his mercurial son was up to the task. "I mean, he's a kid in this game. We're from Canada, too, not California or Florida, where baseball's in the DNA. I mean, look at me: a rugby guy. All I tell people is: give the kid a chance, and when he's 24? Look out."

The history of the Blue Jays since the 1993 World Series has been a continual struggle to recapture the old magic, that special something that turned the organization from expansion team to pretender to gold standard. This is a team both haunted and teased by its history, a team that has been playing catch-up ever since an absentee Belgian brewery stood still as the economic game passed it by. There have been bold signings and bold trades and bold pronouncements, all attempting to replicate the accomplishments of men such as Cito Gaston, Pat Gillick, Paul Beeston, Joe Carter and Roberto Alomar. Know this: the game in Canada is all grown up. Time, now, for its major league franchise to catch up.

REFERENCES

INTRODUCTION

Brunt, Stephen. *Diamond Dreams: 20 Years of Blue Jays Baseball*. Toronto: Viking, 1996.
Howell, Dr. Colin. Interview with author, November 29, 2012.
Shearon, Jim. *Canada's Baseball Legends*. Kanata, ON: Malin Head Press, 1994.

CHAPTER 1

Brunt, Stephen. *Diamond Dreams*.
Gaston, Cito. Interview with author. September 11, 2012.
Gillick, Pat. Interview with author, October 22, 2012.
Martinez, Buck. Interview with author, October 1, 2012.
Morris, Jack. Interview with author, October 2, 2012.
Ward, Duane. Interview with author, September 26, 2012.

CHAPTER 2

Alomar, Roberto. Interview with author, 2012.
Blair, Jeff. "Alomar's Induction a Celebration for Jays, Puerto Ricans." *Globe and Mail*, July 25, 2011.
Giuliotti, Joe. "Eckersley Plagued by Sore Elbow." *Boston Herald*, October 14, 1992.
Jacobson, Steve. "Winfield Legacy: All Business." *Newsday*, February 9, 1996.
Smith, Claire. "This Toronto Team Isn't Afraid of Ghosts." *New York Times*, October 12, 2012.
Toronto Star staff. "La Russa Defends Eck's Fist Pump." October 13, 1992.
Ward, Duane. Interview with author, 2012.

CHAPTER 3

Carter, Joe. Interview with author, October 27, 2012.
Gaston, Cito. Interview with author.
Gillick, Pat. Interview with author.
Milton, Steve. "Devo's Grab Turns Game Around; The Catch Goes Down In History." *Hamilton Spectator*, October 21, 1992.

Perkins, Dave. "White's Spectacular Catch Equal to Mays' Grab in '54." *Toronto Star*, October 21, 1992.

Slater, Tom. "Pinch Me! Sprague Tags Game-Winning Shot as Jays Even Series Score." *Toronto Star*, October 11, 1992.

CHAPTER 4

Campbell, Neil A. "Jays Wise to Frowzy Phils: Behind the Façade Lies a Tough, Talented Philadelphia Team." *Globe and Mail*, October 16, 1993.

Carter, Joe. Interview with author.

Daley, Ken. "A Wild Thing Goes to Blue Jays: Toronto Pulls Out 15–14 Win for 3–1 Lead on Philadelphia." *Los Angeles Daily News*, October 21, 1993.

Dwyer, Timothy. "Quoth the Wild Thing: 'Awesome' Williams, Cornered Amid Champagne, Was Unabashedly Proud of His Worst-to-First Team." *Philadelphia Inquirer*, October 14, 1993.

Gaston, Cito. Interview with author.

Gillick, Pat. Interview with author.

Hentgen. Pat. Interview with author, 2012.

Toronto Star staff. "Blue Jay Butler First Canadian in Series Since '75." *Toronto Star*, October 17, 1993.

Weir, Tom. "Williams Born to Be Wild Thing." *USA Today*, October 21, 1993.

CHAPTER 5

Beeston, Paul. Interview with author, May 15, 2012.

Blair, Jeff. Column. Globesports.com, June 9, 2003.

Blair, Jeff. "The Clemens-McNamee Story Began in Toronto." *Globe and Mail*, February 13, 2008.

Carter, Joe. Interview with author.

Gillick, Pat. Interview with author.

Hentgen, Pat. Interview with author.

Lind, Phil. Interview with author, September 14, 2012.

Maloney, Tom. "Drug Use by Ball Players Raises Some Questions." Southam News, August 24, 1998.

CHAPTER 6

Beeston. Paul. Interview with author.

Canadian Press staff. "Jays President and CEO Balks at Suggestions Rogers Is Ready to Dump Team." April 20, 2002.

Godfrey, Paul. Interview with author, May 22, 2012.

Lind, Phil. Interview with author.

Rogers, Ted. *Relentless: The True Story of the Man Behind Rogers Communications*. Toronto: HarperCollins, 2008.

Viner, Tony. Interview with author, December 15, 2012.

CHAPTER 7

Ash, Gord. Interview with author, August 21, 2012.

Baseball Prospectus. *Baseball Prospectus, 2005*. New York: Workman Publishing Company, Inc., 2005.

———. *Baseball Prospectus, 2006*. New York: Workman Publishing Company, Inc., 2006.

Blair, Jeff. "Godfrey Defends Delgado Contract as Selig Frets." *Globe and Mail*, October 23, 2000.

Law, Keith. Interview with author, July 16, 2012.

Ricciardi, J. P. Interview with author, June 5, 2012.

CHAPTER 8

Baseball America staff. "The Great Debate." January 7, 2005.

Blair, Jeff. "Athletics Become Example to Follow." *Globe and Mail*, February 21, 2004.

Fitz-Gerald, Sean. "Godfrey Gets an A for Economic Hire of Blue Jays GM." *National Post*, November 15, 2001.

Godfrey, Paul. Interview with author.

Law. Keith. Interview with author.

Lewis, Michael. *Moneyball: The Art of Winning An Unfair Game*. New York: W. W. Norton & Company, Inc., 2003.

Ricciardi, J. P. Interview with author.

CHAPTER 9

Blair, Jeff. "Trade Steals Martinez's Thunder." *Globe and Mail*, July 2, 2002.

Blair, Jeff. "Mondesi Deal Just Good Business." *Globe and Mail*, July 2, 2002.

LaCava, Tony. Interview with author. October 27, 2012.

Law. Keith. Interview with author.

Ricciardi, J. P. Interview with author.

CHAPTER 10

Braunecker, Darek. Interview with author, October 16, 2012.

Delgado, Carlos. Interview with author, December 14, 2012.

Godfrey, Paul. Interview with author.

Law, Keith. Interview with author.

Ricciardi, J. P. Interview with author.

Viner, Tony. Interview with author.

Wells, Vernon. Interview with author, November 27, 2012.

CHAPTER 11

Beeston, Paul. Interview with author.

David, Shi. "Blue Jays Livid About Article Which Insinuates Team is Racist." Canadian Press, June 28, 2003.

Davidi, Shi. "Blue Jays Players Say There Are Problems in Clubhouse, Gaston Says There Aren't." Canadian Press, October 2, 2012.

Gaston, Cito, Interview with author.

Ricciardi, J. P. Interview with author.

Viner, Tony. Interview with author.

CHAPTER 12

Anthopoulos, Alex. Interview with author, November 30, 2012.

Law, Keith. Interview with author.

Lott, John. "R. A. Dickey on Blue Jays: I'm Going to Pitch My Guts Out." *National Post*, December 18, 2012.

CHAPTER 13

Abraham, Peter, and Nick, Cafardo. "Henry Confirms John Farrell Is New Blue Jays Manager." Boston.com, October 24, 2012.

Anthopoulos, Alex. Interview with author.

Farrell, John. Interviews with author 2012; pre-game news conferences, 2012.

Simmons, Steve. "Vizquel's Parting Advice/Retiring Veteran Sees Promise for the Jays but Feels Letting Mistakes Slide Has to End." *Toronto Sun*, September 28, 2012.

CHAPTER 14

Anthopoulos, Alex. News conference, September 29, 2013; interviews with author.

Buehrle, Mark. Interview with author.

Bautista, Jose. Pre-game interview.

DeRosa, Mark. Interview with author.

Dickey, R. A. Post-game interview.

Gibbons, John. Interview with author.

CHAPTER 15

Ash, Gord. Interview with author, January 15, 2013.

Burrows, Walt. Interview with author, January 14, 2013.

Butterfield, Brian. Interview with author, May 17, 2012.

DeRosa, Mark. Interview with author.

Farrell, John. Interviews with author; pre-game news conferences.

Lawrie, Brett. Interview with author, October 2, 2012.

Lawrie, Russ. Interview with author, January 14, 2013.

Simpson, Alan. Interview with author, November 29, 2012.

Wilson, Charlie. Interview with author, January 14, 2013.

ΛCKNOWLEDGEMENTS

SO, THERE YOU ARE. I'VE WRITTEN A BOOK. THIS wouldn't have happened without my literary agent, Rick Broadhead of Rick Broadhead & Associates, who for the better part of three years kept checking in to see if I had book ideas and who in fact presented me with this project, and without Paul Taunton, my editor at Random House of Canada, who somehow thought the words I was capable of generating would do justice to one of his ideas. Both gentlemen provided counsel, and Paul's editing skills not only made the product better but also inspired a great deal of confidence for a first-time author who needed to learn how to run into dead ends and get back out.

I'd also like to thank everyone at Random House of Canada, where I was lucky to have a lineup as long as the '93 Jays, including Anne Collins, Louise Dennys, Marion Garner, Carla Kean, Ruta Liormonas, Brad Martin, Deirdre Molina, Terra Page, Andrew Roberts and Matthew Sibiga. Additional thanks to Liba Berry, Angelika Glover and Linda Pruessen.

Several people gave a great deal of their time, either for interviews or on- and off-the-record consultations—in particular, Paul Beeston, Paul Godfrey, J. P. Ricciardi, Alex Anthopoulos and Gord Ash. Former players Buck Martinez, Duane Ward, Jack Morris, Roberto Alomar, Joe Carter and Carlos Delgado, and manager Cito Gaston, were tremendous storytellers and provided the type of honesty so common to baseball people. No wonder I love covering this game so much. The Blue Jays public relations department, Jay Stenhouse and Mal Romanin, put up with my badgering. Howard Starkman told stories and provided clarity on several matters. Phil Lind, Tony Viner and Keith Pelley made themselves available. So, too, did others who asked not to be mentioned. There have been more trials and tribulations than championships for the Blue Jays since 1993. I hope all those involved will see this book as fair treatment, because that was my aim.

I am lucky because I have two employers, the *Globe and Mail* and Sportsnet 590 The Fan, that provide me an outlet to do the work I love in my own, er, unique fashion. Thanks to Tom Maloney and editor-in-chief John Stackhouse. Thanks to Don Kollins, program director at Sportsnet 590 The Fan. You all have my undivided attention again.

This book came together quickly, less than a year from idea to index, and was written on planes and trains, in hotel rooms, press boxes and coffee shops in Toronto, Hamilton, London, Newcastle, Coventry, Detroit and San Francisco. Most of the work was done at home, however, which means the ultimate debt of gratitude is owed to my wife, Shelley, and daughter, Emma Rose. Their full-time husband and dad became a pinch-hitter for the past year; time now to reclaim my spot in the everyday lineup.

Hamilton, Ontario
January 2013

INDEX

Adams, Russ, 153, 155, 243
Adams, Terry, 139
Alderson, Sandy, 119, 127, 172
Alexander, Doyle, 18
All-Star Break, 109, 141, 240
All-Star Game, 166, 176, 194, 242 (*See also* Midsummer Classic)
All-Stars (hockey), 77
All-Stars (baseball), 32, 37, 42, 58, 108, 109, 136, 169, 176, 179, 181, 193, 199, 216, 220, 243, 254
Alomar, Roberto, 5, 25–26, 27, 28, 29–30, 31, 34–36, 37–38, 41, 45, 49, 51, 52, 55, 56, 57, 58, 59, 60, 61, 63, 64, 74, 158, 166, 185, 221, 261
Alomar, Sandy, Jr., 35
Alomar, Sandy, Sr., 35, 36, 38, 226
Alou, Felipe, 22, 48–49, 58, 189
Alou, Moises, 55
Alvarez, Henderson, 208
American League Championship Series, 19–20, 26–29, 30, 32, 41, 42, 44, 45, 48, 57, 64, 115
American League Comeback Player of the Year, 169
American League East, 2, 4, 14, 30, 57, 70, 87,108,115, 152, 157, 166, 170, 174, 194, 222, 229, 232, 259
American League West, 115
American League Wild Card, 3, 108, 149,150, 166, 205
American League, 6, 26, 37, 48, 56, 58, 60, 64, 69, 72, 136,157, 166, 181, 193, 199, 219, 229, 234 (*See also* National League)
Ameriquest Field, 141
Anderson, Larry, 62
Anderson, Sparky, 33
Andrews, Dr. James, 75, 181
Angelos, Peter, 82
Anthopoulos, Alex, 1, 2, 4, 88, 101, 118, 128, 129,156, 166, 170, 176, 177, 178, 183, 185–95, 213–27, 229, 230, 232, 235, 236, 244, 260
Anthopoulos, John, 187
Arencibia, J. P., 2, 100, 129, 208, 230, 231, 234, 254

Arizona Diamondbacks, 36, 62, 121, 138, 139, 158, 192
Arizona Fall League, 22
Arizona State University, 232
Arnsberg, Brad, 160, 161, 163
Arvada West High School, 193
Ash, Gord, 73, 74, 77, 80, 103, 105, 107–8, 110–12, 113, 115, 116, 121, 122, 123, 127, 131, 154, 158, 244, 253, 254, 255, 256, 257
Atlanta Braves, 18, 20, 28, 31, 36, 41, 45, 47, 49, 50, 51, 58, 59, 75, 78, 117, 128, 147, 248
Atlanta–Fulton County Stadium, 45, 78
Avery, Steve, 50, 51
Aviles, Mike, 1, 21, 214

Babe Ruth, 8
Baltimore Orioles, 36, 43, 44, 57, 62, 80, 82, 112, 115, 117, 124, 129, 139, 157, 169, 189, 207–8, 209, 226, 232, 243
Baltimore Stallions, 120
Bane, Eddie, 125
Barajas, Rod, 169
Barclays Premier League (soccer), 8
Barfield, Jesse, 20
Barrow, Ed, 8
Baseball America, 125, 153, 252
Baseball Canada, 239, 245, 239, 242, 245, 251, 253, 255, 258, 259
Baseball Halls of Fame. *See* Canadian Baseball Hall of Fame; Manitoba Baseball Hall of Fame; National Baseball Hall of Fame
Baseball Prospectus, 150, 151
Baseball Weekly, 131
Basketball Hall of Fame, 229
Batista, Miguel, 139, 158
Batista, Tony, 109, 112
Battle, Howard, 242
Bautista, Jose, 100, 129, 180, 183, 195, 198, 203, 207, 220, 231–32, 233, 236, 240, 254
Bavasi, Peter, 14, 116
Bay, Jason, 243
Baylor, Don, 247
BC Premier League, 8–9, 251

Beachcombers, The, 254
Beane, Billy, 117, 118–19, 121–22, 123, 124–25, 155, 172, 174, 175, 188–89, 225
Beane, Casey, 119
Beane, Tara, 119
Beckett, Josh, 160–61, 200
Beeston, Paul, 2, 4, 5, 7, 13–14, 17, 18, 20, 21, 23, 43, 44, 47, 52, 70–71, 76, 77, 78, 80–82, 83, 86, 92, 97–100, 104, 107, 122,164, 169, 170–71, 173, 174, 180, 182, 185, 192–93, 194, 203, 214, 220, 223, 224, 225, 236, 241, 243, 261
Beinfest, Larry, 161
Bell Media, 96
Bell, Buddy, 113
Bell, Derek, 48
Bell, George, 14, 20, 21, 23, 58, 70, 144
Beltran, Carlos, 99, 220, 221
Bernhardt, Josephang, 154
Berryhill, Damon, 45, 49
Bevington, Terry, 138
Biggio, Craig, 190
Bill James Handbook, The, 191
Blanco, Henry, 2
Blauser, Jeff, 49
Blue Jays Level of Excellence, 143
Blue Jays Player of the Year award, 129
Blue Ribbon Panel, 71
Blyleven, Bert, 25
Bobby Mattick Training Center, 205
Boggs, Wade, 46
Bonds, Barry, 72
Bonds, Bobby, 65
Bonifacio, Emilio, 186, 218, 219, 222, 223, 231, 232, 234, 237
Boras, Scott, 241, 252
Borbon, Pedro, Jr., 132
Borders, Pat, 29, 47
Boston Globe, 200
Boston Herald, 27
Boston Red Sox, 4, 13, 20, 27, 30, 37, 42, 63, 66, 70, 71, 87, 104, 117, 119, 123, 126, 129, 131, 132, 136, 138, 139, 149–50, 151, 153–54, 156, 160, 162–63, 165, 166, 173, 199, 200, 210–11, 212, 214, 215, 222, 227, 229, 230, 233, 235, 242, 244, 246, 250
Boudreault, Stefan, 185
Bramson, Lenny, 17
Brandon Greys, 9
Brandon League, 220
Brandon Wheat Kings, 17
Brascan, 80
Braunecker, Darek, 163–64, 165
Bream, Sid, 49
Brett, George, 13
Brochu, Claude, 76, 82

Bronfman, Charles, 76
Bronner, Jim, 104
Brooklyn Dodgers, 8
Brown, Dana, 190–91
Brunt, Stephen, 15
Buchholz, Clay, 201, 211
Buck O'Neil Lifetime Achievement Award, 36
Buck, John, 219, 223–24
Buckner, Bill, 52, 66
Buehrle, Mark, 1, 186, 219, 230, 232, 233, 234
Buffalo Bills, 93
Buhner, Jay, 44
Burke, Brian, 182
Burnett, A. J., 159–65, 167, 178, 194
Burnett, Karen, 163, 164
Burrows, Walt, 229, 241, 242, 243–44, 239, 252, 253, 254–57
Bush, David, 158
Bush, George W., 257
Butler, Rich, 242
Butler, Rob, 242
Butterfield, Brian, 226, 230, 246–47

Cabrera, Melky, 1, 87, 186, 219, 235, 237
Caisse de dépôt et placement du Québec, 89
California Angels, 30, 36, 108, 129, 242
    (*See also* Los Angeles Angels of Anaheim)
Caminiti, Ken, 72
Canada Cup, 255
Canada Customs, 165
Canada Games, 260
Canadian Baseball Hall of Fame, 8
Canadian Baseball League, 3
Canadian Football League, 120
Canadian Imperial Bank of Commerce, 13, 90
Canate, Willie, 62
Canseco, Jose, 72–73
Cape Cod League, 117
Carnegie Mellon University, 125–26
Carpenter, Chris, 109, 221
Carter, Gary, 2, 3, 5, 6, 175
Carter, Joe, 3, 5, 6, 10, 13, 26, 28, 29, 30, 35, 37, 46, 49, 51, 52, 53, 55, 56, 58, 59, 60, 61, 63–66, 74, 75, 78–79, 112, 115, 116,158,166, 185, 221, 261
Carter, Joe, Sr., 66
Carter, Jordan, 66
Catalanotto, Frank, 140, 180
Caudill, Bill, 74
CBC-TV, 254
CBS Sports, 44
Cecil, Brett, 207
Central Scouting Bureau, 190
CFTO-TV, 85
CFTR (radio), 89
Chacin, Gustavo, 167

Chapin, Allan, 80–81, 82
Chapman, Aroldis, 193
Cheek, Tom, 6, 140–41
Cherington, Ben, 117
CHFI-FM, 85
Chicago Cubs, 28, 69,117, 177, 179
Chicago White Sox, 36, 57, 58, 111, 112, 115,
   177, 181, 205, 216, 220, 223
Chippola Junior College, 241
Cincinnati Reds, 6, 55, 251
Citi Field, 235
Clancy, Jim, 43
Clark Sports Center, 25
Clemens, Roger, 46, 69–72, 73, 79
Clement, Matt,162
Cleveland Forest Cities, 7
Cleveland Indians, 35, 65, 121, 122, 129,
   153–54, 158, 166, 214, 220
Cochrane, Tom, 45
Cohen, Alan, 95
Collins, Tim, 127–28, 129
Colon, Bartolo, 220
Colorado Rockies, 6, 104, 113, 155, 243
Community College of Rhode Island, 128
Cone, David, 29, 43, 47, 55, 74, 79
Conseco, Jose, 72, 73
Cooper, David, 243
Cooperstown, 25, 26, 36, 37, 38 (*See also*
   National Baseball Hall of Fame)
Cox, Bobby, 18, 19, 20, 45, 49, 51
Credit Suisse Boston, 120
Crosby, Sidney, 239–40
Cruz, Jose, Jr., 109, 113
Cy Young Award, 1, 6, 26, 69, 122,186, 193,
   216, 221, 226, 235

D'Addario, Silvio, 96
d'Arnaud, Travis, 194, 195, 117, 217, 221, 235
Dalton, Harry, 117
Darvish, Yu, 88, 202, 203, 205, 213
Daulton, Darren, 58
Davidson, Bob, 49, 50
Davis, Bryan, 185
Davis, Chili, 42
DeFreites, Arturo, 189
Deglan, Kellin, 7
Delgado, Carlos, 105–8, 109, 112, 113, 123,
   131, 133, 135–38,139, 140,141–44, 148,
   149, 176,182
Dempster, Ryan, 252, 254–55
DeRosa, Mark, 229, 233, 249
Detroit Tigers, 14, 18, 20, 29, 31, 33, 42, 113,
   120, 158, 166, 193, 229
DeWitt, William, 159–60
Diamond Dreams (Brunt), 15–16
Diaz, Robizon, 195

Dickey, R. A., 1, 2, 5, 87, 156, 186, 195, 216–18,
   219, 231, 232, 235–36, 246
Diefenbaker, John G., 85
Disney, 242
Dodgers. *See* Brooklyn Dodgers; Los Angeles
   Dodgers
Dombrowski, David, 35, 120
Double-A baseball, 17, 140, 203, 225
Drabek, Kyle, 194, 205, 207
Ducey, Rob, 242
Duncan, Mariano, 59
Dunedin (training site), 77, 151, 162, 246
Dunn, Adam, 140
Dunston, Shawon, 18
Duquette, Dan, 70, 117
Dykstra, Lenny ("Nails"), 58, 59, 63

Eagles Nest Golf Club, 5
Eckersley, Dennis, 26–28, 38, 48, 64, 185
Eichhorn, Mark, 242
Eisenreich, Jim, 60
Eliopoulos, Jake, 241–42
Elliott, Bob, 226
Encarnacion, Edwin, 129, 180, 231, 233, 236
Epstein, Theo, 162–63, 200
Erickson, Scott, 42, 43
Escobar, Kelvim, 109–10
Escobar, Yunel, 127, 128, 196, 212
ESPN, 44, 66, 148, 166, 171
Exhibition Stadium, 32, 93

Fall Instructional League, 253
Famous Players theatres, 90
Farrell, John, 1, 2, 13, 20, 21, 35, 200, 206–7,
   208, 210–15, 225, 226, 229, 230, 244, 245,
   246, 249–50
Felix, Junior, 30
Fenway Park, 131, 210, 229, 233
Fernandez, Tony, 30, 37, 61, 139
Ferreira, Fred, 189–90, 191
Fielder, Prince, 176–77, 202
Flanagan, Mike, 43
Florida Auto Exchange Stadium, 230
Florida Marlins. *See* Miami Marlins
Florida State League, 190
Foothills-Wheatbelt League, 9
Forbes magazine, 91, 97
Ford C. Frick Award, 36,141
Fox Broadcasting Company, 100
Francis, Jeff, 243, 255
Francona, Terry, 200, 226–27, 250
Fraser, Willie, 30
Frasor, Jason, 213
Fregosi, Jim, 64, 66, 108–9, 110
Frum, Murray, 81–82, 92
Fullmer, Brad, 109, 132

Gagne, Eric, 6, 243
Gammons, Peter, 139
Gant, Ron, 49
Garner, Phil, 113
Gaston, Cito, 4, 21–23, 28, 30–31, 32, 33, 34, 35, 46, 47, 48–49, 51, 52–53, 56, 57–58, 60, 61, 73–74, 77, 135, 167, 169, 170, 174–75, 180, 195–96, 198, 215, 261
Gaylord Opryland Hotel, 216
Gedman, Rich, 117
Gehrig, Lou, 76
Giambi, Jeremy, 188–89, 214
Gibbons, John, 2, 35, 117–18, 139, 140, 150, 156, 164, 169, 174, 175, 176, 177, 178, 195, 217, 224–26, 229, 230–31, 232, 233, 234, 254
Gibbons, Walter Lee, 9
Gibson, Kirk, 47–48
Giles, Brian, 159
Gilhooley, Bob, 104
Gillick, Pat, 4, 5, 9, 14, 15, 16, 17, 18, 19, 22–23, 25, 28, 30, 32–33, 37–38, 42, 43, 44, 47, 52, 55–56, 60, 65, 74, 75, 80, 95, 105, 115, 116, 118, 156, 175, 186, 221, 222, 241, 243, 244, 261
Gillis, Jack, 139
Girardi, Joe, 226
Giuliotti, Joe, 26–27
Glaus, Tony, 158, 166, 194
Globe and Mail, 13, 96, 182, 211
Gnat, Albert, 82, 92
Godfrey, Paul, 91, 92–94, 95, 98, 104, 107, 113, 116, 118–19, 120, 121, 122, 123, 130, 131, 132, 140, 147, 154, 157, 159, 163, 169–70, 172, 173, 174, 177, 179, 182, 192
Goins, Ryan, 232, 234
Gold Glove Award, 25, 59, 176
Golden Era Committee, 36
Gonzalez, Alex, 103–4, 123, 132
Gooden, Dwight, 18
Gordon, Joe ("Flash"), 37
Gose, Anthony, 195
Gossage, Richard Michael ("Goose"), 16
Grand Prairie AirHogs, 241
Grapefruit League, 205, 229, 231
Green, Shawn, 107, 131, 158
Greenberg, Peter, 218
Gretzky, Wayne, 239–40, 259
Grieve, Ben, 113
Griffey, Ken, Jr., 199
Griffin, Alfredo, 19, 20
Gross, Gabe, 158
Gruber, Kelly, 14, 45, 50, 55
Guerrero, Epy, 154
Guerrero, Vladimir, 189
Guzman, Juan, 31–32, 38, 43, 59, 62
Gwynn, Tony, 36

Hale, DeMarlo, 226
Halladay, Roy, 47, 69, 109, 110, 135, 136, 139, 140, 149, 150, 162, 163, 165, 178, 193–94, 221
Halls of Fame. *See* Basketball Hall of Fame; Canadian Baseball Hall of Fame; Manitoba Baseball Hall of Fame; Sons of Italy Hall of Fame
Hamilton, Greg, 239, 245–46, 253, 254–56, 258, 259–60
Hamilton, Joey, 122
Hampton, Mike, 104
Harbour Light Centre (Toronto), 63
Hardy, Peter N. E., 13, 14, 15–16, 17, 18, 23, 81, 164
Hargrove, Mike, 226
Harper, Bryce, 3, 249
Harper, Tommy, 22
Hart, John, 121, 122
Harvard University, 118, 119, 125
Hayhurst, Dirk, 234
Hechavarria, Adeiny, 193, 221
Helton, Todd, 155
Hemond, Roland, 36–37, 117
Henderson, Paul, 5
Henderson, Rickey, 5, 26, 46, 60, 62, 63, 64, 115–16
Hendricks, Alan, 70
Hendricks, Randal, 70
Henke, Tom, 17, 29, 34, 55, 56, 74
Henry, John, 196
Hentgen, Pat, 15, 43, 56, 59, 69, 75, 140, 163, 166, 206, 221
Hernandez, Pedro, 15
Herrera, Jose, 64, 115
Hill, Aaron, 149, 169, 170, 198–99
Hillenbrand, Shea, 169,178, 225
Hollins, Dave, 61
Holy Name High School, 117
Home Run Derby, 176
Honda Hit, Run and Throw Program, 245
Horn, Al, 91
Hot Stove, Cool Music (radio), 139–40
Houston Astros, 7, 78, 97, 177, 195
Howarth, Jerry, 41
Howell, Dr. Colin, 260
Hoyer, Jed, 117
Hudson, Orlando, 158
Hunter, Brian, 49
Huntington, Neal, 117
Hutchison, Drew, 205, 207

Ilitch, Mike, 120
Incaviglia, Pete, 58, 252
Inge, Brandon, 208
Innes, Jan, 156

Interbrew SA, 4, 80–81, 82, 90, 96, 105, 106, 111,
Intercounty Baseball League, 240, 259
International Baseball Federation, 254
International Olympic Committee, 259
Izturis, Cesar, 104, 242
Izturis, Maicer, 219, 231, 232, 234, 237

Jackson, Bo, 58, 75
Jackson, Danny, 59, 60
Jackson, Zach, 158
Jacobs Field, 110
Jacobson, Steve, 31
Janssen, Casey, 129, 211, 213
Jenkins, Ferguson, 7
Jenks, Bobby, 181
Jeter, Derek, 246
Jocketty, Walt, 164
John Labatt Limited, 4, 13, 14, 16, 80, 81, 90, 95 (*See also* Labatt Breweries)
Johnson, Davey, 110, 124
Johnson, John, 218
Johnson, Josh, 1, 186, 221, 232, 235, 237
Johnson, Kelly, 198
Johnson, Randy, 62, 115
Johnson, Tim, 108, 180
Jordan, Ricardo, 242
Juiced: Wild Times, Rampant 'Roids, Smash Hits and How Baseball Got Big (Conseco), 72, 73
Julio, Jorge, 157
Jumbotron, 50, 96
Justice, David, 50

Kansas City Royals, 2, 3, 16, 18–19, 28, 29, 47, 97, 112, 113, 128,140, 179, 225, 231, 234
Kapstein, Jerry, 16
Karsay, Steve, 64, 115
Kauffman, Ewing, 13
Kawasaki, Munenori, 232
Keeler, Wee Willie, 8
Kellogg, Ryan, 242
Kelly, Roberto, 189
Kelly, Tom, 33
Kent, Jeff, 43
Key, Jimmy, 55
Knoblauch, Chuck, 71
Koch, Billy, 132
Koskie, Corey, 149,151–52, 180, 194, 242
Kruk, John, 58, 59
Kubski, Gil, 16

La Russa, Tony, 27–28, 247
Labatt Breweries, 44, 244 (*See also* John Labatt Limited)
LaCava, Tony, 129–30, 154, 195

Lackey, John, 200
Lajoie, Nap, 8
Lalonde, Jon, 190
LaLoosh, Nuke, 160
LaMacchia, Al, 14
Lamont, Gene, 58
Landry, Greg, 194
Langley, BC, 7
Lang Michener LLP, 92
Langford, Rick, 108–9
Law, Keith, 125–26, 130, 138, 148, 151–55, 165, 175, 176, 187
Lawrie, Brett, 1, 100, 193, 199, 203, 208, 209, 220, 231, 232, 233, 239, 240–41, 242, 243, 244–50, 251, 252, 254, 256, 258, 259, 260
Lawrie, Danielle, 245
Lawrie, Russ, 240, 245, 254, 260
Lee, Carlos, 177
Lee, Cliff, 163, 220
Lee, Manny, 14, 48
Lefebvre, Joe, 175
Leible, Chris, 218
Leiter, Al, 59, 70
Lenihan, Ken, 239
Lester, Jon, 200
Lewis, Michael, 118, 124
Leyland, Jim, 229, 247
Liebrandt, Charlie, 51
Lilly, Ted, 150, 178, 179, 225
Lincecum, Tim, 216
Lind, Adam, 206, 209–10, 211, 230, 233, 248
Lind, Phil, 82, 86–87, 88, 89, 90, 92, 93
Loewen, Adam, 243, 259
Lofton, Kenny, 35, 56
Lopes, Davey, 113
Lopez, Felipe, 104
Loria, Jeffrey, 82–83
Los Angeles Angels of Anaheim, 125, 177, 181, 196, 209, 220 (*See also* California Angels)
Los Angeles Dodgers, 6, 32, 97, 107, 120, 122, 131, 158, 177, 241, 242
Lovullo, Torey, 230
Lowell, Mike, 160
Loyello, P. J., 188
Lucchino, Larry, 200

Maddon, Joe, 226
Madison Square Garden, 80
Major League Baseball (MJB), 45, 52, 69, 71, 91, 96, 107, 178, 185–86, 189, 190, 202, 240, 252
Major League Baseball Players Association, 33, 71, 79, 214, 240
Maldonado, Candy, 47, 49, 51, 52, 55
Maloney, Tom, 72
Manager of the Year Award, 21, 175
Man-Dak League, 9

Manfred, Rob, 157, 177
Manitoba Baseball Hall of Fame, 9
Maple Leaf Sports and Entertainment
  Limited, 96
Marcum, Shaun, 193, 220, 244
Maris, Roger, 72
Marisnick, Jake, 221
Markwell, Diegomar, 154
Marriott Hotels, 95
Martin, Russell, 243, 255, 259
Martinez, Buck, 14–15, 16, 18, 19, 20, 32–33,
  41, 46, 74, 110, 111, 113, 123, 138, 176
Martinez, Edgar, 44
Martinez, Pedro, 151
Mathis, Jeff, 223–24
Matthews, Gary, Jr., 177
Mattick, Bobby, 14, 15,128, 141
Mays, Willie, 50
Mazeroski, Bill, 64
McCleary, Tim, 72
McDonald, John, 198, 232
McDougall, Don, 17, 81
McGinnis, Bo, 217
McGriff, Fred, 30, 37
McGuirk, Terry, 147
McGwire, Mike, 72
McIlvaine, Joe, 37
McKay, Dave, 242
McMaster University, 187
McNamee, Brian, 71, 72, 73
Meche, Gil, 178, 179
Melvin, Doug, 36, 107, 121, 192, 245
Mench, Kevin, 149
Miami Marlins, 2, 4, 55, 83, 87, 97, 120, 143,
  144, 160–62, 186, 188, 193, 216, 218–24, 232
Midsummer Classic, 58 (See also All-Star
  Game)
Milken, Michael, 86
Miller, Bill, 208, 209, 247
Milwaukee Brewers, 29, 31, 48, 61, 107, 113,
  117, 118, 121, 152, 158, 169, 177, 180, 192,
  193, 231, 245
Minasian, Perry, 217
Minaya, Omar, 190–91, 220
Minnesota Twins, 6, 25, 28, 29, 33, 41, 42,
  47, 50, 79, 85, 110, 120,139, 149, 151,
  181, 242
Mirvish family, 81
Mitchell, George, 71
Mitchell, Kevin, 225
MLB Network, 41
MLB.AM, 178
Mohamed, Nadir, 97, 99, 180
Molitor, Paul, 5, 31, 55, 56, 57, 58, 60–61, 63,
  64, 79, 110, 156, 166
Molson family, 89

Mondesi, Raul, 131,132, 133, 138
Moneyball (book), 118, 119, 120, 123, 124,
  153, 191
Moneyball (film), 118, 191
Montreal Canadiens, 81, 89
Montreal Expos, 3, 4, 6, 7, 36, 48, 51, 58,
  82–83, 107, 117, 120, 129, 175, 185, 188,
  189, 190, 191, 214, 215, 220, 241, 252
Montreal Royals, 8
Morgan, Gareth, 7, 259
Morneau, Justin, 7, 243, 244, 255, 258, 259
Morris, Jack, 18, 27, 30, 32–34, 41–43, 45, 46,
  50, 51, 56, 62, 156
Morrow, Brandon, 205, 206, 220, 232, 236
Moseby, Lloyd, 20
Most Valuable Player Award, 6, 7, 26, 37, 60,
  62, 72, 136, 160, 161
Mottola, Chad, 248
Mulholland, Terry, 58, 59
Mulliniks, Rance, 48
Murphy, Dwayne, 195
Muser, Tony, 113
Myers, Greg, 242

Nash, Steve, 239
Nathan, Joe, 221
National Baseball Hall of Fame, 5, 7, 25, 26,
  34, 36, 37, 43, 60, 108, 115, 117, 141,156,
  175, 180, 212, 226 (See also Cooperstown)
National Baseball Institute (NBI), 253
National Basketball Association (NBA), 239
National Basketball Association Hall of
  Fame, 239
National Football League (NFL), 92, 93, 96
National Hockey League (NHL), 77
National League Championship, 59
National League East, 58
National League West, 58
National League Wild Card, 3
National League, 1, 6, 47, 51, 58, 64, 72,186,
  216, 219 (See also American League)
NCAA, 241
Ndungidi, Ntema, 243
Negro Leagues, 9
New England Small Colleges Athletic
  Association, 117
New England Sports Network (NESN), 166
New York Mets, 43, 47, 61, 66, 108, 117,127,
  143, 144, 151, 157, 158, 172, 175–76, 217,
  219, 225, 235
New York Times, 30, 118
New York Yankees, 4, 8, 21, 32, 37, 46, 48, 55,
  57, 62, 63, 64, 69, 71, 72, 74, 75, 87, 108,
  115, 118, 121, 123, 126, 129, 131, 136, 138,
  140, 148, 151, 156, 159, 161, 165, 166, 173,
  174,189, 200, 195, 222, 246, 252

Newsday, 31
Nicolino, Justin, 206, 221
Nippon Professional Baseball, 202
Nippon-Ham Fighters, 202
Nixon, Otis, 50, 51–52, 53
Northwest League, 3

O'Neill, Tip, 8
Oakland Athletics, 26, 27, 28, 29, 30, 32, 45,
    55, 64, 113, 115, 118, 120, 121, 123, 126,
    130, 132, 140, 153, 154, 155, 172, 191, 195,
    244, 252
Oakland–Alameda County Coliseum, 26,
    41, 248
Olerud, John, 59, 60, 61, 74, 166, 252
Olympic Stadium, 83, 185, 188, 214
Olympics, 78, 248
Onex (investment co), 80
Ontario Baseball Association, 9
Overbay, Lyle, 158, 169, 170

Pan Am Games, 7
Park, Chan Ho, 162
Pavano, Carl, 151
Paxton, James, 241
Peavy, Jake, 220
Peladeau, Pierre Karl, 89
Pelley, Keith, 101
Pence, Hunter, 222
Pendleton, Terry, 45, 50
Perez, Luis, 205
Perfect Game USA, 252
Perkins, Dave, 85
Pettite, Andy, 71
Philadelphia Phillies, 5, 6, 19, 22, 58–65, 109,
    190, 194, 205, 222, 242
Phillips, Bill, 7–8
Phillips, Brandon, 220
Piniella, Lou, 21, 175
Pittsburgh Pirates, 3, 64, 117, 129, 153, 255
Plesac, Dan, 132
Pollock, Sam, 81, 111
Premier League soccer, 8
Prentice, Bob, 244
Prieto, Ariel, 155
Princeton University, 253
Progressive Conservative Party, 85
Project Macdonald-Cartier, 89
Prokopec, Luke, 242
Providence Grays, 8
Puhl, Terry, 7

Quantrill, Paul, 132, 242
Quebec Nordiques, 77
Quebecor, 89, 93
Queen, Mel, 109, 193

Ramirez, Hanley, 160
Ramirez, Manny, 104
Rasmus, Colby, 234
Reagins, Tony, 220
Real Sports Bar & Grill, 229
Reardon, Jeff, 47, 48, 51
Reed, Rick, 28
Reilly, Mike, 49
Renteria, Edgar, 151
Reyes, Jose, 2, 4–5, 186, 218, 219, 222, 231,
    232, 233, 234
Ricciardi, Dante, 127, 172
Ricciardi, Diane, 117, 171
Ricciardi, J. P., 22, 101, 105, 113, 115–18,
    121–22, 123–33, 135, 138–44,147–56,
    157–59, 162–63, 164–65, 166, 167,
    169–83, 186,191, 192,194, 195, 198,
    200, 210, 215, 216, 218, 225, 236, 242,
    243, 244, 260
Ricciardi, Johnny, 116
Ricciardi, Mariano, 127, 172
Richview Collegiate Institute, 6
Ricketts, Chad, 242
Rickey, Branch, 124
Rios, Alex, 166, 167, 176–77,180, 216
Ripken, Cal, Jr., 76
Ripken, Cal, Sr., 13, 57
Rivera, Luis, 233, 248
Rivera, Mariano, 156
Robinson, Frank, 22
Robinson, Jackie, 8, 9
Rodgers, Buck, 160
Rodriguez, Alex, 44, 104, 136
Rodriguez, Francisco, 181
Roger Dean Stadium, 190
Rogers Broadcasting, 89
Rogers Cablesystems Limited, 86, 90
"Rogers Campus," 156, 180
Rogers Centre, 2, 13, 38, 83, 85, 87, 93, 94, 99,
    107, 163, 178, 185, 193, 212, 220, 235, 236,
    237, 245 (*See also* SkyDome)
Rogers Communications, 20, 82, 86, 99, 103–4,
    105, 106, 107, 111, 112, 119, 135, 138, 156,
    170, 172–73, 181, 237
Rogers Media, 86, 89, 96, 99, 101, 237
Rogers Sportsnet. *See* Sportsnet
Rogers, Esmil, 214
Rogers, Ted, 82, 85–87, 88–94, 96–97, 101, 112,
    118, 147–48, 150, 151, 156, 159, 173, 174, 179
Rogers, Ted, Sr., 89, 94
Rolen, Scott, 170
Romero, Ricky, 100, 129, 155, 199, 206, 208,
    219, 232
Rookie League, 257
Ryan, B. J., 155–56, 157, 158, 159, 163, 164,
    166, 170, 173–74, 176, 180–81, 182, 186, 194

Ryan, Nolan, 108, 202
Ryan, Terry, 120

Sabean, Brian, 192, 216
Saint Mary's University's Centre for the Study
    of Sport and Health, 260
San Diego Padres, 30, 32, 36, 37, 38, 61, 72,
    97, 99–100, 154, 159, 221, 225, 257
San Francisco Giants, 26, 78, 177, 178, 192
Sanchez, Anibal, 160, 206, 218, 221
Sanders, Deion, 49, 50
Santos, Sergio, 205
Sartori, Jay, 222
Saunders, Michael, 258
Schilling, Curt, 59, 61, 62–63, 66
Schoeneweis, Scott, 150
Schuerholz, John, 117
Schwartz, Gary, 80, 81
Scott, Dick, 139
Seattle Mariners, 44, 80, 115, 118, 178, 232,
    241, 258
Selig, Bud, 3, 71, 83, 93, 94, 97, 106, 122, 154,
    157, 177, 190, 192, 202
Shapiro, Mark, 122–23
Showalter, Buck, 121, 138–39, 226
Simpson, Allan, 252, 253
Single-A baseball, 3, 17, 175, 206
Sirotka, Mike, 111–12
680 News, 89
Sizemore, Grady, 220
SkyDome, 4, 5, 6, 29, 30, 33, 34, 50, 59, 64,
    70, 78, 81, 83, 85, 90, 94, 95–96, 112, 136
    (*See also* Rogers Centre)
Sloane, David, 107
Smith, Lonnie, 50, 51
Smoltz, John, 49
Snider, Travis, 153, 193
Sojo, Luis, 30
Sons of Italy Hall of Fame, 116
Sony Centre, 94
Soriano, Alfonso, 177
Sosa, Sammy, 72
Sotomayor, Justice Sonia, 77
South Atlantic League, 175
Southam News, 72
Sports Illustrated, 13, 72
Sportsco International LP, 94, 95, 112
Sportsnet 590 The Fan, 139, 211
Sportsnet, 90, 99–100, 101
Sprague, Ed, 27, 47–48, 61–63
St. Louis Cardinals, 3, 63, 153–54, 159,
    163,164, 220
St. Peter-Marian High School, 117
Stanford University, 117
Stanley Cup, 52
Stark, Jayson, 166

Starkman, Howard, 76
Stavros, Steve, 86
Steinbrenner, George, 13, 21, 32, 131
Stewart, Dave, 30, 55, 56, 59, 60, 63, 108–9,
    111, 122, 123
Stieb, Dave, 41–42, 43, 144
Stocker, Kevin, 59
Stottlemyre, Todd, 43, 59, 73–74
Strasburg, Stephen, 3
Strawberry, Darryl, 175, 225
Sturtze, Tanyon, 129
Summit Series (1972), 5
Sun Media, 93
Syndergaard, Noah, 206, 217, 221, 235

Tampa Bay Rays, 9, 25, 99, 113, 209, 226,
    233
Tapani, Kevin, 42, 43
Taylor, Brien, 252
Taylor, Michael, 195
Team Canada, 231, 259
Telemedia, 17
Terry, Ralph, 64
Texas Rangers, 7, 66, 97, 104, 121, 122, 136,
    141, 149, 162, 177, 202, 203, 217, 252, 254
The Fan 590. *See* Sportsnet 590 The Fan
Thole, Josh, 2
Thomas, Frank, 180, 194
Thompson, Ryan, 43
Tiger Stadium, 33
Timlin, Mike, 51, 52
Torborg, Jeff, 161
Toronto Argonauts, 52, 237
Toronto Maple Leafs, 8, 52, 86, 182
Toronto Mets, 241
Toronto Star, 85, 123, 182
Toronto Sun, 34, 93, 182, 224, 226
Torre, Joe, 46
Tosca, Carlos, 138–39, 140, 175, 176
Towers, Kevin, 192
Triple Crown, 6, 37, 69
Triple-A baseball, 3, 17, 135, 160, 207, 234
Tulowitzki, Troy, 155
Turner Broadcasting, 147
Turner Field, 78
Turner, Ted, 85

University of British Columbia, 243
University of California, Berkeley, 243
University of Oregon, 37
University of Wisconsin, 242
Upper Canada College, 85
Upshaw, Willie, 14, 19
US Justice Department, 71–72
US Marine Corps Color Guard, 45
US Supreme Court, 77

Valentine, Bobby, 210, 250
Valenzuela, Fernando, 62
Van Horne, Dave, 36
Van Poppel, Todd, 252
Vancouver Canadians, 3
Vanier College, 188
Vaughn, Mo, 190
Veterans Stadium, 60, 66, 109
Videotron, 88–89
Viner, Tony, 86–87, 89–90, 91–92, 94–95, 147–48, 170, 173–74, 179
Vizquel, Omar, 212–13, 233, 250
Votto, Joey, 6, 9, 243, 251, 258

Wagner, Billy, 157
Wainhouse, David, 7
Wakamatsu, Don, 226
Wakefield, Tim, 246
Walken, Harvey, 95
Walker, Larry, 6, 7, 241, 243, 244, 247, 258, 259
Wallace, Brett, 195
Wallach, Tim, 226
Walton, Bruce, 206
Ward, Duane, 17–18, 29, 34, 35, 48, 49, 56, 57, 61–62, 73–76, 166
Washington Nationals, 3, 205, 249, 257
Washington State University, 252
Weaver, Earl, 124
Webster, Howard, 13, 44, 81
Wednesdays With J. P. (call-in show), 139
Welcome Back, Kotter (TV show), 5
Welke, Tim, 112
Wells, David, 43, 56, 109, 110, 111, 140
Wells, Vernon, 136, 139, 166, 169, 176, 177–78, 179, 180, 219, 220
Wertz, Vic, 50
White, Devon, 26, 27, 30, 31, 49–50, 56, 74, 166
Whitt, Ernie, 16, 19
Widdrington, Peter, 13, 16–17, 18, 81
Widmar, Al, 23
Wiggins, Scott, 131

Wild Card. *See* American League Wild Card; National League Wild Card
Wilken, Tim, 111, 130
Williams, Bernie, 189
Williams, Jimy, 20–21, 51
Williams, Kenny, 112, 223
Williams, Mitch ("Wild Thing"), 5, 6, 29, 58–59, 61, 63–67, 78, 116
Williams, Ted, 37
Wilner, Mike, 140
Wilson, Charlie, 256-57, 258
Wilson, Mookie, 66
Wilson, Roger, 93
Wilson, Willie, 18–19
Winfield, Dave, 5, 30–32, 34–35, 42, 48, 49, 51, 55, 57, 60
Winnipeg Giants, 9
Winnipeg Jets, 77
WIP (radio), 109
Wolfe, Brian, 180
Worcester Telegram, 116
World Baseball Classic, 2, 7, 231, 236, 248, 255, 259
World of Sport facility (Disney), 254
World Series, 1, 3, 5, 10, 13, 14, 17, 19, 22, 25, 28, 29, 31, 32, 33, 34, 37, 41, 42, 44–53, 55–67, 70, 73, 74, 76, 77, 78, 83, 101, 105, 106, 108, 110, 115, 116, 120, 121, 122, 135, 143, 144, 156, 160–61, 165, 167, 175, 179, 224, 226, 229, 241, 242, 250, 261

Yankee Stadium, 38, 106, 140, 161, 166, 175, 208, 212, 248
Yankees Entertainment and Sports Network (YES), 166
Yawkey, Jean, 13
Yawkey, Tom, 13
York University, 105

Zaun, Greg, 180, 234
Zito, Barry, 178

JEFF BLAIR has more than 30 years of experience in sportswriting and broadcasting. The *Globe and Mail*'s sports columnist and host of *The Jeff Blair Show* on Sportsnet 590 The Fan in Toronto has covered Olympics, World Series, Stanley Cups and earthquakes while working in Winnipeg, Calgary, Montreal and Toronto. But his first love is baseball, which he covered from 1989–97 as a beat reporter with the *Gazette* and has covered since then as a columnist with the *Globe and Mail*. Blair grew up in Morden, Manitoba, and attended the University of Manitoba. He lives in Hamilton with wife, Shelley, and daughter, Emma Rose.